The Esoteric Investor

The Esoteric Investor

*Alternative Investments for
Global Macro Investors*

Vishaal B. Bhuyan

Vice President, Publisher: Tim Moore
Associate Publisher and Director of Marketing: Amy Neidlinger
Executive Editor: Jim Boyd
Editorial Assistant: Pamela Boland
Operations Manager: Gina Kanouse
Senior Marketing Manager: Julie Phifer
Assistant Marketing Manager: Megan Colvin
Cover Designer: Alan Clements
Managing Editor: Kristy Hart
Project Editor: Lori Lyons
Copy Editor: Gayle Johnson
Proofreader: Water Crest Publishing, Inc.
Indexer: Larry Sweazy
Compositor: Nonie Ratcliff
Manufacturing Buyer: Dan Uhrig

This book is sold with the understanding that neither the author nor the publisher is engaged in rendering legal, accounting, or other professional services or advice by publishing this book. Each individual situation is unique. Thus, if legal or financial advice or other expert assistance is required in a specific situation, the services of a competent professional should be sought to ensure that the situation has been evaluated carefully and appropriately. The author and the publisher disclaim any liability, loss, or risk resulting directly or indirectly, from the use or application of any of the contents of this book.

FT Press offers excellent discounts on this book when ordered in quantity for bulk purchases or special sales. For more information, please contact U.S. Corporate and Government Sales, 1-800-382-3419, corpsales@pearsontechgroup.com. For sales outside the U.S., please contact International Sales at international@pearson.com.

Company and product names mentioned herein are the trademarks or registered trademarks of their respective owners.

Printed in the United States of America

First Printing June 2011

ISBN-10: 0-13-248507-9
ISBN-13: 978-0-13-248507-4

Pearson Education LTD.
Pearson Education Australia PTY, Limited.
Pearson Education Singapore, Pte. Ltd.
Pearson Education Asia, Ltd.
Pearson Education Canada, Ltd.
Pearson Educatión de Mexico, S.A. de C.V.
Pearson Education—Japan
Pearson Education Malaysia, Pte. Ltd.

Library of Congress Cataloging-in-Publication Data

The esoteric investor : alternative investments for global macro investors / Vishaal B. Bhuyan.
  p. cm.
ISBN-13: 978-0-13-248507-4 (hardback : alk. paper)
ISBN-10: 0-13-248507-9
1. Life insurance. 2. Viatical settlements. 3. Longevity. 4. Fisheries—Finance. 5. Water supply—Finance. 6. Portfolio management. I. Title.
HG8771.B46 2011
332.63—dc22
                    2011013399

This book is dedicated to all my cousins, especially Shivam Shah.

Contents

Acknowledgments

I would like to acknowledge Joseph L. Shaefer, Richard Ellis, and Frank X. Diebold for their assistance in putting together this book.

About the Author

Vishaal B. Bhuyan is Founder and Chief Investment Officer of Nariman Point, LLC, a New York-based investment management firm focusing on demographic-driven instruments, with expertise in insurance and longevity/mortality instruments. Prior to launching Nariman Point in early 2011, Bhuyan was an independent consultant providing family offices, private equity funds, and hedge funds with market insight and quantitative analysis on the life linked asset class. During that time he published "The Wave Report," a monthly newsletter to clients providing a firsthand market perspective on the life markets.

Bhuyan is the author and editor of *Life Markets: Trading Mortality and Longevity Risk with Life Settlements and Linked Securities* and *Reverse Mortgages and Linked Securities: The Complete Guide to Risk, Pricing, and Regulation*. He has spoken at various hedge fund and insurance conferences in Tokyo, Vienna, New York, Orlando, London, Nice, Monaco, and Hong Kong. His book *Life Markets* was referenced in the U.S. Securities and Exchange Commission report on life settlements.

Bhuyan graduated from the University of Pennsylvania in 2005 with a degree in History and Sociology of Science, where he was vice president of the Phi Delta Theta fraternity.

Contributing Authors

Richard Ellis is one of America's leading marine conservationists and is generally recognized as the world's foremost painter of marine natural-history subjects. His paintings of whales have appeared in *Audubon, National Wildlife, Australian Geographic, Encyclopedia Britannica*, and numerous other national and international publications. His shark paintings have been featured in *Sports Afield, Audubon, Sport Diver, Nautical Quarterly, Reader's Digest*, and his own *Book of Sharks*, now in its seventh printing and called the most popular book on sharks ever written. Ellis has been asked to advise on many museum installations. In 1978 he completed a 35-foot-long whale mural for the Denver Museum of Natural History. The Smithsonian Institution selected 106 of his paintings to form a traveling exhibit of the marine mammals of the world. These paintings are now in the permanent collection of Whaleworld, a museum in Albany, Western Australia. In 2005, in conjunction with the publication in Italian of his *Encyclopedia of the Sea*, Ellis was given a one-man show of his drawings at the Museo del Mare in Genoa. Ellis is a special adviser to the American Cetacean Society, a member of the Explorers Club, and a research associate at the American Museum of Natural History. From 1980 to 1990, he was a member of the U.S. delegation to the International Whaling Commission.

Joseph L. Shaefer, B Gen, USAF, Ret., has had a varied and unique career, both military and civilian. He entered active-duty service in Army Psychological Operations in 1970. He served as a Special Forces A-Team XO and CO from 1971 to 1976, first with the 5th, and then with the 20th (NG) Special Forces.

He joined the USAFR as an intelligence analyst and command briefer, and later he served as a HUMINT (human intelligence) officer, an interrogator and strategic debriefer, and an interrogation and debriefing instructor. Later assignments included the NATO, South America, and Southeast Asia country desks; commander of the Mobile Interrogation Teams in operations Desert Shield and Desert Storm; air attaché to Rangoon, Burma; commander of the language detachment at the Presidio of Monterey; and senior political/military affairs officer, Office of the Deputy Chief of Staff for Air and Space Operations, Headquarters U.S. Air Force, Washington, D.C.

Positions as a general officer include service as the reserve chief for the A2 and the acting A2 during Operation Allied Force (Kosovo) at Air Combat Command; a member of the AF Intelligence Crisis Action Team after 9/11; reserve chief for the J2, U.S. Strategic Command; and reserve chief for the Director, Defense Intelligence Agency.

In his civilian career, Shaefer entered the securities industry in 1972 and later founded his own brokerage, which was subsequently bought by Charles Schwab & Co. He was a regional and senior VP at Schwab until he retired to found Stanford Wealth Management, an SEC-registered investment firm. He was one of the charter members of the CIA's Project Prophesy regarding the use of market intelligence (MARKINT) to discern possible terrorist activities, and he contributed to a number of research papers as author or editor.

Shaefer currently is professor of global and security studies (counterterrorism, the intelligence community, illicit finance) at American Military University/American Public University. After being awarded his undergraduate degree in international relations at UCLA, he earned a master's in military studies with honors in unconventional warfare from AMU/APU.

Introduction

The Esoteric Investor is the product of research I did for my own investment management firm, Nariman Point, LLC. My firm focuses on making investments that are demographic in nature and completely unusual. This book is not meant to offer any stock tips, or investment philosophies or anything of the sort. It is simply a 10,000 foot view at a variety of interesting opportunities that exist due to dramatic changes occurring around the world. One example is finding opportunities that relate to aging populations in developed nations. I have spent the past six years focused on the *life markets* (see my biography). These markets are composed of longevity and mortality risk instruments such as life settlements, reverse mortgages, longevity reinsurance, and, in some cases, extreme mortality bonds. On one level these products are all linked to insurance, but on a macro level they are about a watershed time in human history when many of us will live to be 100 years old, and the economic impact that fact carries. As populations live longer they create a drag on retirement systems, which needs to be addressed. Unfortunately, as the baby boomer generation begins retiring (baby boomers make up almost one-fourth of the U.S. population), longer-living retirees can destroy the fiscal soundness of governments and companies. I believe we are headed for a violent and catastrophic pension collapse in the Western World as well as in Japan. These topics are covered in detail in this book. The theme of demographics is an important one, and the word is changing before our eyes. Markets have become overcrowded and volatile due to the modern era of rapid dissemination of information. Furthermore, understanding and predicting where regulation and taxation are going in the U.S. seems as difficult a task as predicting where regulation and taxation are going in India, or in another emerging economy. The end result of all this is that the vast majority of professional and retail investors are chasing the same few easy ideas, which makes most of these ideas *not* interesting. So, the real purpose of this book is to offer something a bit different in the way of analysis. I don't make any stock recommendations. Stocks may be mentioned to highlight that some equities do exist that pertain to the topics discussed in the book; however, these are not recommendations, and I probably do not own any of them.

For years I have been interested in a few investments: fisheries, water, and human demographics. Although I made the last one into a career, I never gave up reading about and researching the other two. Tuna was interesting because I often came across headlines such as "Tuna sells for $400,000 in Tokyo." I never understood why there was not a standardized futures contract that allowed for the hedging of tuna prices. It turns out that there is a form of tuna futures contract, but not in the same sense. Tuna also starting piquing my interest when I learned that certain types of bluefin tuna were nearing extinction due to overfishing. Generally, aquaculture (the practice of breeding and farming fish) became of considerable interest to me because I found it shocking that the majority of commercial fishing that occurs today is for the purpose of catching smaller fish to feed raised fish such as salmon and tuna. Simply, we eat mostly farmed fish that is raised for consumption by corporations, not fish caught in the wild by a guy wearing a yellow raincoat. Then I learned about the Tuna Wranglers and Tuna Kings of Australia, who were making millions of dollars catching and trapping large schools of bluefin and selling them to the Japanese. Coupled with seeing Tsukiji fish market in Tokyo for myself, I had to take this further.

Regarding water, my interest stemmed from my frequent trips to India growing up and even recently, although India has changed quite a bit during that time. What I never understood was that in nations such as India—countries that need water more than anyone (over 1 billion people)—water was treated the absolute worst. It was highly polluted, contaminated, and filled with waste. In Hinduism, the concept of restricting beef in the diet arose from cherishing the cow, which provided milk to the people. In the same way, water is the absolute and literal lifeblood of the human race, yet it is abused and misused, especially in India. When I began to explore water as a commodity, I reached a tentative conclusion that perhaps that this misuse of our water resources can be attributed to a mispricing of water. Water is considered "free" right now and therefore is treated as if it belongs to no one.

With help from my coauthors and researchers Richard Ellis, a highly respected marine conservationist, and Joseph Shaefer, a retired USAF Brigadier General/Special Forces-turned-wealth manager, I delved into these interesting topics of the plight of the bluefin tuna and how valuable water really is. In addition, this book covers topics such as longevity and mortality risk, which, again, is my specialty. I sincerely hope that you enjoy reading this book as much as I enjoyed putting it together.

Part I

Investing in Demographics

The *life markets* are one of the most interesting and innovative markets in existence today. They consist of the secondary market for life insurance (life settlements), reverse mortgages, and longevity and mortality risk. Part I explains each of these markets in the context of global macro investing, as opposed to a more technical structural finance perspective. However, some basic quantitative concepts are necessary to fully understand the asset class. When examining these assets, it is important to understand the economic backdrop and the need for such markets. In this regard, the life markets can be broken into two distinct buckets: reverse equity transactions and longevity-mortality risk. Demographics is the common theme of both of these market segments as large numbers of baby boomers and seniors head toward retirement, creating a number of tangential economic problems.

1

Building the Demographic Framework

Demographics are one of the most important factors when analyzing the future economic prospects of any geographic area. Nations
such as India have large young populations (only 5.2% of India's population is older than 65) and therefore have a tremendous amount of
future potential due to a growing labor force and a growing pool of
consumers. In contrast, nations such as Japan, where 22% of the
nation is older than 65, face a serious threat to their economy and will
suffer from a shrinking labor force for the next several decades. In the
U.S., more than 12% of the nation is over 65; in the UK, that number
is 16%. Moreover, since 2006, an astonishing 330 people turn 60
every hour in the U.S. By 2050, Korea will have lost roughly 38% of
its population, and Japan and Russia will have lost over 20%.

It is important to consider that although growing and large populations are important for economic growth, adequate infrastructure is
required to support them. In India, for example, although the demographics are promising, the nation still faces unimaginable poverty,
and basics such as fresh water are scarce. Figure 1.1 illustrates India's
rise as the most populated nation in the world by 2030, ahead of
China, which is currently at an optimum demographic point. Hope-
fully by that time, the nation will have taken steps toward adding sufficient schools, hospitals, highways, roads, and other public utilities to
accommodate the extra bodies. The country must also address the
high illiteracy rate, which currently stands at roughly 61% according
the CIA World Fact Book. Although this rate is low, in 1947, when
India achieved independence, only 12% of the nation was literate.
The point is that demographics are the fundamental drivers of
economies.

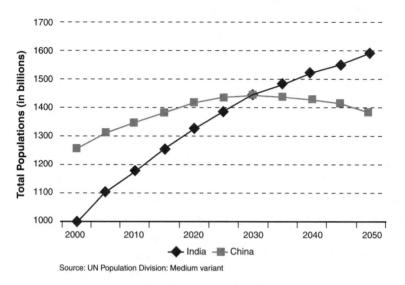

Figure 1.1   India's population versus China's

Source: United Nations

Japan, which is referenced quite a bit in this book, suffers from a crippling demographic decline. According to several government sources, and as illustrated in Figure 1.2, Japan is at peak population as of 2010. This creates a number of issues for the nation. The shrinking workforce will face difficulties in manufacturing and exporting products for the West at the same pace as it once did. This is only one of the issues facing the country as a result of its demographic problem. Japan is discussed in further detail later in this chapter and the next.

Aging populations have historically been a positive sign of economic prosperity and flourishing developed societies. However, from an economic standpoint, longer-living populations can put a tremendous strain on retirement and health care systems:

> In the U.S., social security and Medicare currently account for roughly 7% of the GDP, but within the next 25 to 30 years these programs will account for nearly 13%, essentially the majority of the entire federal budget. Proposals have been made to prevent these disasters, such as opening borders to

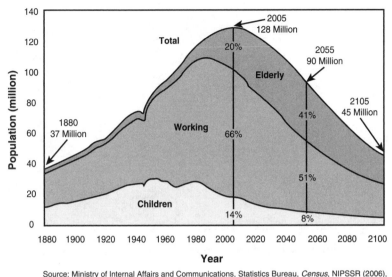

Source: Ministry of Internal Affairs and Communications, Statistics Bureau, *Census*, NIPSSR (2006), Population Projection for Japan: 2006-2055.

Figure 1.2   Japan's population 1880–2100

immigrants to prop up the work force, privatizing government programs, and increasing the retirement age from 65 to 71. These proposals, however, have failed to adequately address the matter and gain widespread acceptance. Plans have been made to extend the retirement age by two years in some countries over a 20-year period, but this is simply not enough. The retirement age should be at least 71 in order to adjust for dramatic increases in life expectancy over the past 100 years relative to a static 60-to-65-year-old retirement age (in some places 55), which has been in place since as far back as the 19th century.

Mass immigration will cause a number of national security problems, and people are simply not fungible assets. Skill and education level must be comparable for immigrants to take on many of the skilled labor jobs the baby boomers will leave behind. Moreover, the sheer number of immigrants necessary to counteract the baby boomer phenomenon would be unthinkable.[1]

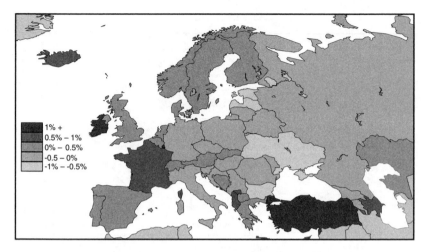

Figure 1.3   Countries' population growth or decline in Europe 2009

Source: Zonu.com

Generally, developed nations are aging rapidly, and their leaders must provide for the increase in health and retirement costs to care for the "gray" population (see Figure 1.3). But even in booming, headline-making nations such as China, demographics are an enormous dark cloud over their economies. China's one-child-per-family policy poses an enormous issue in terms of the nation's dependency ratio, or the ratio of younger workers supporting the elderly (see Figure 1.4). China is currently in a "sweet spot" of dependency ratios; however, every year moving forward China's elderly will become a larger percentage of the overall population. According to the Chinese government, the nation prevented roughly 250 million births between 1980 and 2000. These 250 million additional young workers could have helped carry the additional financial burden of aging and retired workers. The low dependency ratio has helped China reduce its economic drag by limiting the number of children who needed to be cared for. However, this policy is shortsighted in the long term. It is projected that the number of Chinese between the ages of 20 and 24 will drop from 125 million in 2010 to approximately 68 million by 2020, or nearly a 50% decrease.[2] China also suffers from a severe gender imbalance because families in rural areas prefer males to females due their ability to generate income or work on the family farm. Because of sex-specific abortions, researchers believe that over the next 15 years, there will be roughly 30 million more marriage-age men than women. And we all know that single, sexually frustrated men are a recipe for disaster! Wang Guangzhou, a Chinese researcher for the *Global Times*, commented: "The chance of getting married will be rare if a man is more than 40 years old in the country-side. They will be more dependent on social security as they age and have fewer household resources to rely on."[3]

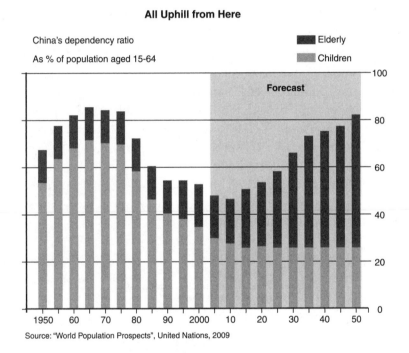

All Uphill from Here

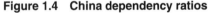
Source: "World Population Prospects", United Nations, 2009

Figure 1.4   China dependency ratios

Source: United Nations 2009

The lighter bars in Figure 1.4 provide some evidence that dependency ratios, especially as a result of sex-specific abortions, have led to China's explosive economic growth. Starting in 2015, the darker bars indicate a dramatic spike in the elderly dependency ratio, which will continue into 2050. Because fewer children are being born, it costs less money to run a family, and therefore more money stays in the economy. The problem now is that those fewer children need to support all the older people who are retiring. The economic result is yet to be seen.

Again we can see that demographics may be used to predict the direction of a particular nation or economy. Granted, China's dependency ratio does not provide much insight into where the Shanghai Stock Exchange (SSE) will trade over the next week, month, year, or even five years. But over the next 10 or 20 years, it provides an excellent picture of the nation's position relative to other nations. India, which many believe is 10 or 20 years behind China at the moment, does not have a large future dependency ratio to worry about. Therefore, India maybe primed to surpass China in economic output over the next 50 or 100 years.

It is no coincidence that major growth in the U.S. coincided with the aging of the baby boomers, the largest generation in U.S. history. Certain market pundits, such as futurist Harry S. Dent, associate peak spending of families with the performance of the U.S. equities market. Figure 1.5 illustrates the various spending habits of different age groups within the U.S. Not surprisingly, people between the ages of 46 and 50 spend the most. They probably are supporting their two teenage, college-bound children, and maybe even their parents. Notice the sharp decline in spending after the children have moved out and entered the working world.

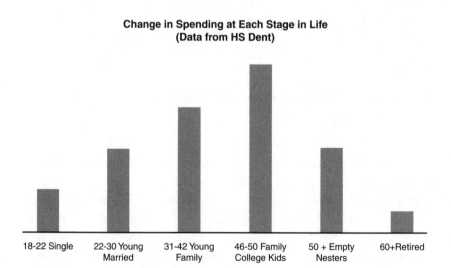

Figure 1.5   Spending life cycle

Source: HS Dent

Figure 1.6 illustrates the concept of "peak spending" as it relates to the performance of the Dow Jones Industrial Average (DJIA). The thick line represents the DJIA, and the shaded area represents the number of people at their peak spending phase of life. Dent theorizes that one of the major reasons for the 2008 market downturn was a decline in peak spending. Furthermore, Dent cities this drop in peak spending as indication that a bear market will persist over the next two decades.

The Spending Wave-Births Lagged for Peak in Family Spending

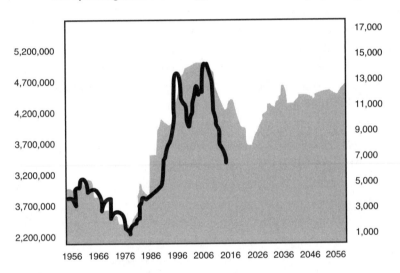

Figure 1.6   DJIA versus peak spending

Source: HS Dent

In summary, demographics are an important element in investment analysis. A 2011 report released by PriceWaterhouseCoopers (PWC) projected that the G-7 economies will be replaced by emerging markets by 2032. The report estimated that by 2028, India will eclipse Japan in economic size, and Brazil will surpass Germany. China has already passed Japan to become the second-largest economy in the world. This sets the stage for a dramatic shift in global power from West to East and old to new. However, historically India and China have been the wealthiest and most powerful nations. Western prominence starting in the late 18th century was merely a blip in

the context of human history. However, do not discount the importance of the unknown. Any competent actuary will admit that actuarial science and population projections are never entirely accurate. On
the other hand, you cannot ignore the baby boomer population as
they begin retiring. Nations and corporations must be prepared for
any swing in population size.

Economic Implications of Longevity and Mortality Risk

Given that demographics play such a significant role in a nation's
economic growth, it is easy to see why corporations must pay close
attention to not only the demographic makeup of their customers,
but also their employees. Pension obligations, if mismanaged or mis-
calculated, can be the downfall of any otherwise fundamentally sound
business. This section examines two major demographic risks facing
governments and corporations: longevity risk and mortality risk.

Longevity risk is the risk that a group of people, whether employees at XYZ Corp. or U.S. citizens, are living longer than originally estimated, and therefore collecting social security for a longer period of
time. Although we use the term "risk," it is more of a certainty that
requires adequate planning. For example, although the retirement
age in many developed countries is between 60 and 67 (see Table
1.1), in many of these nations, the average life expectancy is well over
75. This means that the average taxpayer collects social security (as
well as any health benefits) for 10 to 15 years. In the U.S., the average
life expectancy is about 78; in Japan, it is 82.6, the highest in the
world.

Figures 1.7 through 1.9 show the exponential increase in human
longevity. As technology rapidly advances, so does our ability to live
longer. Life expectancies have increased dramatically since 1840 due
to the eradication of smallpox and a general improvement in health
conditions. Thereafter, life spans increased at an average rate of 2.5
years per decade for the next 160 years. By 1900, the highest average
life expectancy was roughly 60, and by 2000 it was over 80.

TABLE 1.1 Retirement Age and Percentages of Employed Older Workers

Country	Early Retirement Age	Normal Retirement Age	Employed, 55 to 59	Employed, 60 to 64	Employed, 65 to 69	Employed, 70 and Over
Austria	60 (57)	65 (60)	39%	7%	1%	0%
Belgium	60	65	45%	12%	1%	0%
Denmark	None	65	77%	35%	9%	1%
France	62	65	51%	12%	1%	0%
Germany	65	67	64%	23%	3%	0%
Greece	57	65	51%	31%	8%	1%
Italy	57	65 (60)	34%	12%	1%	0%
Netherlands	60	65	53%	22%	3%	0%
Norway	62	67	?.	?.	?.	?.
Spain	60	65	46%	22%	0%	0%
Sweden	61	65	78%	58%	5%	1%
Switzerland	63 (61), [58]	65 (64)	77%	46%	7%	2%
United Kingdom	None	65	69%	40%	10%	2%
United States	62	67	66%	43%	20%	5%

Source: Organization for Economic Cooperation and Development (OECD)

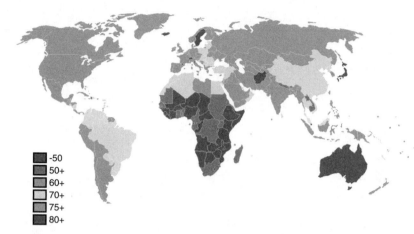

Figure 1.7   Global life expectancy in 2009

Source: CDC

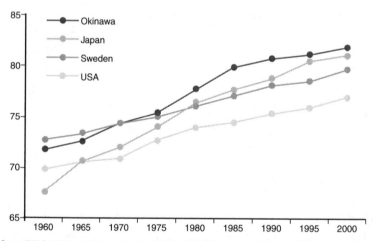

Source: W.H.O. 1996; Japan Ministry of Health and Welfare 2004; US Department of Health and Human Services/CDC 2005.

Figure 1.8   Life expectancy since 1960 in long-lived populations and the U.S.

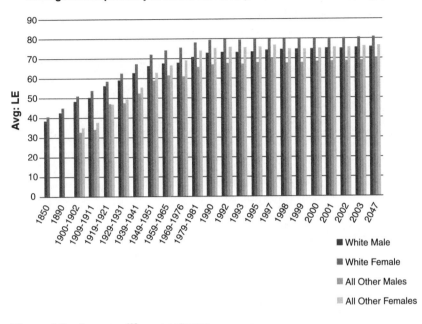

Figure 1.9 Average life expectancy

Between 1960 and 2002, average life expectancy rose from 36 to 71 in China, from 56 to 71 in Latin America and the Caribbean, from 47 to 69 in the Middle East and North Africa, and from 44 to 63 in South Asia.[4]

Given that each additional year of life expectancy after age 65 adds roughly 3% to the present value of pension liabilities, the cost of providing pensions in 2050 may be 18% higher than currently expected.[5] For many pension funds, this uncertainty is a substantial and unquantifiable risk, leaving them unprepared to address future obligations (see Figure 1.10).

The first pension fund was created by Otto von Bismarck, the Prime Minister of Prussia from 1862 to 1890, under the Old Age and Disability Insurance Bill of 1889. This program used tax revenues to make annuity payments to seniors who reached the age of 70. Average life expectancy at birth during this time was 46. In 1918, the German government lowered the eligibility age from 70 to 65, where it remains, more or less, even though average life expectancy in Germany has skyrocketed to 80.

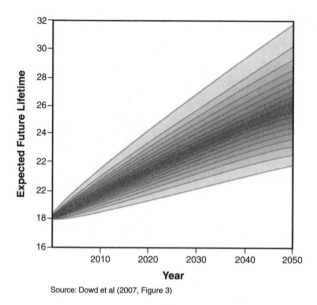

Source: Dowd et al (2007, Figure 3)

Figure 1.10   Pension deficits and surpluses (UK-based defined benefit pensions)

Source: Pension Protection Fund

Retirement ages should have been hiked decades ago around the world; however, any politician who suggested doing so was met with disdain by party rivals and voters. In 2010, when French parliament raised the retirement age from 60 to 62, workers took to the streets in violent protests. The same occurred in Greece after the nation announced that it plans to increase the retirement age to 63 from 61 and ban early retirement.

Coupled with the recent economic crisis, which has left major U.S. corporations with $400 billion in underfunded programs (from a $60 billion surplus at the end of 2007), the risk of longer-living populations is substantial. Uncertainty in retirement programs has resulted in the growth of *reverse equity* markets such as life settlements and reverse mortgages. These allow seniors to sell their life insurance policies or equity in their homes in exchange for an upfront lump sum. Moreover, the number of working seniors has more than doubled over the past 20 years (see Figure 1.11) due to the destruction of the nest egg.

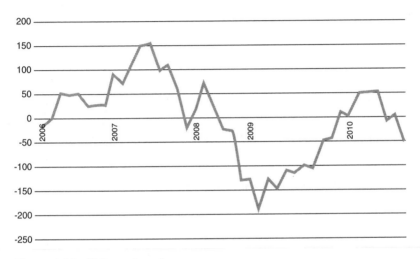

Figure 1.11   U.S. workers by age

Source: U.S. Bureau of Labor Statistics

Even though increased life expectancy is the logical result of improvements in modern medicine, life expectancies have become increasingly uncertain (see Figure 1.12). Many factors can hinder longevity and cause life expectancy to fall. For example, obesity rates in the U.S. for both children and adults are at alarming levels (and the rest of the world is following suit). Perhaps we as a society take our health for granted and rely too heavily on medicine to bail us out.

Figure 1.13 (a-f) is a state-by-state mapping of body mass index (BMI) levels in the U.S. Keep in mind that this data includes lower-income individuals. The disparity in life expectancy estimates between individuals of higher and lower socioeconomic levels, as well as between white and black Americans, is significant. On the other hand, the disparity between men's and women's life expectancies is actually narrowing.

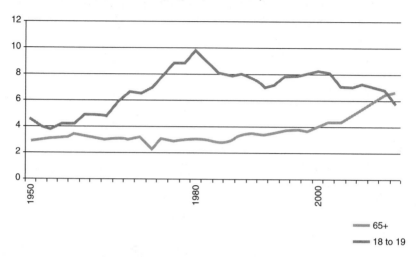

U.S. Workers by Age 1950 to 2009 (monthly average for each year; in millions)

65+
18 to 19

Figure 1.12   Longevity fan chart at age 65

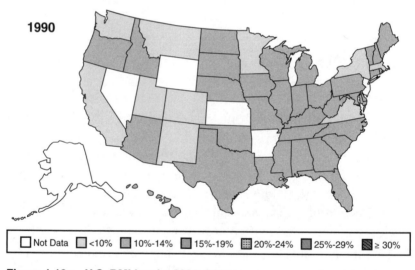

Not Data   <10%   10%-14%   15%-19%   20%-24%   25%-29%   ≥ 30%

Figure 1.13a   U.S. BMI levels, 1985–2008

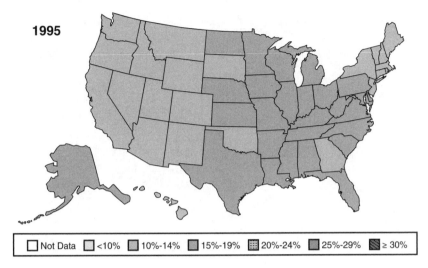

Figure 1.13b   U.S. BMI levels, 1985–2008 (continued)

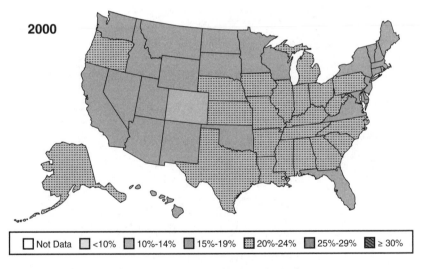

Figure 1.13c   U.S. BMI levels, 1985–2008 (continued)

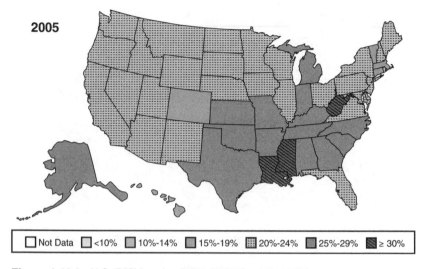

Figure 1.13d   U.S. BMI levels, 1985–2008 (continued)

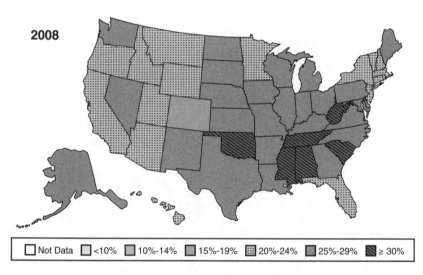

Figure 1.13e   U.S. BMI levels, 1985–2008 (continued)

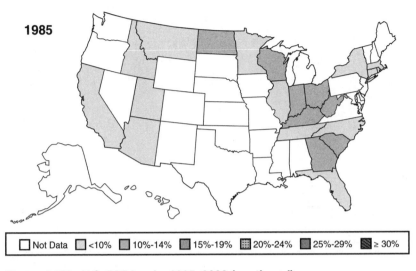

1985

Not Data ☐ <10% ☐ 10%-14% ■ 15%-19% ▦ 20%-24% ■ 25%-29% ▨ ≥ 30%

Figure 1.13f   U.S. BMI levels, 1985–2008 (continued)

Historically, developed nations have experienced a general mortality improvement rate of roughly 1% per annum, with a "mortality shock" ranging from plus or minus 3%, with 5% being an absolute extreme. A positive mortality improvement shock could result from, for example, a cure for cancer. A negative mortality improvement shock could result from the spread of a new disease or an unforeseen side effect of artificially grown foods. The last major mortality shock was the Spanish influenza pandemic of 1918, which lasted from 1917 to 1920. Almost 3% of the world's population (50 million) died of the disease, and 28% (500 million) were infected. This disease was unique in that infections in younger people were more fatal than those of their older counterparts. This has also been the case to a much lesser extent in outbreaks occurring in 1976, 1988, 1998, and 2007. Figure 1.14 shows typical mortalities among various ages from 1911 to 1917 compared to the mortality distribution in 1918.

Generally, *mortality risk* is the inverse of longevity risk. It is the risk that a group of individuals dies before and unexpectedly relative to estimates. As mentioned, longevity "risk" is actually more of a given that requires adequate planning. In contrast, unexpected mortality is a risk in the more traditional sense because it is unforeseen. For example, whereas a pension fund's obligations increase as life expectancy increases (longer-living retirees mean the pension must

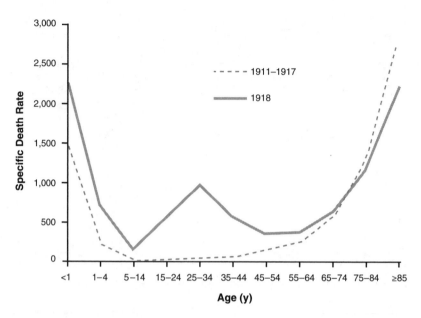

Figure 1.14 Mortality disparity of the Spanish flu

Source: CDC

make more payments), a life insurance company may be subject to the risk of substantial numbers of early deaths. In the latter example, the life insurance company would have to pay more claims than expected and would experience a reduction in premium inflows. Table 1.2 shows the relationship between longevity risk and mortality risk and lists organizations that may be exposed to each.

TABLE 1.2 The Relationship Between Longevity Risk and Mortality Risk

	Longevity Risk	Mortality Risk
Definition	The group lives longer than estimates	The group dies prior to estimates
Actuarial notation	1–qx	qx
Exposure	Corporate-defined benefit pension programs, annuity providers, social security (governments), life settlement investors, reverse mortgage lenders	Life and health insurance companies, pharmaceutical companies, municipalities reliant on wealthy elderly residents

The next chapter provides more details on why certain groups are exposed to either longevity or mortality risk.

Endnotes

[1] Bhuyan, Vishaal B. "Riding the Demographic Wave: Pension Busts and Market Booms," Global Macro EconoMonitor. March 19, 2009.

[2] Weinschenk, Matthew. "The Dependency Ratio: Use This Number to Find the Best International Investments," Stock Blog Hub, January 29, 2010: issue 1186.

[3] "Chinese gender imbalance will leave millions of men without wives." *The Telegraph*, January 11, 2010.

[4] Jamison, D.T., Breman, J.G., Measham, A.R., et al., editors. *Priorities in Health*. Washington (D.C.): World Bank, 2006.

[5] David Blake. The Pension Institute, Cass Business School.

2

Longevity and Mortality Risk Markets

Through a variety of structures including swaps, indices, bond structures, and reinsurance, institutions can offset their exposure to any issues related to demographics. The following lists further explain such issues. Figure 2.1 illustrates how longevity risk impacts net returns for institutions exposed to either longevity or mortality risk. For example, an annuity provider loses money as its customers live longer than expected. Inversely, a life insurance company would benefit from longer living customers as it would mean more premium in flows over time.

Organizations Exposed to Longevity Risk

- **Defined benefit (DB) pensions:** A DB pension plan uses a formula based on an employee's age, tenure, and income to create a formula for providing a prescheduled monthly income to retired employees until death. These plans use actuarial analysis to underwrite the scheme because the longer a retiree lives, the more payments the corporation must make to him. Social security in many regards is a DB program. These plans, which used to be commonly offered by corporations, are now on the brink of extinction due to longer-living retirees and large unfunded obligations that will create a massive drag on profit. According to actuarial firm Watson Wyatt, in 1985 89% of Fortune 100 companies had DB pension programs. By 2007, the number of such programs fell to just 28%. Globally, roughly $25 trillion of longevity risk is held by defined pension programs.

- **Annuity providers:** A life annuity is a contract between a purchaser and an annuity provider (typically a life insurance company) that provides monthly lifetime payments in exchange for an upfront cost. For example, a 65-year-old would make an upfront payment to Acme Insurance Corp. and in return would receive some nominal amount every year for the rest of her life. The longer the senior lives, the more payments the annuity provider must make to her. So if she surpasses the estimated life expectancy, Acme's returns on capital would decrease and possibly become a loss.

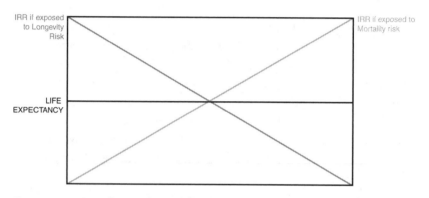

Figure 2.1   Longevity mortality risk

- **Life settlement investors:** A life settlement is the sale of a life insurance policy from a senior older than 70 to a third-party investor. The longer the senior lives, the more premium payments the investor must make to the insurance carrier, which decreases the return on investment.

- **Reverse mortgage lenders:** Similar to a life settlement, a reverse mortgage uses life expectancy and real estate value projections (not typical FICO scores) to underwrite loans to seniors age 65 and over collateralized by their homes. Unlike traditional loans, these loans are not repaid until the senior dies or moves out of the home. One common reverse mortgage format is to provide monthly income to the senior for the extent of the loan. This means that the longer the senior (borrower) lives, the more payments must be made.

Organizations Exposed to Mortality Risk

- **Life insurance companies:** Life insurance companies generate profits by investing monthly premiums over a long period of time and, through "the law of large numbers," paying a lesser number of claims. A couple may purchase life insurance at age 35 when they have young children and then maintain their whole-life policies for 30 years. At that point their children are adults, and they no longer see a need for the policies, so they let them lapse. The carrier in this scenario would collect 30 years of premiums and have to offer only a small amount to the seniors when they surrender the policies. With lapse ratios above 90%, the carrier relies on these long-term cash flows to pay any claims. Therefore, if an unforeseen outbreak of a virus killed 2% of their customers, a spike in claims would need to be paid out, and less lifetime cash flow would be received.

- **Health insurance companies:** Similar to a life insurance company, a health insurance company would be severely negatively affected if a virus broke out, because carriers would have to pay for a large increase in medical treatments.

- **Pharmaceutical companies:** Drug companies generate a substantial amount of profit from older and elderly individuals. A lifetime of illness is the golden goose in the pharmaceutical industry. If a large number of their customers were to die unexpectedly, that could mean a huge drop in company revenue.

- **Municipalities:** Municipalities with a larger number of older residents (pick any town in Florida) rely on tax income from a group that at some point will all die around the same time. This would mean growing expenditures and possibly a sudden and significant drop in tax receipts.

- **Third-party investors:** Hedge fund or other investors may have a view that longevity or mortality is underpriced or overpriced and therefore make investments to generate yield uncorrelated to other markets. This is similar to players in the credit default swap (CDS) markets, who need not actually be exposed to default risk to purchase or protection.

- **Products:** Investors in these risks, whether for hedge purposes or not, have a number of different vehicles in which to access the market.

Longevity swaps are one way to hedge longevity risk, or merely invest in it. Similar to any other type of swap contract (credit default or interest rate), fixed and floating cash flows are exchanged at predetermined dates. In a standard interest rate swap, the counterparty

accepts a floating rate and makes a fixed one to edge against any fluctuations in interest rates. In a credit default swap, a protection buyer
would pay a fixed amount—say, 125 basis points—annually to receive
$10 million of credit protection on some reference company.

In a longevity swap, fixed and floating cash flows are exchanged
based not on interest rates or default risk but on life expectancy. XYZ
Pension Fund and ABC Investment Bank may identify a specific
cohort by which to analyze their expected mortality probability. Sup-
pose that, out of a group of 5,000 seniors above the age of 65, .5%
matures in year 1, 1.5% in year 2, 3% in year 3, and so on. The pension fund would then pay some fixed coupon to the investment bank
based on these *expected* mortality probabilities, and the investment
bank would pay the pension fund based on *actual* mortality probabilities. Throughout the duration of the swaps contract, each counterparty may also be required to post collateral based on actual and
expected mortalities quarterly or annually.

Pension funds have historically looked at freezing their pension
plans or turning to pension buyout schemes, whereby a third party
assumes the assets and liabilities of a pension program under the
Employee Retirement Income Security Act of 1974. ERISA governs
company-run pension plans, establishes a set of standards and protocols, and requires that the assets be invested with "care, skill, pru-
dence, and diligence." Due to large pension deficits incurred from
the credit crisis, this is an unattractive proposition to buyout firms.
This has further bolstered the longevity swaps business, although it
should be noted that some investors view longevity swaps as a synthetic exposure to pension buyouts.

The first such longevity swap deal was transacted between Babcock International in the UK and Credit Suisse in 2009. The deal was
written to limit Babcock's Davenport Royal Dockyard defined benefit
liabilities to roughly $482 million. The firm plans to insure an addi-
tion $750 million. In this structure, the pension scheme will make
fixed monthly payments to Credit Suisse in exchange for mortality-
contingent payments from a pool of 4,500 retirees.

Steven Dicker, senior consultant at Watson Wyatt, which acted
as lead adviser, said: "This flagship deal heralds the launch of a new

market in longevity risk. Longevity swaps have been talked about for years but, until now, there was no precedent of a satisfactory contract being drawn up. By demonstrating the technical obstacles can be overcome, a dockyard better known for supporting the Royal Navy's battleships and submarines has boosted the armory of trustees and employers who want to reduce pension risks."

Another major deal was closed between Deutsche Bank's Abbey Life subsidiary and BMW in 2010. BMW purchased roughly $4.8 billion worth of longevity insurance from Deutsche Bank in February 2010, which was the forth such deal in two years. This landmark deal also contributed to the $11 billion of longevity protection written at the time, which was double the value of traditional pension buyouts.

Longevity bonds (see Figure 2.2) offer yet another way to participate in the longevity markets. These bonds, issued by a reinsurance company or investment bank, make a floating payment based on the survival of a specific population cohort. The coupon is set to the number of surviving individuals in that cohort in any given year. For example, a bond issued on January 1, 2011 may offer an 8% coupon based on a cohort of 1,000 individuals age 65, living in the UK, and composed of an equal mix of males and females. By January 1, 2016, this cohort has all turned 70, but roughly 500 have passed away in this five-year period. So the coupon would have declined annually in proportion to the number of deaths in the pool to its current level of 4%. The bond will continue to pay some coupon until all of the 1,000 reference individuals have passed away, which could take more than 15 years. Longevity bonds can be conceptualized as an inverse life annuity and therefore can act as a hedge for annuity providers.

Although the longevity market has experienced a tremendous amount of growth, clear barriers still exist. For example, longevity swaps, unlike other derivative transactions, are not yet governed through documents drafted from the International Swaps and Derivatives Association (ISDA), but the group is making an effort. Moreover, transparent and accurate longevity data is necessary because it is the underpinnings of all these transactions. In recent years, to provide further clarity on the market, several investment banks and reinsurance companies have started publishing life-linked indices:

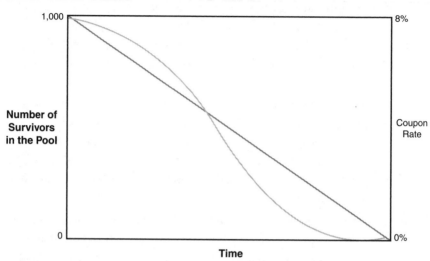

Figure 2.2   Sample survival curve versus a bond coupon

- **The Credit Suisse Longevity Index^sm:** Released in December 2005, this is the first index designed to enable the structuring and settlement of longevity risk transfer instruments such as longevity swaps and longevity structured notes. The Index is intended for use by institutional and retail investors, insurance companies, reinsurance companies, providers of post-retirement benefits, and other longevity and mortality risk managers. By providing market participants with a single, transparent reference tool, Credit Suisse believes the Index, SubIndices, and underlying mortality rates will spur the development of a liquid, tradeable market in longevity risk. Credit Suisse and Milliman, the Index calculation agent, will release the CSLI annually. It is based on government mortality and population statistics, initially for the U.S. population.

- **The LifeMetrics Index^sm:** Launched by J.P. Morgan in March 2007, this is a toolkit for measuring and managing longevity and mortality risk, designed by J.P. Morgan for pension plans, sponsors, insurers, reinsurers, and investors. LifeMetrics enables these risks to be measured in a standardized manner, aggregated across different risk sources, and transferred to other parties. It also provides a means to evaluate the effectiveness of longevity/mortality hedging strategies and the size of residual risk. LifeMetrics advisors include Towers Watson and the Pensions Institute at Cass Business School.

- **ICAP market derivatives that reference vivaDex^{sm} defined-pool longevity indices:** Defined-pool longevity indices, first engineered by SwapsMarket^{sm}, reference pensions, annuities, life settlements, and other life-contingent assets or liabilities affected by alpha- and beta-longevity risk. The underlying pools can be an investor's aggregation of life settlements or can be synthetic pools of insured grouped with similar characteristics, such as health impairment or cohort (age bracket). An example might be "75- to 77-year-old non-smoking males, table 8-10 impairment." Defined-pool swaps are collateralized with cash margin and expire every year for the expected life of the pool. When strung together, the swaps allow market participants to hedge exposures as short as two years and as long as 15 years, as well as enable yield-conversion strategies.[1]

Goldman Sachs also created a longevity index known as the QxX index, but it was discontinued in 2010 due to minimal to nonexistent activity.

Longevity swaps and bonds are basically forms of reinsurance designed to protect against the very slow-moving economic risk of longer-living retirees. Extreme mortality bonds (also called XXX bonds) protect against random, completely unforeseen spikes in human mortality. Unlike longevity link instruments, mortality structures are not focused on simply elderly individuals, but on the broader population. Similar to the structure of a typical natural catastrophe bond ("cat bond"), which offers insurance coverage against certain losses caused by hurricanes, floods, windstorms, and so on, mortality bonds provide coverage against bird flu, swine flu, or any other pandemic that would create havoc in the financial sector.

The structure of these bonds in their simplest form is as follows: An investor purchasing a morality bond would receive an annual coupon payment for a specified amount of time, possibly a bond that costs $100 and pays 7% for five years. Attached to the bond is a pre-determined threshold of mortality linked to the bond seller's books. If the bond issuer (or seller) is a life insurance company, for example, the mortality threshold could be estimated losses the carrier would suffer if swine flu killed 5% of its customers. In such an extreme event, the carrier may not have the funds to make good on the life insurance policies owned by its customers, so an extreme mortality hedge is necessary. In the event of extreme mortality, the bond buyer's funds would be used to pay the insurance carrier's losses. If no such event occurs during the five-year period, the investor would have his principal returned and would have earned the 7% annual coupons for five years. The thresholds on these bonds can be defined in a number of ways:

- **Indemnity:** Triggered by the issuer's actual losses.
- **Modeled loss:** As opposed to actual losses, use modeled simulations to determine a hypothetical threshold.
- **Indexed to industry loss:** Total loss of a specific industry or through the use of a longevity mortality index.
- **Parametric:** The degree to which the extreme mortality would occur.
- **Parametric index:** More applicable to natural catastrophe bonds, rather than extreme mortality bonds.

Although covered separately in this section, pools of life settlement policies are sometimes grouped as mortality bonds; however, their uses differ from what was just described. Figure 2.3 groups both but still accurately reflects the growth in the XXX bond category.

On November 24, 2009, Swiss Re sold roughly $75 million of mortality bonds, which insured against potential losses triggered by the swine flu or terrorist attacks. According to a statement, investors will receive 6.17% above a benchmark rate provided that mortality rates do not exceed a predetermined "trigger" level.

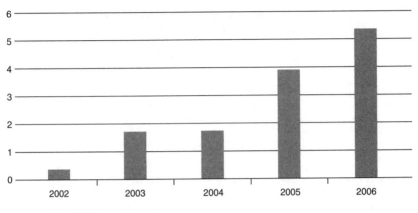

Figure 2.3   XXX bond issuance

Source: Fitch Ratings

Longevity Risk: The Nail in Japan's Coffin

In my opinion, there is no better example of the economic implications of an aging society than Japan, the oldest and most indebted nation on the planet. Although some of the problems facing Japan's economy were mentioned in the preceding chapter, this section provides a more detailed view of the negative effects of longevity and mortality risk when it is misunderstood and poorly managed. Japan's problems are nothing new and have been written about extensively by economists and research analysts. In fact, many have even tried to bet against Japan—namely, through Japanese government bonds (JGBs)—wagering that close to 0% interest rates would rise through the 1990s and even the early part of the 2000s. These investors have almost always been wrong, and many within the hedge fund community deemed this kind of trade "the widow maker." But the missing component in all the analysis is demographics. Not that anyone ignored the demographic component, but 10 or 15 years ago the population was, well, 10 or 15 years younger. As mentioned in Chapter 1, starting in 2010, Japan's population has been in secular decline. In addition, people are living much longer in Japan; it has one the longest average life expectancies in the world. This growing number of seniors is putting a tremendous strain on public and private retirement systems. And because these seniors are the largest lenders to the Japanese government, any change in the financial stability of this cohort could spell disaster for the country as a whole. Although demographers have seen Japan's demographic problem coming for years, it's a very difficult dilemma to solve, so the problem has not been addressed in any material way. More than anything the nation has severe leadership issues, shuffling through several financial ministers and other key government posts in only a few years.

Fiscal Troubles: An Economic Background

Comparing Japan's GDP to other financial statistics helps us evaluate the effectiveness of monetary policy in line with current and future growth prospects. Throughout the early 2000s, Japan and the U.S. have been running relatively large fiscal deficits—approximately 6% and 3–4% of the GDP, respectively. These numbers, while important to consider, do not seem outrageous by themselves. Looking at the countries' debt-to-GDP ratios, however, reveals a much different story. In 1991, Japan's debt-to-GDP ratio stood near the average for all the G7 countries, but it was lower than the ratio for Italy, Canada, and the U.S. Ten years later, Japan led the G7 nations with a ratio of approximately 120%. This number would continue to grow at a rate of 10% a year, further separating Japan's indebtedness from that of the rest of the world. As of February 2011, Japan has above a 190% debt-to-GDP ratio. It is projected to surpass 200% by the end of the year. That would make it the highest debt-to-GDP ratio seen out of wartime by any developed country. Japan's debt-to-GDP ratio is almost double that of Greece, whose ratio stands at 115.1%. Interestingly, Greece, Portugal, Spain, and Ireland receive the majority of attention regarding the likelihood of sovereign debt defaults. These "Club Med" nations have contributed far less value to the global economy than Japan, the third-largest economy in the world with a GDP of roughly $5.39 trillion. China surpassed Japan as the second-largest economy ($5.75 trillion) at the end of 2010, a trend that is sure to continue.

In Hubbard and Ito's 2005 "Overview of the Japanese Debt Question," the authors point out the importance of considering net liabilities as opposed to simply "gross" domestic product.[2] In other words, the government of Japan has a number of assets on its balance sheet, such as its own government and agency bonds as well as other securities, natural resources, foreign currencies, and so on. Japan owns roughly $1 trillion for foreign exchange reserves, of which about $882 billion is held in U.S. Treasuries. It is also important to note that, in contrast to other largely indebted nations such as the U.S., Japan has very little in the way of natural resources. Crude oil reserves in Japan are a marginal 45 million barrels as of 2010. To put that into perspective, Canada and the U.S. have some 179 and 21 million barrels of crude oil in reserves, respectively. Japan's buffer of assets is limited to the securities owned by the government. When we take these assets into account and look at the ratio of net debt-to-GDP ratio, the fiscal problems in Japan look much less severe. In 2004, the net debt-to-GDP ratio was only 80%. Even when looking at the net ratio, however, the Organization for Economic Cooperation and Development (OECD) predicted last year that Japan's 2010 net debt-to-GDP ratio would reach 104.6%. According to many economists, any nation with a gross debt-to-GDP ratio is at severe risk of default, let alone a net number.

When analyzing the fiscal health of any business, especially one that carries a substantial amount of debt, a prospective investor or lender attempts to gauge the company's ability to service its debt. It also would look at how much revenue would need to be generated to turn a profit after satisfying its interest payments. A nation is no different. If a business issues 10-year debt around 1% on average but still struggles to meet its financial obligations, I believe a lender would start running in the other direction. In the case of Japan, this is not hypothetical but rather economic fact.

Japan's outstanding debt has nearly tripled in the last three decades. Yet the government has enjoyed the privilege of paying extremely low interest on its debt to investors—less than 1% in most cases. Although the average rate paid in 1970 was approximately 6%, the number dipped below just 1.5% in 2009. Additionally, the spread between 10-year and 2-year JGBs has narrowed from more than 170 basis points in 2004 to less than 50 basis points last year. Now, add to

the picture the fact that well over 90% of all outstanding JGBs are
held by domestic investors. The Bank of Japan (BOJ) itself holds
upwards of $500 billion in bonds on its balance sheet. According to
Hugh Pym, chief economics correspondent for BBC News Tokyo,
"risk-averse small savers, pension funds, and institutions"[3] are the
main groups that are content to hold JGBs. The fact that nearly all
JGB subscribers come from within Japan acts as a sort of cover-up for
the mountain of debt that has been steadily increasing over the years.
In other words, in terms of debt issuance, the Japanese government
has never had to worry about the global perception of its fiscal state.
This is clearly no longer the case, as many problems have begun to
surface on a public (both national and global) scale. The fact that six
different officials have been elected Minister of Finance since 2008
signals that Japanese leaders recognize the need for change—an issue
we will cover in depth while assessing the need for social change. In
addition, the savings rate for both corporations and households has
fallen to all-time low levels as the result of an aging population.
Although the Japanese historically have been considered to be the
world's greatest savers (as measured by the amount saved as a percentage of household income), today this is not the case. Throughout
the mid-1970s, the internal savings rate was approximately 20% of
disposable income. In 2009, this number was just above 2%, in a year
in which the fiscal deficit stood at around 7% of GDP. Such a low savings rate means that the internal demand for JGBs will inevitably
decrease, because citizens will no longer have the money to purchase
government assets. In fact, it has already begun to do so. With average yields on 2-, 5-, 10-, and 30-year JGBs at 0.19, 0.43, 1.21, and
2.12%, respectively, it will be difficult to attract a meaningful number
of outside investors without significantly raising interest rates to levels competitive with the U.S. and Germany. So what does this mean?
Harvard economist Martin Feldstein describes the situation as a "vis-
cous spiral of rising deficits and debt that would be likely to push
interest rates even higher, causing the spiral to accelerate."[4] Furthermore, the growing deficits will ultimately have a crushing effect on
Japan's current account surplus. A country's current account equals
its balance of trade (exports less imports) net interest payments and

government transfer payments. For years, Japan has maintained a current account surplus because of its high private savings rate, an achievement on which it will no longer be able to rely. Feldstein makes it clear that "[Japan's] cycle of rising deficits and debt will soon make national savings negative."

In addition to the falling (near zero) savings rate, the nation has suffered from a tremendous decline in tax revenues (see Figure 2.4). Japan's tax revenues, a nation's lifeline, are at the same level as 1986, whereas its debt has tripled during the same time. A strengthening yen, which is fatal for an export-based economy such as Japan, a shrinking workforce, and the negative impact of the recent economic crisis all play a role in the declining tax revenue. Furthermore, as the yield on the government's debt rises, more of the tax revenue must be allocated to servicing interest payments. According to the 2010 budget, 25% of the government's expenditures are debt service, and rates hover around 1%. Moreover, an additional 30% or so is allotted to social security (see Figure 2.5)!

The problem does not stop here. Japan's dire outlook will also have a negative effect on a number of major nations across the globe. As of November 2010, Japan is the world's second-largest holder of U.S. Treasuries, with over $768 billion worth of American bonds on its books. Only China and the U.S. Federal Reserve own more. At some point, Japan will need to sell its foreign exchange reserves to purchase yen to fund its yen-denominated obligations. The largest of these obligations would be maturing debt and social security for retirees. Ironically, if the BOJ needed to swap U.S. dollars, euros, and pounds for yen, it might strengthen the yen, which would further cripple Japanese exports, further weakening the economy. Net selling of U.S. Treasuries by Japan would have a negative effect on the U.S., which currently maintains an approximately 85% debt-to-GDP ratio. If Japan liquidates a sizable portion of its foreign holdings, it could possibly send prices tumbling. This would increase the borrowing cost of the U.S. government, which faces its own looming social security crisis.

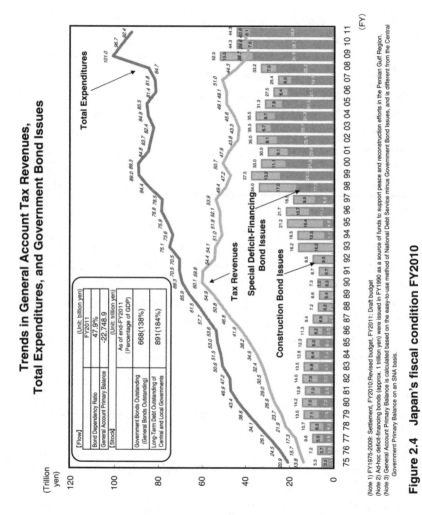

Figure 2.4   Japan's fiscal condition FY2010

Source: Japanese Ministry of Finance

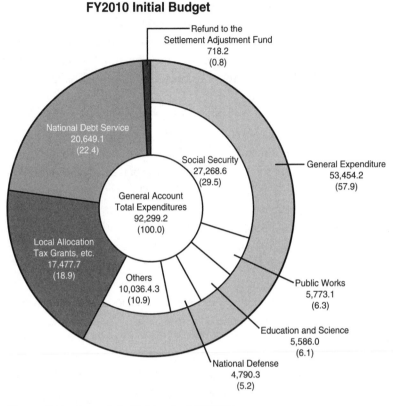

FY2010 Initial Budget

Refund to the
Settlement Adjustment Fund
718.2
(0.8)

National Debt Service
20,649.1
(22.4)

Social Security
27,268.6
(29.5)

General Expenditure
53,454.2
(57.9)

General Account
Total Expenditures
92,299.2
(100.0)

Local Allocation
Tax Grants, etc.
17,477.7
(18.9)

Others
10,036.4.3
(10.9)

Public Works
5,773.1
(6.3)

Education and Science
5,586.0
(6.1)

National Defense
4,790.3
(5.2)

Figure 2.5   Japan's initial budget FY2010

Source: Japanese Ministry of Finance

As mentioned earlier, another serious concern involves the appreciation of Japan's currency. The Japanese yen (JPY) reached a 15-year high against the U.S. dollar (USD) in October 2010. Ultimately, a strong currency makes Japanese exports more expensive for other countries and, therefore, significantly less competitive on a global stage. Japan's recovery from the 2008 recession is considered by many to be entirely dependent on the return in demand for its exports. Its most prominent exports are automobile and motor-related equipment, machinery, and vehicles; semiconductors and other electrical computing supplies; and pharmaceutical and medical equipment. In a September 2010 speech, Japanese Minister of Finance Yoshihiko Noda warned that "recent movements [in the yen] will have adverse effects on the stability of economic and financial conditions." Noda's finance ministry and the BOJ have proven that they will not shy away from artificial stimulus. However, the late-August 2010 meeting of the BOJ involved discussions and an eventual implementation of currency intervention. Adding to the JPY dilemma is, yet again, the fact that it is far from isolated. This issue must be considered a global issue instead of one confined to Japan or the Far East. Successful and impactful monetary intervention requires the cooperation of all nations involved, whether via trades and exports, foreign exchange reserves, or political motivations. Because domestic demand for its most popular products has been relatively dull for the past decade, Japan largely depends on its high-growth neighbor, China, and the distant U.S. for economic prosperity. Major Japanese-based global conglomerates such as Sony and Toyota depend on a healthy export economy (external demand) to maintain respectable levels of profitability. The recent sovereign debt crisis in Europe coupled with the slow recovery in the U.S. will make it extremely difficult for Japan to stir up external demand. It should be noted, however, that a weaker yen also lowers the cost of importing, which helps make up for Japan's utter lack of natural resources. Despite the advantages of cheaper oil and other imported commodities, at the moment the costs of a strong yen far outweigh the benefits. Although the many fiscal issues could indeed be cause for concern individually, this is only the contextual backdrop for analyzing a more significant matter—demographics (in particular, longevity risk).

Demographics

Chapter 1 highlighted the importance of demographics through concepts such as "the spending life cycle" and other ways in which demographics can influence economies. This chapter has examined how corporations and governments can use the longevity/mortality risk markets to hedge the impact of population change—namely, longer-living populations. The economic issues plaguing Japan, which have already been highlighted, are compounded exponentially by Japan's severe demographic problem—longevity risk. Unfortunately, demographics cannot be changed by economic policy.

According to traditional demographic standards, a society in which 7% of the citizens are age 65 and older is considered to be "aging," and a society in which 14% of the people are older than 65 is termed "aged." Although it has taken many of the world's developed countries between 50 and 100 years to transform from aging to aged—more than 65 years in the U.S. and 115 years in France—Japan's transition has occurred in just 24 years. One of the main reasons for this short time frame has to do with the extreme lengthening of life expectancies in Japan post-World War II. Between 1947 and 1970, the life expectancy for males in Japan increased from 50.1 to 69.3 and from 54 to 74.7 for females. In many ways, the longer life spans were the result of what historians have called Japan's postwar "economic miracle"—the fiery growth of the country's economy. This resulted from foreign investment, vertical integration of large corporate enterprises, and industry-wide cooperation. Additionally, substantial American investment and economic intervention allowed for enormous growth and, in turn, unforeseen technological and medical development. During this period, individuals and families saw drastic increases in both their personal and cumulative household incomes. Ultimately, Japanese citizens were able to take better care of themselves and live healthier and more productive lives. Japan's National Institute of Population and Social Security Research (NIPSSR) has published a series of fascinating charts depicting the country's "population pyramid"[5] (see Figures 2.6 through 2.8). In 1950, the vast majority of the country's population was younger than 55. As with any baby-boom decade, most are under the age of 20. By 2010, however, the visualization looked quite different—more like a diamond than a pyramid, a change indicative of the population's upward age shift. Here, more than 50% of Japanese citizens are between 25 and 65 years of age. NIPSSR predicts that the chart will take on the shape of a kite by 2050, as more people age and the percentage of young people continues to decline. Between the years 2045 and 2055, it is forecast with high probability that Japan's working-age population will shrink to a size smaller than its 1950 levels, with four out of 10 citizens over the age of 65.

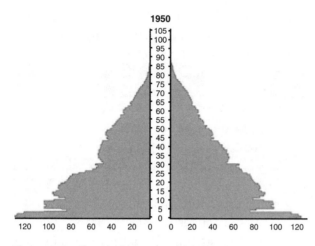

Figure 2.6   Population pyramid 1950

Source: NIPSSR

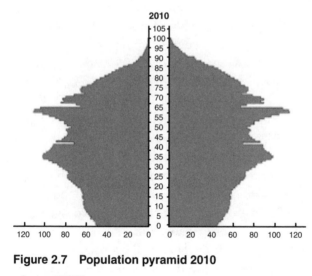

Figure 2.7   Population pyramid 2010

Source: NIPSSR

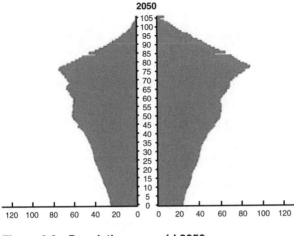

Figure 2.8 Population pyramid 2050

Source: NIPSSR

Because of Japan's aging population—indeed, Japan is now the oldest country in the world, with three people of working age for every person of pensionable age (a ratio expected to increase to 1:1 by 2040)—an overall decrease in population size has already started to occur. This decrease is largely due to a mortality rate that is higher than the current fertility rate. Despite efforts by the Japanese government to increase the birth rate throughout the 1970s, Japan's current level of 1.3 children per woman solidifies its status as one of the lowest-birth-rate countries in the world. Due to the almost unbreakable relationship between childbirth and marriage, it is especially difficult to increase procreation rates in Japan's modern society. A growing number of younger women are deciding to marry later in life or to remain unmarried indefinitely. Another problem is that private companies rarely reserve positions for women who want to return to work following a maternity leave. Therefore, women who want to reenter the workforce usually accept temporary or irregular positions, often backtracking in terms of job prestige and qualifications. For these reasons, it is clear that childbearing at a young age is neither attractive nor realistic for the vast majority of Japanese women. The fact that Japan's population is both aging and shrinking, then, is a dual threat to the world's third-largest economy. Ultimately, the working-age-versus-pensionable-age ratio, or dependency ratio, is one of the most important tools when determining the effect of demographics on economic growth. Economists around the globe agree that a healthy working-age population is necessary for any sort of meaningful productivity; put simply, GDP requires labor to grow.

Japan's historically high savings rate and its resulting investment in productive capacity are useless without a workforce in place to utilize them. When compared to the other G7 nations, Japan's working-age population has been diminishing by the largest percentage per year since 1995. It's expected to decrease by just under 1.5% between 2035 and 2045. This statistic alone is enough to predict that Japan's economic growth due to labor productivity will lag far behind the rest of the developed world and ultimately will be responsible for meager if not negative GDP growth.

Some people hope that immigration may be able to save Japan, but most consider this idea far-fetched for such a closed society. Japan's immigration policy has historically been one of the strictest in the world. The 1952 Immigration Control Law was the first prominent legal framework for solidifying immigration policy in postwar Japan. Although not explicitly stated in writing, it became clear that in many ways it was designed to prevent the permanent settlement of foreigners in Japan. This veiled implication seems to have made its way into the revised immigration policy in place today. In 2004, the Justice Ministry amended the Immigration and Control and Refugee Recognition Act to further decrease the number of foreigners allowed into the country. As a result, only a quarter of a million new immigrants enter each year. The main disadvantage of importing foreign labor as a solution to the declining working-age population is that this would simply postpone the problem. Also, immigrant labor has its costs. As Kotlikoff and Fehr argue in their 2004 paper titled "The Role of Immigration in Dealing with the Developed World's Demographic Transition," "Immigrants are not free. They require public goods and services, and they also demand the same transfer payments as the indigenous population."[6] The authors ultimately conclude that using immigrants to solve productivity-related economic issues would "likely cost the Japanese fiscal authorities almost as much as they would generate in additional revenues." Similar conclusions are found by McKinsey & Co. in a study examining the household savings rate in Japan: "Increasing immigration, even at the highest levels projected by government statistics, is not large enough to change overall demographic structure, and thus does not materially impact net financial wealth accumulation." When looking at the historical numbers of immigrants, one might become justifiably skeptical when assessing the possibility of a changing attitude toward immigration. Between the years of 1975 and 2001, total immigration accounted for less than 1.5% of the total 2001 population. This minimal percentage of new entrants into Japan highlights the magnitude of change necessary to combat the looming demographic threats.

The major issue with a demographic problem, such as the one in Japan, is that it hinders future growth as well. Not only are current assets eaten away by ballooning pension and debt liabilities, but the shrinking workforce stifles future progress. Japan's bread and butter has been technology—the ability to export cutting-edge appliances and electronics to the rest of the world. Why can't Japan simply innovate its way out of its problems? Unfortunately, Japan's population is shrinking much faster than any potential gains would arise. Who would manufacture these novel technological products? Possibly Korea? China? But other Asian nations are creating their own technologies that are more currency-friendly to the West and that are of equal if not better quality. LG, a South Korean company, is an excellent example. Moreover, outsourcing production will do little for Japan.

Although technological advancement could potentially relieve some of the pension and health care obligations that come as a result of the aging epidemic, it is by no means guaranteed that Japan's political and financial leaders would act accordingly. It is extremely difficult to accurately measure the rate of technological growth in an industry, local economy, or country. A widely accepted method is to use the measure of the Solow residual—a number describing the growth in an industry or economy that cannot be explained by the accumulation of capital or other factors such as an increase in land or labor.

According to Kato, "a 1% difference in the annual rate of technological progress results in a substantial difference in future GDP over the relevant horizon."[7] Technological progress in Japan as measured by variations of the Solow residual has hovered around zero for the past 20 years. Kato's projections show that a 1% reduction in the rate of technological progress can produce an approximately 18% fall in per capita income—a significant statistic to consider when evaluating the effectiveness of instituting nationwide technology-boosting programs. Bessho, Ihori, et al.'s general equilibrium model predicts that an expansion of future technological progress both helps increase GDP and "results in an increase in the future equilibrium interest rate." This rise in the interest rate is a particularly important finding because of its unavoidable association with rising interest payments on Japanese government debt. The authors suggest that a significant raise in the consumption tax rate will be necessary to finance the massive amount of outstanding debt. The issue of openness, although already discussed in terms of immigration, has much to do with technological development as well. Many U.S. and European conglomerates accumulate talent from around the globe to develop the most innovative and advanced products. They realize that brilliant entrepreneurship is both a finite and limited resource and that an outward-looking attitude is a prerequisite for success. On the contrary, the Japanese rely almost solely on homegrown scientists and engineers to conduct any sort of extensive research and development programs.

When looking at Japan's aging problem, we must step back and realize that, as an isolated topic, longer life spans for Japanese citizens is primarily a good thing. This means that the population is healthy and has access to world-leading medical technologies, and that the overall quality of life is superior to many other countries. As expressed by Henry J. Aaron in his Brookings Institution working paper titled "Medium-Term Strategies for Long-Term Goals," "rather than being bad news, increased longevity is the culmination of human efforts spanning centuries to extend the duration and quality of life."[8] Surely Japan cannot morally consider diminishing the budget for medical development and life-saving pharmaceutical innovations. Aside from the two major propositions discussed in this chapter, a number of minor yet certainly plausible suggestions have been put forward.

First, we consider the effect of increased female presence within Japan's working-age and elder workforce population. 1968 marked the first year since World War II in which the younger working-age population began to decline (particularly those aged 20 to 39). Here,

Japanese companies turned to a new source of labor to fill the rapidly enlarging gaps—middle-aged women. Less than a decade later, in 1976, the percentage of employed women aged 40 to 54 would begin to increase. The salaries of these women were tremendously low compared to industry averages, however, and firms invested most of these low-pay-related savings into automation techniques. It was widely believed at the time that the automation of rudimentary tasks would lead to indefinitely sustainable increases in firmwide productivity. However, there is a certain level of capital intensiveness, K, where production output starts to flatten and value added begins to decrease. Each level of capital intensiveness beyond point K continues to see linearly rising production costs. Since the mid-1970s, Japan has operated to the right of the capital intensiveness threshold—to the right of K—artificially pushing production beyond the healthy levels supported by a combination of human and automated labor. Such irrational corporate behavior is largely responsible for sluggishness in any sizable economy. According to a 2008 report by the OECD, Japan is in last place in terms of utilizing the available pool of well-educated female workers. The report calls Japan's gender-related hiring practices a "considerable waste of valuable human resources...which need to be addressed urgently, notably in the actual context of population aging." This inefficient and discriminatory labor usage is particularly surprising in light of the fact that Japanese women are as a whole better educated than in nearly all other OECD countries. (Only Canada and Finland have a greater percentage of women with university degrees.) While the OECD average of women with college degrees stands around 28.5%, over 42% of Japanese women possess such academic qualifications.

A November 2010 special report in *The Economist* highlights the gap between male and female workforce participation as being "larger than any other developed country." This has much to do with the fact that women are not given the same opportunity to succeed via firm-specific managerial programs—programs designed to nurture talent internally and develop future executives. More often than not, males are considered to be the ideal candidates for such "managerial fast track" programs. Gender-biased hiring practices can be seen at all levels of the corporate world. As of 2011, only 16 female executives exist within Japan's equivalent of the Fortune 100.

Japan will need to devote serious effort to finding a feasible solution sooner rather than later. Of course, this will be a combination of efforts instead of a single, solve-all proposition. We have not yet discussed Japan's pension system, which, as it turns out, is one of the nation's top issues—a culmination of the problems related to labor shortages and an aging society. Along with the title of the oldest population in the world comes a tremendous strain on Japan's pension and health care systems, as well as the potential change in both corporate and personal tax structure. Because of unprecedented economic growth throughout the 1960s and 1970s, the Japanese pension system was globally renowned as one of the world's most generous. Accordingly, a pay-as-you-go scheme was most appropriate for a booming economic climate and favorable demographic composition. However, after decades of economic stagnation throughout the late 1990s and 2000s, change would become necessary. If benefits were to remain at their 1960s and 1970s levels, Japanese citizens would have to contribute more than one-fourth of their annual income. Because of the severely depressed savings rate of the average Japanese household, this would be demographically impossible. Therefore, the 2004 pension revision sought "to delicately balance benefits and contributions over the next century." This particular revision established that Japanese citizens would contribute a growing percentage of their income each year until 2017, at which point the rate would be frozen at 18.3% of income. Also, the age at which citizens may receive pension benefits was set to gradually increase over time. This pension structure is predicted to decrease benefits by approximately ¥350 trillion by 2100. According to Kohei Komamura's 2007 study in the *Japanese Journal of Social Security Policy*, such a reduction would move the ratio of pension expenditures to GDP below its current level to 9% by the year 2025.

Despite the steps taken to prevent a collapse of the outdated pension system, much of its success is only predicted or hypothetical. We have yet to see how it will fare when placed alongside the other economic issues. A November 30, 2010 article in the *Financial Times* titled "Japan Looks at Pension Fund to Cover Shortfall"[9] is a perfect example of a potential impediment to the success of pension system reform. With the government expected to pay half of all pension benefits, extracting capital from the pension reserve fund could prove to be an irreversible mistake. Ultimately, the government faces the formidable challenge of devising a pension scheme that increases old-age benefits with the aid of a shrinking working-age population. According to Yoshihiko Noda, "it will be extremely difficult to secure the ¥2,500 billion (approximately $300 billion) in financing needed to meet the treasury's obligation."

Social/Cultural Issues

Japan's fiscal and demographic problems will ultimately trigger the need for social change as well. Corporate rigidity, seniority-based compensation, and lifetime employment guarantees are just a few traditional Japanese customs requiring revision if Japan is to move from economic stagnation to consistent growth. As Akihiko asserts in *Shrinking Population Economics: Lessons from Japan*: "The demographic change under way in Japan thus mandates fundamental change in economic policy and in business management."[10] We will explore this change in management, business processes, and leadership.

The practice of "lifetime employment" has been used by many major Japanese firms since the nation's period of unprecedented economic growth post-World War II. As argued by Chiaki Moriguchi and Hiroshi Ono in their 2004 paper "Japanese Lifetime Employment: A Century's Perspective," the practice is "[both] an economic [and] a social institution"[11] that is "characterized by an implicit contract and reciprocal exchange of trust, goodwill, and commitment between employers and workers." Emphasis must be placed on the social forces at play, because Japanese cultural standards and traditions are held to be of the utmost importance. In economic terms, many scholars have argued against lifetime employment as an effective practice, mainly stating its inability to coexist with financial uncertainty. That is, guaranteed lifelong employment leaves minimal room for labor flexibility in a fluctuating business climate. Ono's 2010 discussion about the actual measurement of lifetime employment statistics in Japan stresses that "the falling birth rate and the rigid employment system are in fact intricately linked." The main reason for this is the difficulty of returning to work following a period of extended absence. Clearly this reality is especially difficult for women returning from maternity leave, and therefore may be considered a significant cause of Japan's rapidly declining fertility rates. As a result, Japanese employers may have to revamp their hiring practices to become both more flexible and attractive to those searching for a reasonable work-life balance.

With the oldest population in the world, Japanese companies will have to evaluate how such a shift in demographics (namely, the change in age structure) will affect their day-to-day operations. Product lines and processes will ultimately need to undergo some major revisions, which will likely involve the streamlining of wasteful operating procedures and the downsizing of the workforce in divisions no longer contributing to the firm's bottom line. Akihiko asserts that lifetime employment "would hinder companies in accomplishing the transformation necessitated by Japan's shrinking and aging population." In line with the changing business landscape, companies will need the flexibility to either increase or decrease their workforce and make selective hiring decisions based on new products and new demand. Japanese firms' hesitancy to stray from such a uniquely Japanese tradition has been the primary blockade to a much-needed social transition.

The dispersion and deflection of responsibility at all levels of Japanese society is another element that does not go well with accepting and embracing the need for change. This is clearly evident when looking at the number of different leaders within the Japanese government since 2006. For example, Junichiro Koizumi, Prime Minister of Japan from 2001 to 2006, is the only prime minister since 1972 to last more than five years in office. Since the end of Koizumi's tenure in September 2006, there have been five prime ministers, 11 agricultural ministers, six foreign ministers, six ministers of internal affairs and communications, seven defense ministers, and eight finance ministers. It should be noted that the term length of each position is four years or less, and legislation states that "no limits are imposed on total times or length of Prime Minister tenures of the same person." A November 2010 article in *The Economist* argues that "any sensible democracy should know that changing ministers so quickly is detrimental to policymaking."[12] This is clearly the case in Japan, because the rapid leadership change will ultimately delay any decision making regarding its dangerous levels of debt and deflation. Additionally, strong and intelligent leadership across all government ministries is necessary to drive internal growth within an elderly society. Change, specifically within the Ministry of Finance, causes significant delays in the country's fiscal initiatives, because coordination between the MOF and the BOJ is crucial for currency interventions and other types of stimulative measures.

Conclusion

Although economists around the globe have had their eye on Japan's economic and fiscal state for a number of years, many have neglected the looming demographic catastrophe. The primary reason for this ignorance is the fact that decades have passed without any truly detrimental consequences. This chapter has shown why Japan's troubles can no longer be postponed. If the various government ministries work together and realize the need for swift and sweeping change, a crisis might be averted. Although other industrialized nations will ultimately face the daunting challenge of an aging population, Japan has the unfortunate privilege of being the first to weather (or fall victim to) the storm.

Endnotes

[1] See Antony Mott, Chapter 15, "Synthetics in Life Markets: Trading Mortality and Longevity Risk with Life Settlements and Linked Securities," 25-31 (Vishaal Bhuyan, ed., 2009), available at http://books.google.com/books?id= UkuzHLKPOW8C&pg=PA25&lpg=PA25&dq=debit+methodology&source= bl&ots=rdiU8mJ072&sig=GAxBEE2tyjnq1QHXIOB75i9xCh0&hl=en&ei= YgehS4nGI4aBlAfq6NCbDg&sa=X&oi=book_result&ct=result&resnum= 9&ved=0CDMQ6AEwCA#v=onepage&q=debit%20methodology&f=false (prerelease form).

[2] Hubbard, R.G. and Ito, T. "Overview of the Japanese Debt Question" (in Kaizuka and Krueger, 2006).

[3] Pym, Hugh. "Japan: Debt, Demographics and Deflation." *BBC News (Business)*. BBC, November 30, 2010. Online. December 10, 2010. http://www.bbc.co.uk/news/business-11867257.

[4] Feldstein, Martin. "Japan's Savings Crisis." *Daily News Egypt*, October 1, 2010. Online. December 10, 2010. http://belfercenter.ksg.harvard.edu/publication/20397/japans_savings_crisis.html.

[5] National Institute of Population and Social Security Research. "Population Pyramid 1955, 2010, 2055." Extracted from NIPSSR website, December 10, 2010. http://www.ipss.go.jp/sitead/TopPageData/Pyramid_a.html.

[6] Kotlikoff, L.J. and Burns, S. *The Coming Generational Storm*. Cambridge: MIT Press, 2004.

[7] Ihori, T., Kato, R., and Kawade, M. "Public Debt and Economic Growth in an Aging Japan." Working Paper, Faculty of Economics, University of Tokyo (2005).

[8] Aaron, Henry. "Medium-term Strategies for Long-term Goals," in *Tackling Japan's Fiscal Challenges: Strategies to Cope with High Public Debt and Population Aging*, edited by Keimei Kaizuka and Anne O. Krueger, International Monetary Fund, 2006, pp. 79-104.

[9] Whipp, Lindsay (for the *Financial Times*). "Japan Looks at Pension Fund to Cover Shortfall." *Financial Times*, November 30, 2010. Online. December 8, 2010. http://www.ft.com/cms/s/0/76330324-fcba-11df-bfdd-00144feab49a. html#axzz18gi4sEER.

[10] Akihiko, Matsutani. *Shrinking Population Economics: Lessons from Japan*. Tokyo: International House of Japan, 2006.

[11] Moriguchi, Chiaki and Ono, H. "Japanese Lifetime Employment: A Century's Perspective." EIJS Working Paper Series No. 205 (2006).

[12] Tricks, Henry (for *The Economist*). "Into the Unknown: A Special Report on Japan." *The Economist*, November 20, 2010.

3

Reverse Equity Transactions

A *reverse equity transaction* is a financial product that allows an individual—in this case, a senior citizen—to extract equity from an asset without the use of credit but rather life expectancy. For the sake of this discussion, reverse equity transactions may be defined as senior life settlements and reverse mortgages. These transactions have become increasingly popular with investors in recent years because they offer returns in the low to mid-teens that are largely uncorrelated to equities, fixed income, credit, real estate, and commodities. On the consumer side, these transactions can provide for health care and retirement costs in a person's golden years.

Many institutional investors (especially hedge funds and private equity funds with expertise in credit) conceptualize life settlements and reverse mortgages as structured financial products. They *securitize* or bundle the underlying cash flows and repackage hundreds of life insurance policies or reverse mortgage loans *en masse*. With the securitization market close to nonexistent, this is a tall order. From the standpoint of global-macro play, these transactions can be better described as a countercyclical value investment that for the purposes of this book hinges on uncertainty in the U.S. social security system. Simply put, as seniors (and baby boomers) approach retirement and find that their retirement funds have been wiped out due to the credit crisis, and social security is unable to honor their obligations, the value of the reverse equity asset class should become apparent.

Life Settlements

A *life settlement* (see Figure 3.1) is the sale of a life insurance policy from a policyholder to an investor (in most cases, a qualified institutional buyer[1]) through a state-regulated originator (provider) for an upfront cash payment. The investor in the policy makes all the subsequent premium payments to the insurance carrier and collects the death benefit upon the senior's death. For example, a 70-year-old man who has a $100,000 life insurance policy would sell his policy to an investor for $25,000 up front. The investor would become the policy's owner and would pay $3,500 per year in premiums to the insurance carrier until the senior's death. At that point, the investor would collect $100,000. Prior to purchasing the policy, the investor would obtain a life expectancy report. It would enable him to model the expected mortality of the insured and calculate how much he is willing to pay for the insurance contract. The transaction process and valuation are discussed later in this chapter. Figure 3.2 shows the cash flows associated with a life settlement from an investor's perspective.

The life settlement market has grown rapidly over the past few decades, growing from $50 million in 1990 to between $14 and $16 billion today (see Figure 3.3). According to Conning Research, in 2008 roughly $16 billion of policies were settled. Future market projections have been set at more than $160 billion over the next 10 to 15 years based on the size of the baby boomer population.

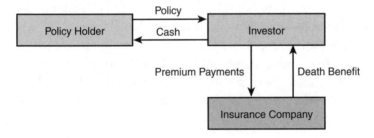

Figure 3.1   Basic life settlement

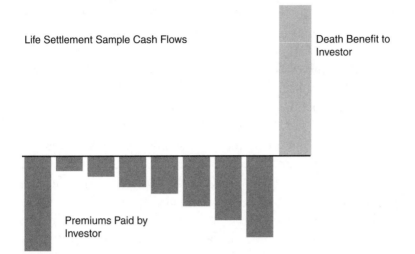

Figure 3.2   Life settlement cash flows

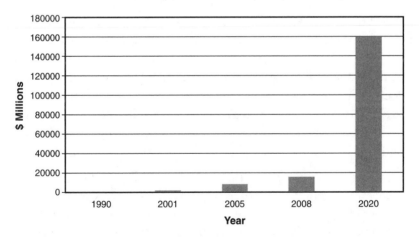

Figure 3.3   Life settlement market size (estimated)

The mainstream media views a life settlement as a macabre investment product. However, the actual mechanics of the transaction are no different from an annuity or pension plan that also has an economic interest in someone's death. The focus should be on seniors' ability to obtain market value for an asset they were not even aware they possessed. Moreover, the life settlement market consistently provides billions of dollars to seniors in exchange for a policy that otherwise would have lapsed. According to the Life Insurance Settlement Association (LISA), life settlements provide seniors with roughly $7 million per day in cash. On average, life settlements provide three to four times more money to senior policyholders than the cash surrender value provided by the insurance company. Life insurance companies in the U.S. enjoy very high lapse ratios; specifically, it is believed that almost 90% of life insurance lapses without paying a single death benefit claim. (Note that for policies purchased by individuals who are older than 65, the lapse ratios are much lower.)

Historical Context

The secondary market for life insurance in the U.S. was created in 1911, when a Supreme Court judge ruled that a life insurance policy should be treated like any other asset, similar to property, gold, silver, and so on. Therefore, a life insurance policy, like property, could be sold and transferred to a third party with no insurable interest[2] in the policy or stake in the well-being of the policy owner. The policyholder could name whomever he wanted as the beneficiary. Moreover, this legislation also allowed an individual to borrow against his life insurance policy. The following is an excerpt from the historic case that provided the foundation of the now multibillion-dollar life settlement market:

> The rule of public policy that forbids the taking out of insurance by one on the life of another in which he has no insurable interest does not apply to the assignment by the insured of a perfectly valid policy to one not having an insurable interest. In this case, *held* that the assignment by the insured of a perfectly valid policy to one not having any insurable interest but who paid a consideration therefore and afterwards paid the premiums thereon was valid, and the assignee was entitled to the proceeds from the insurance company as against the heirs of the deceased.[3]

Throughout the 1980s, life settlements were known as *viatical settlements* (see Figure 3.4). This term is used for life settlements in

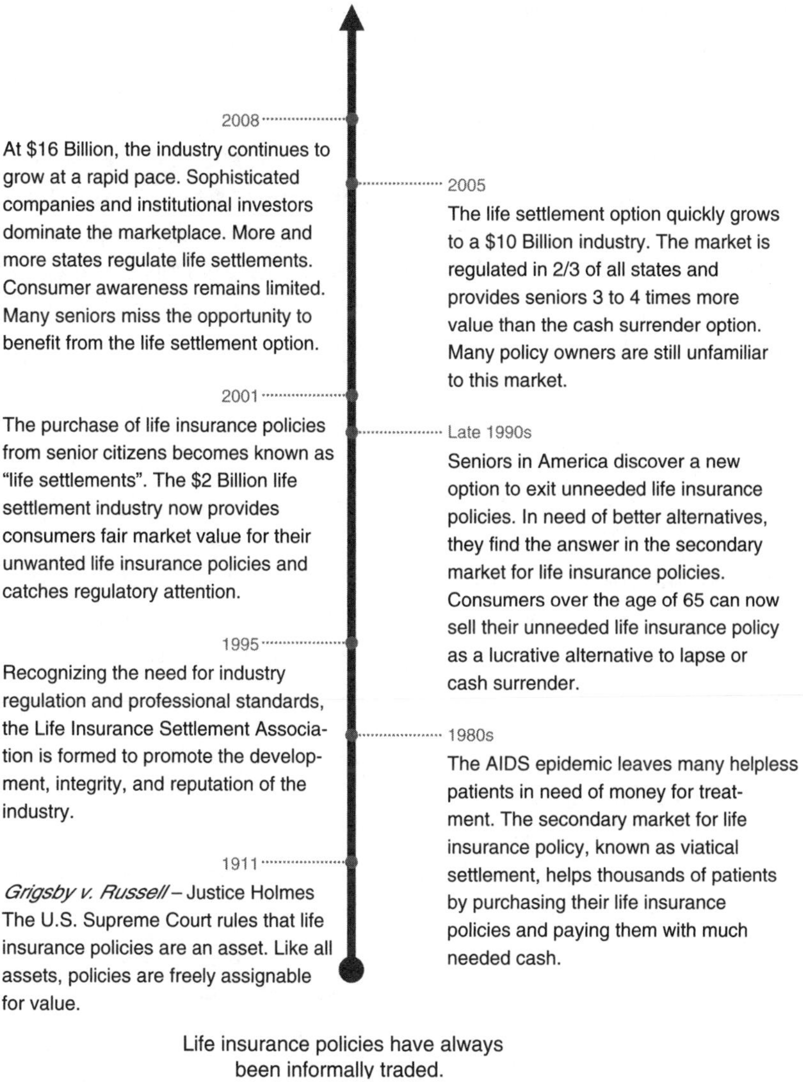

2008

At $16 Billion, the industry continues to grow at a rapid pace. Sophisticated companies and institutional investors dominate the marketplace. More and more states regulate life settlements. Consumer awareness remains limited. Many seniors miss the opportunity to benefit from the life settlement option.

2005

The life settlement option quickly grows to a $10 Billion industry. The market is regulated in 2/3 of all states and provides seniors 3 to 4 times more value than the cash surrender option. Many policy owners are still unfamiliar to this market.

2001

The purchase of life insurance policies from senior citizens becomes known as "life settlements". The $2 Billion life settlement industry now provides consumers fair market value for their unwanted life insurance policies and catches regulatory attention.

Late 1990s

Seniors in America discover a new option to exit unneeded life insurance policies. In need of better alternatives, they find the answer in the secondary market for life insurance policies. Consumers over the age of 65 can now sell their unneeded life insurance policy as a lucrative alternative to lapse or cash surrender.

1995

Recognizing the need for industry regulation and professional standards, the Life Insurance Settlement Association is formed to promote the development, integrity, and reputation of the industry.

1980s

The AIDS epidemic leaves many helpless patients in need of money for treatment. The secondary market for life insurance policy, known as viatical settlement, helps thousands of patients by purchasing their life insurance policies and paying them with much needed cash.

1911

Grigsby v. Russell – Justice Holmes The U.S. Supreme Court rules that life insurance policies are an asset. Like all assets, policies are freely assignable for value.

Life insurance policies have always been informally traded.

Figure 3.4   Life settlement market time line

Source: LISA

which the policy owner has a life expectancy of less than two years. The viatical market, which is what cast the entire market in a negative light, was created by seedy investors purchasing the policies of those diagnosed with HIV or AIDS, which at the time were not understood the way they are today. People diagnosed with the virus sold their life insurance policies to pay for the high costs associated with treating their illness. When it turned out that people could live with HIV/ AIDS for several years, many investors lost money. These viatical settlements turned the institutional investment community off the life insurance market for roughly the next 15 years. The mid-1990s saw a rebirth of the market when European investors, especially from Germany, began to invest in traditional life settlements due to favorable tax treatment of death benefits in Europe. Soon other institutions followed, and the market began its journey to becoming an accepted and understood part of the financial sector.

Market Participants

A life settlement transaction has several parts, making it complex for investors with no previous experience with structured finance. However, the trend is toward efficiency. To break down a life settlement transaction, first we need to understand who is involved at the single policy level. Every life settlement transaction has seven main players:

- The policyholder, also known as the *viator*, seeks to sell his or her policy.
- The financial planner, CPA, attorney, estate planner, life insurance broker, or life settlement broker may or may not be registered with the state.
- The provider or originator acts as a buy-side broker and needs to be licensed in every state in which it purchases policies.
- Life expectancy (LE) underwriter.
- Securities intermediary, escrow agent, or verification agent.
- Investors are most often qualified institutional buyers with at least $100 of assets under management (pension funds, insurance companies, hedge funds, private equity funds, family offices).
- The policy servicer makes all premium payments on behalf of the investor for the duration of the policy, collects the death benefit, obtains and stores all medical and policy records, and sweeps the social security database to track for policy maturities.

Figure 3.5 shows how the various service providers operate in concert.

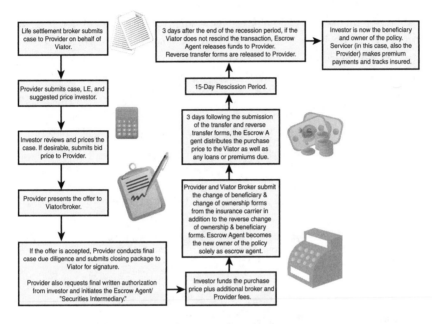

Figure 3.5   A detailed view of the life settlement process

Underwriting

In a life settlement transaction, investors typically obtain life expectancy certificates from independent medical underwriters, which are used to determine a policy's price. In short form, these LEs provide a median life expectancy for an individual, which takes into account a mortality multiplier, or essentially the excess mortality probability of an individual relative to a group of contemporaries. One method used to determine this mortality multiplier is the modified debit methodology. Hypothetically, given that a baseline mortality probability in a single year of the life of a 75-year-old is 200 deaths per 1,000 people, a certain illness could result in 100 additional debits. This translates into this individual's having a mortality probability that is 300% of the baseline. The median life expectancy is then the point at which roughly a 50% mortality probability exists. Interestingly, life insurance and life settlements use a very different set of assumptions to price the very same product (see Figure 3.6). Life insurance carriers assume much longer life expectancies, whereas an owner of a portfolio of life settlements assumes much shorter life expectancies. This is simply due to differences in business models. For a life insurance carrier to project strong future earnings, it is in the carrier's best interest to model an ideal scenario in which its customers purchase policies in their mid-30s, and 90% of them lapse in their 80s. This would allow the carrier to reinvest premiums for 50 years! A life settlement fund also wants to project strong future returns, so it models to its investors purchasing policies of 75-year-olds who pass away at 80. Actual mortality probably leans more toward the carrier's models.

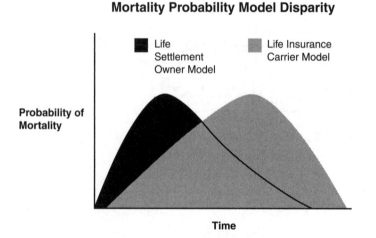

Figure 3.6   Life expectancy perspectives

From the life settlement perspective (as well as reverse mortgages), underwriting is done by analyzing life expectancy data on older policyholders, who often have some degree of illness or impairment. Data on this group of policyholders is thin because only recently has anyone seen value in tracking insurance data for individuals older than 70. Life expectancy data for life insurance carriers is much more robust than data for a life settlement investor. Carriers have over a hundred years of data on tens of thousands of policies to pull from, although this data mostly tracks younger individuals.

Figure 3.7 shows the mortality curve generated on a group of 300 individuals.

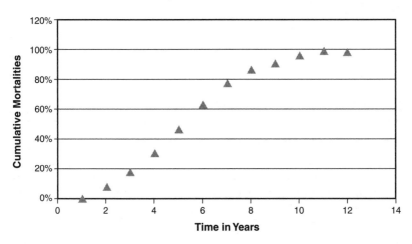

Cumulative Maturities of Fund

Figure 3.7   Cumulative maturities for a life settlement fund (300 policies)

Pricing

Investors can employ one of three methodologies when valuing a life settlement asset: deterministic, probabilistic, or stochastic. In a deterministic approach, a finite LE is simply entered into a discounted cash flow model, as shown in Figure 3.8. A probabilistic methodology determines the expected discounted value of a premium payment and death benefit in a given year. A stochastic approach, or Monte Carlo simulation, is most commonly used to generate the expected return on a pool of life settlements.

In addition to life expectancy assumptions, an investor must have the following pieces of information to value a life settlement:

- Policy type. Whole life,[4] universal,[5] convertible term,[6] regular term,[7] and variable policies[8] are rarely purchased in the secondary market. Term policies have very short durations, and variable life policies are treated as securities by the U.S. Securities and Exchange Commission (SEC).
- Premium mode. Fixed or floating.

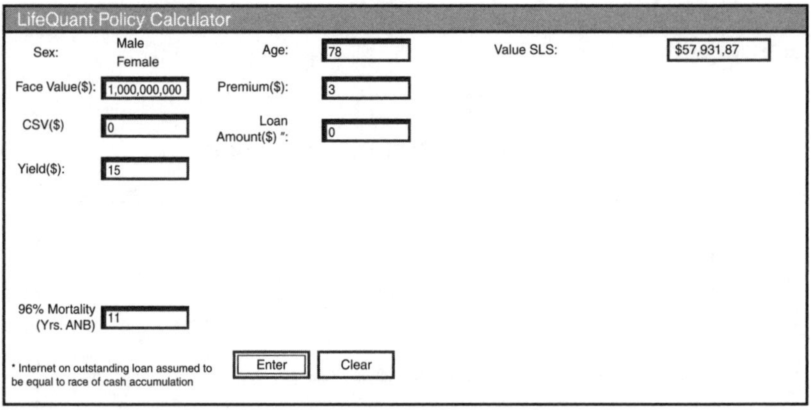

Figure 3.8   Deterministic calculator

- Death benefit or coverage amount of the life insurance policy. Some policies offer a guaranteed death benefit rider, which protects the total coverage amount of the contract.

- The age, sex, and smoking status of the insured.

- Life expectancy estimate.

- Cash surrender value. The cash value a policy can build up over the life of the policy. Although it is simply added to the purchase price of a life settlement, the cash value (if sufficient) can be applied to premium obligations, making the policy self-sustaining.

- Outstanding loans against the policy. Any loans taken out against the policy may affect the total available cash in the policy, as well as the policy's death benefit.

- Premium illustrations to age 100. A premium illustration is simply a schedule provided by the insurance carrier of all future obligations the policy owner must make to keep the policy active. The premium and cost of insurance (COI) can rise over the duration of a contract, so investors must consider a rise in COI when modeling a policy's value.

The deterministic approach is used to price a single life settlement policy, but it can be grossly inaccurate. Rarely can a single person's life expectancy be predicted.

Figure 3.9 shows the expected mortality distribution of 10 different pools of life settlements. Predicting the probability of mortality for any one individual is extremely difficult. But through the law of large numbers, constructing models and portfolios using a larger number of lives (more than 300) produces more accurate modeling and return assumptions, as shown in Figure 3.10.

Maturities of Ten Modeled Portfolios

□0-10 □10-20 □20-30 □30-40 □40-50 □50-60

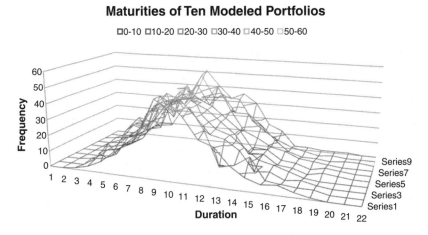

Figure 3.9   Monte Carlo simulation of 10 different pools of lives

Distribution of Annualized Net Returns (5,000 Simulations)

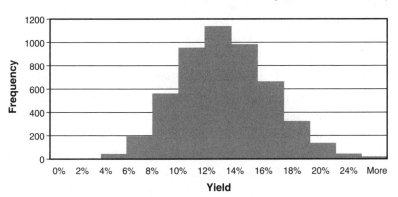

Figure 3.10   Stochastic simulation of returns

Generating life expectancies, which in turn affects pricing, also relies heavily on which mortality table is used. Among the tables are several classes from which to choose. Figure 3.11 shows how the mortality curve of a 76-year-old female nonsmoker differs by class in the context of the 2008 Value Basic Table,[9] which is the most notable mortality table produced by the Society of Actuaries (SOA).[10] The various classes (left) range from 70 to 160 and in this case move from conservative to more liberal.

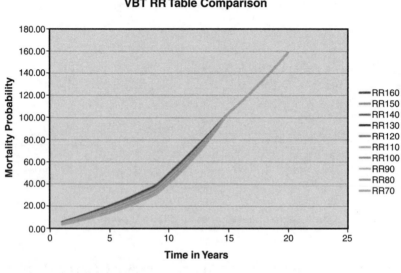

**76 Yr Female Non-Smoker ANB-2008
VBT RR Table Comparison**

Figure 3.11   2008 VBT class comparisons

Source: Society of Actuaries

Figure 3.12 illustrates the disparity between male and female life expectancy. Delving into the mathematics and details of actuarial science and pricing methodologies for life-linked assets such as life settlements or reverse mortgages is outside of the scope of this book. Two books that discuss more of the quantitative elements of life settlement pricing in great detail are *Life Settlements and Longevity Structures: Pricing and Risk Management* by Jim Aspinwall, Geoff Chaplin, and Mark Venn (John Wiley & Sons, Inc., 2009) and *Life Markets: Trading Mortality and Longevity Risk with Life Settlements and Linked Securities* by Vishaal Bhuyan (John Wiley & Sons, Inc., 2009).

76 Yr M/F RR 70 Non-Smoker ANB Comparison - 2008 VBT

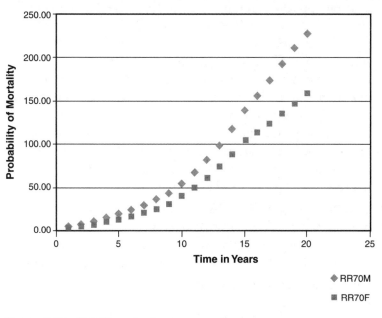

Figure 3.12   Male/female class comparison

Source: Society of Actuaries

Risks

Investors in life settlements are exposed to set of unique risks:

- **Origination and insurable interest risk:** The first two years of a life insurance policy are known as the *contestability period,* in which an insurance carrier reserves the right to cancel a policy and rescind a claim due to fraud and misrepresentation. Although it is rare, contestability risk can have a negative impact on an investor. It is also important to note that contestability period in many states is being increased from two to five years. One reason for doing this is to prevent the practice of stranger-originated life insurance (STOLI). In a STOLI transaction, someone purchases a life insurance policy on a senior, without having any insurable interest, with the intent to sell that policy on the open market. In many cases, investors keep the policy for the duration of the contestability period.[11] STOLI is also called "wet paper." Inversely, policies that have passed the contestability period are known as "dry" or "seasoned" paper. Although regulation of STOLI varies at the state level, most institutional investors shy away from these deals due to the insurable interest risk. An insurance carrier can cancel a policy and return the premium on any policy if it believes the original policy purchaser did not have insurable interest at origination. In a traditional life settlement, because the original policyholder had insurable interest at the time of purchase, she may assign the policy to whomever she wants.

- **Purchase price risk:** Miscalculating the life expectancy of an insured can result in overpaying for a policy. Given that an investor has negative carry in a life settlement for several years, a miscalculation of the upfront cost can mean less margin for error.

- **Cost of insurance/premium risk:** The true "cost" of a life settlement policy is making premium obligations for almost a decade to collect the death benefit. If an investor does not fully understand how to plan for rising premium costs, the total return on the investment can be hurt substantially, especially coupled with any longevity risk or incorrect purchase price.

- **Longevity risk:** Longevity risk ties together premium and purchase price risk, because it is the risk that the insured surpasses modeled expectations. Using conservative mortality estimations and tables is one way an investor can mitigate this risk. Moreover, by building a large-enough portfolio of life settlements, investors can be more prepared for how their portfolios will behave over a 10- to 15-year time frame. Some investors rely heavily on purchasing policies of those who are impaired. This can be a riskier endeavor. Such policies would cost much more to acquire due to shortened life expectancies and are in direct opposition to modern medicine. This is a side I would not want to take.

- **Ramp-up risk:** Building a portfolio of 300 policies or so takes time and may not be possible due to capital or market restraints. Holding a portfolio of a small number of policies over a long period of time may create tremendous volatility in investors' returns.

- **Carrier default risk:** Prior to the credit crisis of 2008, this risk seemed far-fetched. However, a carrier risks defaulting on a policy if a systemic financial meltdown occurs, as we have seen in recent years. That being said, no policy in U.S. history has ever gone unpaid. In most cases, a failing carrier's book of policies is sold to another carrier. Moreover, death benefits of $500,000 and cash values of $250,000 are insured by state insurance funds,[12] although in some states if a policy is transferred from one owner to another, this guarantee becomes void. Typical life settlement investors purchase only policies issued by at least BB-rated carriers (rated by A.M. Best Company). Diversifying across carriers is another way to hedge this risk, as well as by purchasing credit protection on a basket of insurance carriers through CDS.

Figure 3.13 illustrates how a portfolio with a larger number of policies can mitigate skewness[13] and kurtosis risk[14] and create more predictable returns.

Example of Life Expectancy Accuracy in a Portfolio of Life Insurance as a Function of Number of Policies

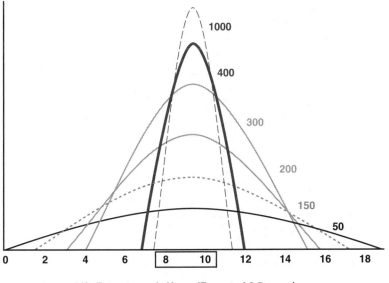

Life Expectancy in Years (Expected 9.5 years)

Figure 3.13   Diversification

Regulation

Currently the SEC doesn't treat life settlements as securities. However, in coming years this might be a strong possibility, because post-financial collapse special life settlement task forces have been created. In 2010, the U.S. Government Accountability Office released a special report pushing for more standardized regulation of life settlements (http://www.lifemarketsassociation.org/documents/GAO_10_775.pdf). Currently life settlements and life insurance on the whole are regulated at the state level by the National Association of Insurance Commissioners (NAIC).[15] Regulation is exactly what the life settlements market needs to attract more institutional capital and consumer protection. Figure 3.14 shows how many states have adopted some life settlement regulation since 1992. Any potential investor in the life settlements market should seek expert legal counsel to fully understand the regulatory environment of the marketplace.

Life Settlement Regulation Time Line

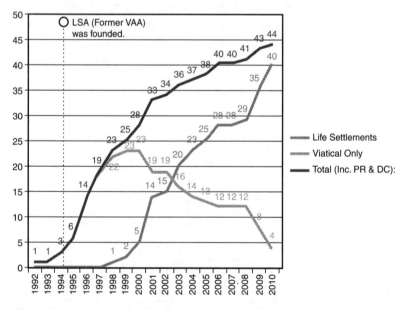

Figure 3.14   Life settlement regulation time line

Taxation

Taxation on life settlements is a complex but important subject that is outside the scope of this book. The LISA website best describes the topic:

> With new clarification from the IRS, some of the proceeds of a life settlement are almost certainly taxable. After a hearing held by the Senate Select Committee on Aging, in 2009, the IRS released Revenue Ruling 2009-13 to "clarify" the issue. Though this ruling is very complex and confusing, and LISA has sought to have it clarified, that information is not yet available, and some issues are sure to be negotiated. The general treatment requires determinations of cost of insurance which are not readily available to consumers. LISA welcomes feedback on this from affected consumers or their representatives. Historically, the amount recouped up to the cumulative premiums paid is tax-free, but the IRS has determined that the "cost of insurance" must be addressed as an issue. Additional money up to the cash surrender value option is to be seemingly treated as ordinary income. Any excess cash above the cash surrender value is apparently to be considered capital gains. The assistance of a professional tax advisor should always be sought. The proceeds of a life settlement could also be subject to the claims of creditors. If the seller is within two years of death, other laws making the proceeds tax-free may apply.

Figure 3.15 shows a life settlement regulation map.

Reverse Mortgages

In addition to life settlements, reverse mortgages will play an ever-growing role in U.S. financial products. Also called "loans of last resort," reverse mortgages are a way for seniors age 65 and older to access the equity in their homes without turning to traditional credit markets. Despite their "loan" characteristics, reverse mortgages are contingent more on life expectancy than credit.

REGULATION OF VIATICAL AND LIFE SETTLEMENTS
As of Dec. 22, 2009

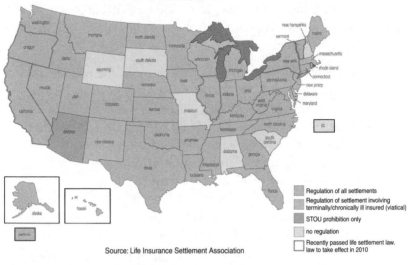

Source: Life Insurance Settlement Association

Figure 3.15   Life settlement regulation map

Source: LISA

History of Reverse Mortgages

Reverse mortgages, which are gaining more attention now than ever before, have been around for more than 50 years. The first reverse mortgage was granted in 1961 by Deering Savings & Loan of Maine. In 1988, the Federal Housing Authority Insurance Program was created, making possible the first federally insured reverse mortgage in 1998, which was distributed by fewer than 50 lenders across the nation. Due to the product's success, the home equity conversion mortgage (HECM) loan program expanded to all lenders in the country. Over the past 20 years, more than 500,000 reverse mortgages have been written by more than 1,000 lenders.[16]

The most common type of reverse mortgage is the HECM,[17] which currently makes up roughly 90% of all outstanding reverse mortgages in the U.S. HECM is a reverse or reverse annuity mortgage in which the U.S. Department of Housing and Urban Development (HUD),[18] through the Federal Housing Authority (FHA),[19] guarantees that the borrower will receive monthly payments from the insurer (FHA) if the lender is unable to make payments to the borrower.[20] HECM reverse mortgages differ from nonconforming reverse mortgages in that the loans are insured and meet certain criteria set by the FHA. The requirements for nonconforming and conforming reverse mortgages differ slightly. Nonconforming mortgages are more flexible by definition.

The requirements for a nonconforming reverse mortgage borrower (as opposed to a HECM loan) are as follows:

- The lender sets the minimum age.
- The borrower must own the property in full or have the proceeds of the reverse mortgage pay off the existing mortgage balance.
- The home must be the borrower's primary residence.

All the basic information on the HECM reverse mortgage program can be found on the FHA HUD website at http://www.hud.gov/offices/hsg/sfh/hecm/hecmabou.cfm.

The FHA HECM borrower requirements are as follows:

- Be 62 years of age or older
- Own the property outright or have a small mortgage balance
- Occupy the property as your principal residence
- Not be delinquent on any federal debt
- Participate in a consumer information session given by an approved HECM counselor

The mortgage is based on the following:

- Age of the youngest borrower.
- The borrower's life expectancy underwriting. In a nonconforming mortgage, more emphasis and better underwriting methodologies may be used.
- Current interest rate.
- Lesser of appraised value or the HECM FHA mortgage limit or the sales price initial mortgage insurance premium (MIP). Your choices are the 2% HECM Standard option or the .01% HECM Saver option.

Here are the financial requirements:

- No income or employment qualifications are required of the borrower.
- No repayment is necessary as long as the property is your principal residence and the obligations of the mortgage are met.
- Closing costs may be financed in the mortgage.

The following eligible property types must meet all FHA property standards and flood requirements:

- Single-family home or one-to-four-unit home with one unit occupied by the borrower
- HUD-approved condominium
- Manufactured home that meets FHA requirements

The FHA HECM Reverse Mortgage Program has five payment options, which can also be applied to nonconforming loans:

- **Tenure:** Equal monthly payments as long as at least one borrower lives and continues to occupy the property as a principal residence.
- **Term:** Equal monthly payments for a fixed period of months selected.
- **Line of credit:** Unscheduled payments or in installments, at times and in an amount of your choosing until the line of credit is exhausted.
- **Modified tenure:** A combination of line of credit plus scheduled monthly payments for as long as you remain in the home.
- **Modified term:** A combination of line of credit plus monthly payments for a fixed period of months selected by the borrower.

Although there are no limits in terms of house value for a HECM reverse mortgage, as determined by an appraisal or recent sale, the maximum loan limit is $625,500. Nonconforming mortgages carry no such limit. In addition, borrowers are charged an upfront insurance premium of 2% of the maximum claim amount for HECM the Standard option and .01% for the HECM Saver option. In addition, there is an annual mortgage insurance premium of 1.25%. Other HECM costs may be added to the total loan and deducted from the mortgage proceeds.

Reverse mortgage fees can be costly for borrowers. HECM lenders typically charge an origination fee of up to $2,500 if the home is valued at less than $125,000. Otherwise, the fee is 2% on the first $200,000 of home value and 1% thereafter. HECM origination fees, however, have a limit of $6,000.

Closing costs for a HECM loan, or nonconforming loan, include the home's appraisal, title search, and insurance, as well as surveys, inspections, recording fees, mortgage taxes, credit checks, and other fees.

HECM borrowers must also pay a MIP as part of the loan. The MIP is charged upfront and is 2% in the HECM Standard option and .01% in the HECM Save option of the lesser of the home's appraised value, the FHA HECM mortgage limit for the area, or the sale price. The MIP is charged annually for the duration of the loan at 1.25% of the balance. This insurance guarantees payments to the borrower and insurances that the total debt on the house can never exceed the home's value.

Servicing includes sending you account statements, disbursing loan proceeds, and making certain that you keep up with loan requirements such as paying taxes and insurance. HECM lenders charge a monthly servicing fee of no more than $30 if the loan has an annually adjusting interest rate and $35 if the interest rate adjusts monthly. At loan origination, HECM lenders set aside the servicing fee and deduct the fee from your available funds. Each month, the monthly servicing fee is added to the loan balance.

HECM and nonconforming borrowers can choose an adjustable interest rate or a fixed rate. Similar to a traditional mortgage, interest rates may adjust monthly or annually. HECM loans that adjust annually cannot adjust more than 2 percentage points per year and not by more than 5 total percentage points over the life of the loan. FHA does not require interest rate caps on monthly adjusted HECMs.

A HECM reverse mortgage must be repaid in full when the borrower dies or sells the home. The loan also becomes due and payable if the borrower does the following:

- Fails to pay property taxes or hazard insurance or violates other obligations.
- Permanently moves to a new principal residence.

- Fails to live in the home for 12 months in a row. An example of this situation would be if you (or the last borrower) were to have a 12-month or longer stay in a nursing home.
- Allows the property to deteriorate and does not make necessary repairs.

Reverse mortgages are attractive from an investment perspective simply because they possess characteristics similar to other credit-linked structures but are not actually linked to credit. FICO scores are factored into the calculations of a reverse mortgage as much as life expectancy is. Unlike life settlements, however, reverse mortgages are not as "uncorrelated" to traditional asset classes, because future home prices play a significant role in the valuation of a reverse mortgage.

From an economic point of view, reverse mortgage backed securities offer a tremendous amount of opportunity as the securitization market seeks new assets from which to generate yield. Assets such as reverse mortgages, which can thrive during poor credit environments, seem ideal for the "new normal." Ginnie Mae has already established a Home Equity Conversion Mortgage Backed Security (HMBS) program by bundling several individual HECM loans.

Figures 3.16 and 3.17 show the total HECM loan issuance from 2000 to 2008 and the volume of the HMBS market.

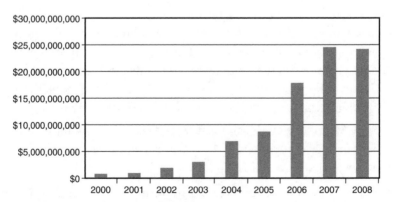

Total Dollar Amount of HECM Loans
FY 00 - FY 08

Figure 3.16   HECM loan issuance

Source: MortgageDaily.com

Ginnie Mae HMBS Volume

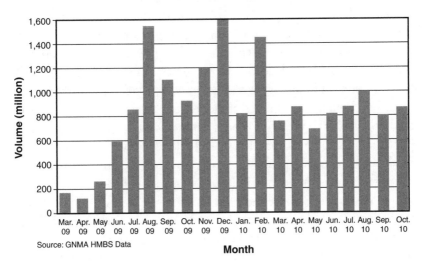

Source: GNMA HMBS Data

Figure 3.17   HMBS volume

Source: GNMA HMBS

Reverse mortgages have an added layer of complexity over a life settlement due to their reliance on housing prices relative to life expectancy, or if the house's value is less than the loan. Although in an FHA, HECM reverse mortgage insurance protection hedges against this risk, also known as *crossover risk*, in a nonconforming mortgage this risk is among the largest in reverse mortgage investing. Here are some other risks:

- **Home price risk:**   If property values depreciate significantly, the crossover point is reached sooner. Geographic concentration can also magnify this risk, as will loan seasoning, because the increase in the loan balance generally outpaces historic home price appreciation.

- **Interest rate risk:**   An increase in interest rates increases the cost of funding in a securitization structure with floating-rate bonds, whereas the increase in the interest rate for the collateral is effectively capped by the property value.

- **Actuarial risk:**   Cash account loans have no stated maturity or term. Therefore, borrowers who remain in their homes for an extended period can cause crossover loss as the loan balance compounds every year going forward.[21]

One other major risk with reverse mortgages at the lender level is *default risk*. For example, if a 75-year-old woman stops paying her property taxes and maintaining her home, a reverse mortgage lender would need to repossess her home because technically she is breaching her contract with the bank. However, this poses an enormous risk for a lender. Nobody wants to be forced to evict an elderly person from her home, and the reputational and image risk in doing this could be irreversible. Finding an incentive for a borrower to maintain her home after she has handed over the keys to someone else is a difficult administrative problem facing any reverse mortgage lender. Moreover, managing a portfolio of homes across the country (on a single-loan basis) could be a nightmare. For all these reasons, structured products linked to reverse mortgages are a cleaner, more liquid method of accessing the benefits of the asset class. Although such products as the GNMA HMBS have a number of drawbacks, such as the life expectancy assumptions made to underwrite the notes, these products will be refined as demand for noncredit-linked yield increases and demographic fundamentals take over.

Conclusion

Given the uncertainty in public and private retirement systems, reverse equity transactions will play a significant role moving forward. Investors looking for a unique way to prepare for a downturn in the U.S. economic system as a result of underfunded pension programs, massive amounts of government debt, and the rapidly growing number of retirees (baby boomer population) should take a deeper look at such products as life settlements and reverse mortgages. The major barrier for entry into the market is expertise and bite size. The important disclaimer when discussing both the life settlements market as well as the reverse mortgage market is that these are negative cash flow assets. Therefore, investors must be prepared or hold some level of cash on hand to make premium payments (in the case of a life settlement) or annuity payments (in the case of a reverse mortgage). By bundling either one of these assets in a securitized pool, investors might be able to circumvent the negative carrying costs. Furthermore, because these assets have variable durations, meaning that the event could happen in two years but also could happen in 20 years, being prepared to maintain an asset longer than expected is of the utmost importance. For many hedge fund investors, this may seem like a terrible use of cash; however, keep in mind that the investment itself is broken down over multiple years. For example, a $30 million commitment to the asset class may mean using $15 million to purchase policies and reserving $15 million for premium payments for four or five years. Premium schedules are maintained to clearly outline future obligations.

For many investors, tying up a substantial amount of capital into life settlements may be difficult, unless a dedicated fund is structured to do so. Regardless, this strategy is more one of risk aversion than generating home-run returns. The demographic and economic fundamentals are certainly apparent, but investors must have long-term investment horizons and be unaffected by severe illiquidity. Life settlements, although there are secondary and tertiary markets, are still difficult to move. That being said, provided that capital reserves are sufficient, a liquidity event need not occur to generate the windfall.

Endnotes

[1] Primarily referring to institutions that manage at least $100 million in securities, including banks, savings and loans institutions, insurance companies, investment companies, employee benefit plans, or an entity owned entirely by qualified investors. Also included are registered broker-dealers owning and investing, on a discretionary basis, $10 million in securities of nonaffiliates. Qualified institutional buyer (QIB) is defined in the U.S. Securities Act of 1933.

[2] An interest in a person or thing that will support the issuance of an insurance policy; an interest in the survival of the insured or in the preservation of the thing that is insured. http://www.thefreedictionary.com/insurable+interest.

[3] U.S. Supreme Court, Grigsby v. Russell, 222 U.S. 149 (1911), Grigsby v. Russell, No. 53, Argued November 10, 13, 1911, Decided December 4, 1911, 222 U.S. 149, CERTIORARI TO THE CIRCUIT COURT OF APPEALS, FOR THE SIXTH CIRCUIT.

[4] A form of life insurance that applies part of the premium payments to build an investment or savings value for the policy owner. The investment or savings value is called the policy's cash surrender value. http://www.americanbanker.com/glossary/w.html.

[5] A form of life insurance that combines term insurance protection with a savings feature. The portion of the funds allocated to the savings feature is invested in a tax-deferred account that typically earns interest at rates comparable to prevailing money market interest rates. http://www.americanbanker.com/glossary/u.html.

[6] Convertible term insurance allows the policyholder to change the face value of the term policy in force into a permanent form of life insurance, such as whole life, universal life, or variable life, without any penalties or evidence of insurability. http://www.allinsuranceinfo.org.

[7] A life insurance policy purchased for a term of years. If the person dies during this term, the beneficiary receives the face amount of the policy. The policy expires at the end of the stated number of years. http://www.pcafoundation.com/main/glossary.htm.

[8] A form of life insurance very similar to whole life insurance. In a variable life insurance policy, the cash value is invested in equity or debt securities. Policyholders can select and switch investment instruments. http://www.americanbanker.com/glossary/v.html.

[9] http://www.soa.org/files/pdf/research-2008-vbt-report.pdf.

[10] SOA is the largest professional organization, dedicated to serving 21,000 actuarial members and the public in the U.S., Canada, and worldwide. SOA's vision is for actuaries to be the leading professionals in the measurement and management of risk. http://www.soa.org/Home.aspx.

[11] The time period during which the insurer is not obligated to pay a claim (usually two years) because of material misrepresentations found in the application. A policy becomes incontestable when the contestability period is over. http://www.smartmoney.com/personal-finance/insurance/life-insurance-glossary-8009/.

[12] http://www.annuityadvantage.com/stateguarantee.htm.

[13] Skewness is a parameter that describes asymmetry in a random variable's probability distribution. http://www.riskglossary.com.

[14] Kurtosis is a parameter that describes the shape of a random variable's probability density function (PDF). http://www.riskglossary.com.

[15] NAIC members are the elected or appointed state government officials who, along with their departments and staff, regulate the conduct of insurance companies and agents in their respective state or territory. http://www.naic.org.

[16] Senior Equity Financial, Inc. http://www.seniorequityfinancial.com/history_of_reverse_mortgages.php.

[17] http://www.hud.gov/offices/hsg/sfh/hecm/hecm—df.cfm.

[18] http://www.hud.gov/offices/hsg/sfh/hecm/hecm—df.cfm.

[19] http://portal.hud.gov/portal/page/portal/HUD.

[20] http://guarantytitlepalatka.com/realestateterms1.html.

[21] For details on reverse mortgage risk mitigation, see Nemo Pererra, Chapter 7 of *Risk Mitigation in Reverse Mortgages and Linked Securities: A Guide to Risk, Pricing, and Regulation*, 68-74 (Vishaal Bhuyan, ed., 2010), available at http://search.barnesandnoble.com/books/product.aspx?r=1&isbn=9780470921517&cm_mmc=Google%20Product%20Search-_-Q000000630-_-Reverse%20Mortgages%20and%20Linked%20Securities-_-9780470921517.

Part II

The Tuna Trade

Big Tuna Fetches Record $396,000 in Tokyo

TOKYO (AP)—A giant bluefin tuna fetched a record 32.49 million yen, or nearly $396,000, in Tokyo on Wednesday, in the first auction of the year at the world's largest wholesale fish market. The price for the 754-pound (342-kilogram) tuna beat the previous record set in 2001 when a 445-pound (202-kilogram) fish sold for 20.2 million yen, a spokesman for Tsukiji market said.

Due to several reasons outside the scope of this book, commodities have experienced dramatic growth since 2000. However, it does not take a doctorate in economics to see that a falling U.S. dollar, uncertainty in global economic policy, and increased demand from China and India play a significant role in the story of commodities. It is not the purpose of this book to provide conjecture on global economic events, but rather to highlight opportunities that seem to have very clear supply/demand imbalances. Whereas commodities such as gold, silver, and crude oil have gained wide acceptance in recent years from the general investing public through exchange traded funds (ETFs), exchange traded notes (ETNs), and a host of indices, these commodities have also become increasingly volatile due to the increase in market participants. This overcrowding has created divergence between fundamentals and price movement. One could argue that this increased volatility has also spurred the high-frequency, or black box, trading industry, which focuses more on capturing incremental price movements as opposed to taking long-term value positions.

Although I believe that high-frequency trading (HFT) is the future of the liquid financial markets, opportunities exist for sophisticated investors to make long-term value investments in the commodities markets without the assistance of an off-the-shelf ETF. Seafood, especially tuna, is one such investment.

Although price data for tuna is sparse, approaching the market from a conservative perspective and viewing other indicators for the broader seafood market should be sufficient to make the argument about tuna's future pricing.

Part II discusses the tuna trade—specifically bluefin tuna, the Tsukiji fish market in Tokyo, and the demand for sushi.

4

The Bluefin Tuna

Price data for tuna is sparse, but approaching the market from a conservative perspective and viewing other indicators for the broader seafood market should be sufficient to make the argument about tuna's future pricing.

At first, it is easy to dismiss the idea of seafood as an investment. It is difficult for investors to access, data is hard to come by, it is illiquid, and overall it is very strange. But it is for these very reasons that seafood has substantial potential. Figure 4.1 is an index of a basket of commodities from December 1995 to October 2010. Note that the index includes global seafood prices (salmon and shrimp) in its calculation. Figure 4.2 tracks the returns of fish products (salmon and fishmeal, dried ground fish used to feed livestock and farmed fish) against crude oil, wheat, and copper over the same time period.

The focus of this chapter is not to discuss the generalities of seafood but rather the specifics of tuna—namely, bluefin, a population that is on the brink of extinction. According to the United Nations Food and Agriculture Organization, 7 of the 23 commercially fished tuna stocks are overfished or depleted, and an additional 9 stocks are threatened.

There are two main geographical areas that need to be understood when understanding the Tuna business; Australia and Japan. Australia, namely places such as Port Lincoln, are at the epicenter of both tuna fishing and farming. Japan, another location where considerable amounts of tuna are caught, also serves as the primary exchange for seafood and giant Tuna. Both Port Lincoln and the Tsukiji market in Tokyo are touched upon in this section.

Commodity Food Price Index Monthly Price

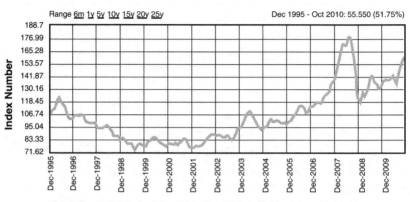

Range 6m 1y 5y 10y 15y 20y 25y   Dec 1995 - Oct 2010: 55.550 (51.75%)

Description: Commodity Food Price Index, 2005=100, includes Cereal, Vegetable Oils, Meat, Seafood, Sugar, Bananas, and Oranges Price Indices

Figure 4.1   Basket of commodities from December 1995 to October 2010

Source: http://www.indexmundi.com

Australia

I was in Australia observing the lifeblood industry of Port Lincoln: the feeding of fish that will be transformed into the town's major export—southern bluefin tuna for Japan.

After an hour, we arrived at the first pen, some 5 miles offshore, east of Boston Island. The five pens clustered together are a part of the 14 maintained by aquaculture company Stehr Group. They are round, floating corrals, 120 feet across, consisting of nets suspended from a ring of stanchions mounted on a circle of floats. Some 50 feet deep, the net corrals each hold between 1,000 and 2,000 half-grown southern bluefin tuna caught in purse seines in the Great Australian Bight to the west. They were transferred at sea to towing cages and, after a 1-knot tow that can take as long as three weeks, were transferred again to these floating pens. These tuna are a precious commodity—which is exactly the right term—and they are pampered and coddled to an extent that would embarrass a purebred Pekinese. Every day of the year, the bait boats make the 5-mile journey to the pens around 6 a.m. and then return to the Port Lincoln marina to pick up another consignment of baitfish to feed the penned tuna. At 2 in the afternoon, they do it again. Stehr Group feeds 60 tons of pilchards a day to their tuna; over the season that adds up to 5,500 tons.

Seafood vs. Other Commodities (Dec '95 to Oct'10)

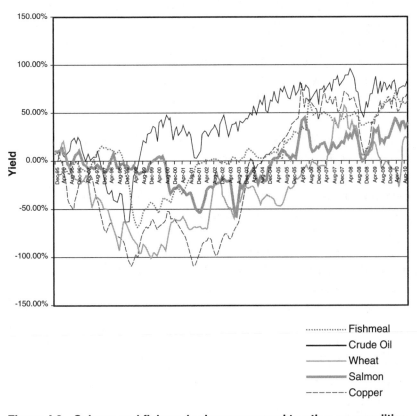

Figure 4.2   Salmon and fishmeal prices compared to other commodities

Source: http://www.indexmundi.com

Frozen blocks of foot-long pilchards, imported from California and eastern Australia, Morocco, and even Europe are fed to these piscine gourmands. When our boat has been made fast alongside the pen, the feeding begins. Just as your pet guppies know when you are about to sprinkle fish food into their tank, the tuna know that the arrival of the bait boat signals a feed. They pick up speed in their endless counterclockwise circling. Sometimes they break the surface with their pointed dorsal and tail fins. Sometimes they roll on their sides to flash a gleam of silver, yellow, and blue and a curiously intelligent glance at the bait boat. The feeding begins as a man tosses one shovelful after another of pilchards into the pen, causing the water to boil with tuna rushing to get their share. So that they do not land in a clump, the shoveler, with his back to the pen, tosses the fish over his shoulder in a graceful arc. Looking down on the feeding frenzy, I notice the bright yellow, horizontal keels at the base of the tail; these yellow markers are the most prominent features of the tuna zooming by underwater. (And, says Jessica Farley of the Commonwealth Scientific and Industrial Research Organization (CSIRO), this may be one of the characteristics that differentiate the southern bluefin from its northern relatives.)

Catching fish to feed fish is an ecologically unsound concept, but tuna are carnivores (more accurately, piscivores), and they would not eat food made from grain. Research is now being conducted to develop a grain + fish products + vitamins pellet that would be the equivalent of the "fish food" sprinkled into your home aquarium. But tuna need fat in their diet to produce the fatty meat that the Japanese prize so highly, and although grain might be used to fatten beef cattle, it doesn't work that well for tuna. (Curiously, the Kobe beef so highly prized by Japanese gourmets looks very much like the best bluefin tuna sashimi (raw fish): rich red in color, marbled with fat to give it the desirable texture and flavor.) So for the moment, thousands of tons of small fish are being caught and exported to Australia to feed the tuna that will end up in the Japanese fish markets and, ultimately, in high-end restaurants, where a piece of uncooked fish can sell for hundreds of dollars.

Southern bluefin tuna, known technically as *Thunnus maccoyii* and commonly as SBT, are born in Indonesian waters. For the next eight years, they leisurely work their way around the west coast of Australia, crossing the Great Australian Bight *en route* to the east coast. There they disperse—some swimming to New Zealand, and others to South Africa. Some of the seven- or eight-year-old fish completely circumnavigate the Australian continent and return to the Indonesian waters where they were hatched to spawn and begin the cycle anew. But many will not make it that far. They will pass unscathed through Western Australian waters and the Great Australian Bight, but then they will find that their migration route has brought them into the perilous seas off South Australia, where boatloads of fishermen with nets are dedicated to keeping them from completing their instinct-inspired journey. (No tuna fishing occurs in Western Australia. The fish are not big enough, so the quotas were sold years ago to South Australian fishers.)

The first Australian tuna fishermen caught their quarry in an old-fashioned, labor-intensive way: They hooked them on a line and jerked them out of the water one at a time. For bigger fish—these fish can weigh over 400 pounds—two men would use a pole each, attached to a single hook. The hooks were barbless, so as the fish were yanked out of the water, the hook pulled out and the fish flopped onto the deck. (Later, a thick foam-rubber "blanket" cushioned the fish's fall so that the valuable tuna would not be damaged.) "Poling" was replaced in the early 1960s by purse seining. A huge net was deployed around a school of tuna and "pursed" to close it around the fish, which were then hauled up on deck. When the Japanese developed a taste for sashimi, Australian fishermen, particularly those in Port Lincoln, labored long and hard to satisfy the Japanese lust for tuna. South Australian fishermen brought the fish to the Port Lincoln docks, where Japanese freezer ships waited with their eager holds agape, ready to carry the frozen carcasses to the Tokyo fish markets. Government scientists, worried that intensified fishing posed a threat to the southern bluefin tuna stocks, imposed such strict quotas on the fishermen that they believed they were being drummed out of business. Tuna farmers to the rescue.

Tuna farming (sometimes called tuna ranching) utilizes the same "feedlot" technology used for cattle, except that it takes place at sea, mostly underwater. Young animals are herded into special enclosures, where they are fed until they reach the desired size and weight, at which point they are slaughtered for human consumption. Spotter pilots locate schools of tuna and radio their location to the waiting "chum boats." Fishermen on these boats throw baitfish into the school, causing the tuna to become excited and follow the boat. The chum boat pulls close to the purse seiner (Australians say "purse seiner" as one word: "per-*say*-ner"). A net is shot around the school of fish and the chum boat. The spotter pilot overhead directs the boat out of the net just before it closes, leaving nothing but fish behind. The net is pursed around the school, perhaps thousands strong. When it is closed and the tuna are trapped, it is drawn alongside the towboat, to which is attached a large net "cage," open at the surface (see Figure 4.3). The cage is used like floating corral to tow the fish to the pens off Port Lincoln. Many net hauls are transferred to a single towing cage, which can hold as much as 150 tons of fish. At the pens, the towing cage is brought alongside. Divers open adjacent panels in the towing cage and the pen, driving the fish into the pen, where they will remain for the rest of their lives. About 150 pens are clustered off Port Lincoln in Boston Bay and off Rabbit Island, each owned by a particular tuna company, which will feed the fish twice daily, every day of the year, until the time comes for them to be killed. Each pen contains anywhere from 20 to 50 tons of fish.

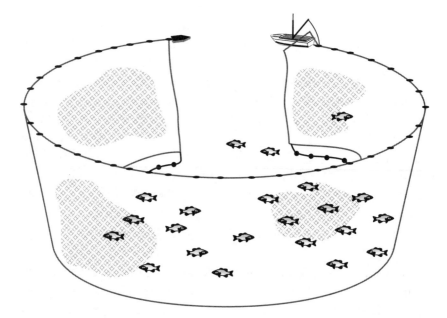

Figure 4.3   Purse seine fishing

Because you cannot easily count fish underwater—much of the school is too deep to be seen even by the spotter pilot—only rough estimates of the school's size can be made. However, experienced spotters can calculate the size of the fish in a given school with remarkable accuracy, so they can advise the catchers as to whether the school is worth pursuing. Kiwi White, a spotter pilot since the 1960s, told me that he can differentiate 17-kilo fish from 19-kilo fish from the air. If the fish are small—say, less than 20 kilos—you can catch more fish in a single haul, but you will have to feed them longer to get them up to market size. Catching larger fish means fewer fish in the cage, but a shorter time to feed them, which means less of the expensive baitfish are required to fatten them up.

Depending on various factors—market price, Aussie dollar versus Japanese yen, abundance of fish, size when caught—the tuna are kept in these fattening pens for several months, or even a year. When the tuna are considered big enough to be slaughtered, a platform is lowered into the pen, and divers in wet suits get ready to kill the fish. One diver shoves a fish up onto the ramp, and another grabs it by the gills and hauls it partially out of the water. While a metal spike is driven into its brain, another metal rod is shoved down its backbone so that the dying fish will not tense up and thus spoil the tender meat. This "humane" method is employed in Australia and other locations where the fish are small enough (less than 100 pounds) to manhandle. In Mediterranean ranches (such as those in Spain) where the tuna are fattened to 250 pounds (120 kg) or more, a man cannot restrain a struggling fish that is much stronger and heavier than he is. So the tuna are herded into a corner of the pen and are shot by men standing on a platform above the pen. "Shooting fish in a barrel" indeed. In Maltese fish farming, the living fish is lassoed around the tail, hauled up out of the water, and shot in the brain, or its throat cut so that it bleeds out.

There are many ways for a southern bluefin tuna to make the long—but often remarkably fast—trip from Port Lincoln to Tokyo. Sometimes the dead fish are taken to factories in Port Lincoln, where they are gutted, iced down—but not frozen—and packed into plastic-lined, coffin-shaped boxes for shipment by air or sea to Japan. Sometimes the fish are transferred directly to waiting Japanese reefers, where they will be gutted and iced down for a sea voyage to Japan. Other times they are loaded into huge bins (again iced but not frozen), trucked from Lincoln to Adelaide, and placed on a plane to Sydney, there to be transferred to a plane to Tokyo. Some of these tuna take only 30 hours to get from Port Lincoln to Tokyo, admirably fulfilling the Japanese requirement for fresh fish. Because they have never been frozen, these 30-hour fish are probably the most desirable at the Tsukiji tuna auctions. But even frozen fish from Port Lincoln's tuna farms, pampered and virtually hand-fed, also demand particularly high prices. So far, the record price for a single fish at the Tsukiji tuna actions is $173,600.

In his 1996 book, *Tuna and the Japanese*, Takeaki Hori claims that the idea for tuna ranching originated with a Japanese tuna auctioneer named Hideo Hirahara. He went to Australia to find somebody to

catch the tuna and put them in some sort of "fish tank," where they
would be fattened for three to six months, killed, frozen, and shipped
to Japan. He found tuna fisherman Dinko Lukin. Even though he was
not the first to "farm" tuna, the Yugoslav-born Lukin is surely one of
the pioneers of the enterprise.[1] At first, the tuna were caught with
baited hooks and transferred to floating pens, but this proved to be
too harmful to the fish. So with Hirahara, Lukin claims to have
devised the scheme whereby they would purse-seine juvenile tuna in
the Great Australian Bight and tow them in underwater cages to the
waters off Port Lincoln. Whether it was Hirahara, Lukin, Joe Puglisi,
or somebody else, whoever thought of tuna ranching rescued a falter-
ing fishery and transformed it into a multimillion-dollar business.
Tuna farming launched the little fishing village of Port Lincoln into
the stratosphere of economic prosperity.

In 1991, only a couple of years after the Australians set up the
first "experimental grow-out project," Takahiko Hamano, a tuna-
farming expert, and Yoshio Koga, a fisheries biologist, were in South
Australia. They were part of a joint $1 million project involving the
Japanese Overseas Fishery Cooperation Foundation (OFCF), the
Australian government, and the Tuna Boat Owners Association of
Australia (TBOAA). Tuna farms were a South Australian innovation,
and it is possible—but not likely—that the Japanese really intended
to raise southern bluefin tuna and "release them into the open sea."
As defined, however, the project was almost circular: breed SBT in
captivity, release the juveniles into the wild, and then catch the juveniles and put them into pens to raise them to adult size so that they
can be killed and shipped to Japan. Obviously, it would be less complicated to raise the tuna from eggs to adulthood in captivity, but that
would require feeding them for eight years or more. It would be
cheaper to let them feed themselves in the open sea, recapture them,
and feed them for only a couple of years.

The 1991 breeding experiment did not work, and no spawning
behavior was recorded, but the tuna farmers of Port Lincoln
expanded their business exponentially anyway. (As we shall see, the
profits made by at least one of the tuna-farming companies have
encouraged them to try again to breed bluefins in captivity, but this
time on a much larger scale.) Capturing half-grown tuna, fattening
them, and selling them for exorbitant prices to Japan was a cash cow

for tuna farmers but a tragedy for tuna. Southern bluefins were so overfished that they became scarce, and some of the larger tuna-fishing companies floundered. Joe Puglisi, now a retired tuna company owner (he sold Australian Bluefin in 2000 for $100 million), was the first commercial tuna farmer in South Australia. As the first president of TBOAA, he has participated in the rise and fall (and rise again) of the economic roller coaster that is the tuna-farming industry. I talked to this genial, white-haired man in his office in Port Lincoln. He claimed that others were taking credit for what he did. But he told me without rancor ($100 million does a lot to dispel rancor) how he had developed the "towing cages" that make the industry possible, and how his company had gone into receivership in October 1992, when "we almost lost everything." With generous refinancing from local banks, however, Puglisi's company bounced back, and within three months, they were out of receivership. In the 1980s, Puglisi was almost alone in supporting the idea of quotas as he was catching close to 20,000 tons in Port Lincoln at the time. If some restrictions weren't in place, the area could become overfished, putting many commercial fisheries out of business. Once on the brink of failure because they were fishing the wild southern bluefins out of existence, tuna ranchers are now wallowing in money. Some of the money comes from the tuna farms, but the bulk of it comes from the individual ownership of quotas, parceled out to the tuna fishermen before the invention of tuna ranching in 1990. Tony Santic, a legendary tuna fisherman, reportedly sold 337 tons of his quota for $72 million, or $214,000 a ton. Even these men recognize that the tuna-ranching boom cannot last, so companies such as Clean Seas are investing heavily in projects designed to breed bluefins in captivity. In the meantime, the tuna millionaires are raking it in.

Port Lincoln is situated on one of the world's largest protected natural harbors, encompassing Boston Bay, which covers an area more than three times the size of Sydney Harbor. The harbor was discovered by Matthew Flinders under his commission by the British Admiralty to chart Australia's unexplored coastline in the ship *Investigator*. Flinders dropped anchor in Boston Bay in February 1802 and named the spot Port Lincoln after his native Lincolnshire in England. Initially considered as the alternative site for the state capital of South Australia, Port Lincoln was rejected in favor of Adelaide because Lincoln lacked an adequate freshwater supply. (Highways running south to Port Lincoln are accompanied by above-ground pipelines that bring in the city's water.) Now home to Australia's largest commercial fishing fleet, Port Lincoln has a thriving tuna-farming industry, but also aquaculture farms for kingfish, abalone, mussels, oysters, and, experimentally, seahorses and lobsters.

There are more millionaires per capita in Port Lincoln than in any other city in Australia, and most of them owe their success to the southern bluefin tuna. New houses, apartments, stores, marinas, hotels, restaurants, and shopping centers are being built at an astounding rate for a town whose population hovers around 14,000. Japanese dealers buy the entire catch of the Port Lincoln tuna fleet—often for astronomical prices. Japanese investments in the various tuna farms provided the capital to develop and implement the sophisticated technology that powered the industry. As the Port Lincoln tuna farmers (now fondly referred to as "tuna barons") prospered, the Japanese were assured of an almost endless supply of the precious red belly meat of the bluefin tuna. It was a win-win situation—unless, of course, you were a fish.

In April 1996, South Australia's tuna industry was crippled by a fierce storm that caused the deaths of thousands of captive fish that would have been worth more than $55 million. The fish, which were kept in floating pens and unable to escape the storm, were suffocated as their gills became clogged in swirling clouds of silt, excreta, and sediment. Between 65,000 and 75,000 tuna died, representing about half the population of Port Lincoln's nine farms in Boston Bay. The mass deaths were a serious setback, but evidently not a lasting one for the booming Port Lincoln tuna-farm industry, which has grown at a phenomenal rate since the first experimental farm was established in 1991. The $100 million fish-fattening industry now comprises a whopping 60% of the Australian tuna industry's 5,200-ton annual quota—and will probably rise even higher.

One unexpected outcome of the disaster of 1996, when most of the season's harvest perished, was the export of Australian expertise to Croatia. When Australians of Yugoslav extraction (such as Dinko Lukin) learned about the tuna farming off Port Lincoln, they realized that there were bluefin tuna in the Adriatic too, and Croatian and Australian businessmen formed a consortium to bring this new industry to Croatia. Aussie divers, net makers, and fishermen advised the

Croatians on the intricacies (and profitability) of tuna farming. By 1997, the Croatian version of Australian tuna farming was up and running. The bluefin tuna of the Mediterranean is not quite the same fish as the SBT—it is Atlantic bluefin tuna (ABT)—but it is similar enough that the same capture techniques can be applied to both species. Italy, across the Adriatic from Croatia, soon initiated its own tuna farming. By 2000, every country on or in the Mediterranean was catching tuna and putting them in offshore pens for fattening and sale to Japan. But the eastern Mediterranean is one of the two known breeding grounds for the Atlantic bluefin, and dozens of countries catching hundreds of thousands of half-grown tuna is the surest way to drastically deplete the population.

The Australian tuna-ranching industry has prospered wildly since its inception in 1991. In 2005 the southern bluefin tuna harvest reached 9,000 tons, the biggest to date. South Australia now has 15 southern bluefin tuna ranches, located primarily in two areas just east of Port Lincoln: Boston Bay and Rabbit Island. (This region is one of the most famous of all locales for great white sharks, and it is not unusual to find one of these man-eaters trapped in a tuna net.) Environmental groups have been lobbying for quotas, arguing that the very stock is threatened. But the tuna-ranching industry claims that a reduction in the catch would put people out of work, and besides, the status of the stock is fine. According to a 2006 report from the Australian Department of Agriculture, Fisheries, and Forestry, the southern bluefin tuna industry now earns an estimated $300 million annually.

Many kinds of fishes are commonly known as tunas: albacore, bigeye, dogtooth, yellowfin, skipjack, longtail, blackfin—and the bluefin, which comes in three varieties: northern (*Thunnus thynnus*), Pacific northern (*Thunnus orientalis*), and southern (*Thunnus maccoyii*). All tuna are scombrids, but not all scombrids are tuna. The family Scombridae includes several species of smaller, bullet-shaped fishes that are (correctly) grouped with the tunas, and also the mackerels, which are essentially smallish tunas without the heft, and without many of the advanced features that characterize the genus *Thunnus*. The blackfin tuna (*Thunnus atlanticus*), for example, is a small, typically shaped tuna, found only in the western Atlantic, from Martha's Vineyard throughout the Caribbean, and along the coast of northeastern South America as far south as Rio de Janeiro. The maximum length is around 40 inches, and the all-tackle record (taken off Key West, Florida, in 1996) is 45 pounds 8 ounces. A pelagic (oceanic) schooling fish that feeds near the surface, the blackfin is blue-black on the back, with a golden yellow band that runs from eye to tail but fades out soon after death. Despite its small size, the blackfin is considered a world-class game fish.

The Spanish mackerels, kingfish, seerfish, and the wahoo—a large, elongated game fish famed for its speed and unwillingness to be landed—are also classified as scombrids. All scombrids are more or less pointed at both ends, with a crescent-shaped tail and a series of finlets on the dorsal and ventral surfaces of the hind end, aft of the second dorsal fin and just before the insertion of the tail fin. The function of these finlets is unknown, but because all scombrids are fast swimmers, they are believed to be somehow connected with speed. (The marlins, swordfish, and sailfishes are as fast as or faster than tunas, but although they have the same lunate tail fin, they lack finlets.) Below the big-tuna designations are several species of bonitos, "little tunas," "bullet tunas," "frigate tunas," the kawakawa, and the cero. Most of the tunas are considered big-game fishes, worthy of being chased by fishermen in big expensive boats. But all the species that can exceed 20 pounds in weight are popular food fishes and are the object of some of the world's most extensive fisheries. Some of the boats used in commercial tuna fishery are *really* big and expensive.

Large or small, cold-water or warm, all tunas have the same basic body shape (plump in the middle and pointed at both ends, rather like a football), generally considered the most advanced design for moving efficiently through the water. The pointy front end would encounter even less water resistance were it not for the tuna's need to move water over its gills by keeping its mouth open. As Richard Brill and Peter Bushnell (2001) wrote, "tunas have high metabolic rates, and are obligate ram ventilators. They suffocate rapidly if prevented from swimming, so special care must be taken to ensure that ventilatory requirements are met during all stages of an experiment."[2] Because they depend on their own motion to pass oxygen-rich water over their gills, tuna can never stop swimming. When they are being as languid as possible, they must move a distance equal to their own length every second. They have no eyelids, so they can't close their eyes, and because stopping is not an option, they might move autonomically through the water, "sleeping" as the water passes over their gills. All fishes need oxygen, which is absorbed into the gills, but oxygen requirements differ dramatically from species to species, depending on the fish's lifestyle. The amount of gill surface on tunas is up to 30 times greater than that of any other fish. In some species, the oxygen-absorbing surface approaches that of the lungs of air-breathing mammals of comparable weight. To transfer oxygen from the gills to the bloodstream and thence to the other tissues, the heart of a tuna is, relative to the body weight, about ten times the size of that of other fishes. A tuna's blood pressure and heart rate are about three times higher. Another factor in oxygen absorption is hemoglobin, the pigment that actually transports oxygen in the blood. The hemoglobin concentration in the blood of tunas is almost as high as it is in humans. A higher oxygen intake contributes to the tuna's stamina and enables these superfish to undertake long-distance migrations, incredibly deep dives, and sprint speed that would do justice to a cheetah.

Also at the end, away from the tail—the cutwater, if you will—are the tuna's large eyes. Unlike the eyes of many other fish species, the tuna's eyes are flush with its head to enable it to pass through the water even more smoothly. The fins all fold flat against the body, and the first dorsal can be completely retracted into a slot. The scales of most tunas are so tiny as to be almost invisible; the great fishes slip through the water like polished torpedoes. All tunas have the same fin arrangement: a spiny, depressible dorsal fin; a second dorsal matched on the ventral side by the anal fin; and pectoral fins, used for steering and lift, that range from short in the bluefins and skipjacks to the long, knifelike blades of the albacore and yellowfins.

Bluefin Tuna

All the smaller tunas, such as skipjack, yellowfin, and albacore, are remarkably efficient animals and are as well-suited for their pelagic, predatory lifestyle as any marine creatures. But bluefins, the giants of the family, have taken every modification to the extreme.

The word "magnificent" is often applied to the bluefins, and it is exquisitely applicable. They are immensely powerful and fast, capable of speeds up to 55 mph. They are mature at about the age of 8, and individuals have been known to live for more than 30 years.

Bluefins spawn in April, May, or June in subsurface waters, but although spawning behavior has been observed in some of the smaller species, it has never been seen in bluefins. We do not know if they spawn once or many times in a season, or even if an individual spawns yearly. It is also unknown whether individuals can spawn in the east and then in the west at different times. Mature male bluefins are somewhat larger than females, which is different from the arrangement in billfishes, where the largest ones are *always* females. (Macho big-game fishermen such as Zane Grey and Ernest Hemingway went to their graves believing that all the big, tough, brave billfish and tuna they caught were males.) In the Western North Atlantic, bluefins mature by age 8. After examining the ovaries of 501 female bluefins from the Mediterranean, Aldo Corriero and (14) colleagues found that maturity for this "population" was reached between 4 and 5 years of age and a length of 54 inches. Females release millions of eggs, which are fertilized by males.

The spawning grounds for western Atlantic bluefins are in the Gulf of Mexico and the Mediterranean. (Spawning areas are identifiable by the presence of females with eggs ready to be broadcast and males with the sperm duct filled with spermatozoa.) Two of the Mediterranean spawning areas have been known for centuries: one just inside the Straits of Gibraltar, around the Balearic Islands, and the second in the Tyrrhenian Sea, from Sicily to the Gulf of Sidra (off Libya). It was not until well into the 21st century that a third spawning area was tentatively identified in the eastern Mediterranean between Turkey and Cyprus (Karakulak et al., 2004). Tagging results (such as Block et al., 2005) have shown that tuna have a definite "homing" instinct: bluefins hatched in a particular area return regularly to the place they were born. But many of the tagged fish do not show up in any of the known spawning areas, which raises a tantalizing question for researchers: Is there another breeding area for North Atlantic bluefins? Mather, Mason, and Jones suggested the possibility of a Gulf Stream spawning ground three decades ago, but so far, confirmation has not been forthcoming.

Tuna spawn only when the appropriate water temperature is reached, which ranges from 75°F to 79°F. For most species, spawning is restricted to warm, tropical waters with high salinity and strong current boundaries. For example, southern bluefins spawn only in a relatively small area off northwestern Australia in the eastern tropical Indian Ocean. Characterized as "reproductive broadcast spawners," mature females lay millions of eggs over a period of months. The eggs are tiny, spherical, and transparent and contain a single oil globule to keep them buoyant. Only a very small percentage of the eggs survive. The larval tuna, which are 2 to 3 mm long, hatch in a few days and begin feeding on plankton smaller than they are. The great majority of larval tuna are eaten by larger predators. It has been estimated that fewer than one in a million survives.

Bluefin tuna migrate on a yearly cycle, arriving in the waters off the northeast coast of North America by June of each year and departing in late autumn. They can be found as far north as Newfoundland in the summer, and they are known to travel as far as 40° south of the equator during the winter. Northern waters provide the fish with rich feeding grounds, where they can grow and store fat as an energy source for migration. Each year, they return to their specific spawning grounds: the Gulf of Mexico and the Mediterranean. It was always assumed that there were two separate North Atlantic populations—one that spawned in the Gulf of Mexico and remained in the western quadrant, and another that spawned in the Mediterranean and swam around in the eastern part of the Atlantic. Starting in 1997, a research team led by Molly Lutcavage of the New England Aquarium in Boston satellite-tagged juvenile bluefins in New England and Canadian waters. The data they collected from the pop-up tags (meaning the tags were designed to pop *off*) revealed some surprising results. None of the tagged fish had appeared in either the Gulf of Mexico or the Mediterranean, the only known spawning grounds for bluefin tuna. It may have been nothing more complicated than that the timed release of the tags was insufficient to detect spawning, but it also might be that there is another breeding area in the central North Atlantic. If that is the case, the ramifications would be enormous. Management of the two North Atlantic stocks, already compromised by the tunas' disinclination to remain in their half of the ocean, would be more than a little complicated if a third breeding population appeared on the scene.

A particularly disastrous alteration of the picture occurred in the waters off northeastern Brazil. Beginning around 1962, a fleet of Japanese longliners began fishing for tuna, and even though the operation was successful at first, it was suspended in 1967. Fromentin and Powers (2005) refer to this as the "Brazilian episode," during which Japanese longliners caught 5,000 to 12,000 tons of Atlantic bluefin tuna (ABFT) in an area where they usually caught tropical tuna. This caused severe overfishing of the large bluefin tuna. Targeting mostly small bluefins, the Japanese took 1,160 tons in 1981 and 2,660 tons in 1982 and reached a high of 4,778 tons in 1992–1993 before quitting. It appears that longlining for bluefins is no longer conducted off Brazil because the big fish are gone. (In the northwestern Atlantic, however, where the biggest bluefins can still be found, fishing continues apace.)

Long thought to consist of localized, discrete populations, the ABFT is actually a single population. It has the "widest distribution of any tuna and is the only large pelagic fish living permanently in temperate Atlantic waters."[3] It now appears that the "giants" come to feed on herring and other small fishes off the coasts of North Carolina, Massachusetts, and Maritime Canada, and move on when the herring are gone. During the course of their wanderings, bluefins display a remarkable range of temperature preferences, from near-freezing waters when feeding (37°F or 2.8°C) to very warm temperatures when breeding (86°F or 29.5°C). Because we saw them there—sometimes feeding voraciously on those herring—we also assumed that ABFT were creatures of surface waters. Not necessarily. Pop-up tags revealed that these fish—ABFT, bigeye tuna, and swordfish—forage at heretofore unsuspected depths, to feed on the small creatures that make up the deep-scattering layer, or perhaps as a means of cooling their overheated bodies. The energy required to maintain a high body temperature is limited, and the tunas cannot remain at depths indefinitely. They have to rise into warmer waters to restore their thermoregulatory balance.

Bluefin tuna were not always venerated. Around the turn of the twentieth century, they were known as "horse mackerel." They were considered a nuisance by herring or mackerel fishermen, because they sometimes followed the small fishes into the nets and, after eating their fill, tore their way out. Evidently the red meat was considered unappetizing then, for they were occasionally harpooned for oil when fish oil was a popular commodity. During the early decades of the last century, fishermen began harpooning the big ones, and land-ings in Maine and Massachusetts reached 94,000 pounds in 1919, 250,000 pounds in the 1930s, and 2 million pounds by 1948.[4] Bluefin tuna are now fished around the world, but a large proportion of the fish caught off Maine, Massachusetts, and California are destined for Japan. North Atlantic bluefins use the Mediterranean as a spawning ground, and fishers from virtually every country with a shoreline on that inland sea catch the tuna there. Countries such as Spain, Italy, Greece, Tunisia, Libya, Malta, and Turkey are now "ranching" blue-fins. They catch juvenile fishes and tow them to a pen, where they are fattened until they reach the size where they can be killed, frozen, and shipped to Japan. It is the Japanese sashimi market that sets the astronomical prices on these fish. They are the source of *toro*, the fatty belly meat that sells in Tokyo restaurants for the equivalent of $50 an ounce. When a big, top-quality tuna is caught in New Eng-land, Australia, or New Zealand waters, it may sell for $100,000 on the dock in Tokyo. By the time it is served in a restaurant, its value may have increased tenfold. Because of these prices, bluefins have been overfished, and their populations are threatened. But few effec-tive protection measures have been taken, because doing so would require unprecedented international cooperation.

As mentioned, at one time it was believed that there were two sep-arate populations of Atlantic bluefins: one that spent time along the east coast of the U.S. and offshore, and another that hung out in the eastern Atlantic and the Mediterranean. In those simpler times, Americans thought they should be able to catch the bluefins of the Western North Atlantic, and Europeans (along with Japanese, Chinese, and everybody else) thought the European tuna (which sometimes entered the Mediterranean) were theirs for the taking. A notable tagging program showed that the population structure was infinitely more complex than was previously thought, and that the Atlantic bluefins paid very little attention to which side of the ocean they were supposed to be on. (An analogous situation occurs in the Pacific. Bluefin tuna born off Japan sometimes swim to California, and if nothing interferes with their round trip (think Mexican purse seiners), they swim back to Japan.)

For purposes of "stock management," the International Commis-sion for the Conservation of Atlantic Tunas (ICCAT) divides the Atlantic tunas into two groups based on their known spawning areas.

One group spawns in the Gulf of Mexico and the Straits of Florida (the spawning areas of swordfish, too), and the other group spawns in the Mediterranean. It was never obvious to ICCAT that the Gulf of Mexico is open to the Atlantic and the Caribbean (except along the Gulf Coast, of course), while the Mediterranean is a huge fish trap—hard to get out of once you're in it—and that therefore the fisheries should be handled completely differently. (The first tuna ranchers, at Ceuta in Spanish Morocco, took full advantage of this fact. They set their trap nets in the 9-mile-wide passage that is the Strait of Gibraltar, snagging the post-spawning tuna on their way out of the Mediterranean.) In response to dwindling catches, ICCAT's 22 member countries divided the North Atlantic into eastern and western sectors, each with its own quota. In 1991, when Sweden submitted a proposal to ICCAT that the bluefin be listed as endangered, it was immediately voted down by the U.S. and Japan, two countries with a strong economic interest in catching tuna. (Japan consumes 36% of all tuna—of all species—caught in the world, and the U.S. follows with 31%.) Conservationists, fishermen, and bureaucrats continued to draft proposals and position papers, while tuna populations plummeted and prices rose. As John Seabrook wrote in 1994, "One reason that the price is so high is that there are so few of them left in this part of the ocean, and one reason that there are so few of them is because the price is so high."[5] In 1995, a 440-pound bluefin tuna sold on the dock in Tokyo for $173,600. If someone is willing to pay $173,000 for a fish, a lot of fishermen will be looking to be the lucky one to cash in.

The tuna of the eastern zone, caught mostly by Europeans, are managed under a strict annual quota set by the European Union. Those of the western Atlantic, targeted by American fishermen, have been managed under strict catch quotas since 1995. Nevertheless, in both areas, the stocks of bluefin tuna have fallen dramatically. An 80% decline in the eastern (European) stock has been seen over the past 20 years, and a 50% drop in the western Atlantic population. ICCAT's persistence in treating the "eastern" and "western" populations as separate stocks will only mean the continued and inexorable decline of Atlantic bluefin tuna. Because the fish of the western sector have been so heavily fished, they have received more of the benefits (such as they are) of ICCAT protection. The recent quotas of 3,000 tons in the western North Atlantic (compared with 32,000 tons in the east) will not benefit the western population if the fish are regularly venturing into the more heavily fished eastern regions. Until ICCAT recognizes that the ABFT is composed of a single, mixed population, the numbers will continue to plummet.

Because of the prices they can fetch, bluefins have been overfished, and their North Atlantic breeding populations are estimated to have declined about 90% in the last 20 years. As with all fish populations, exact counts are impossible. Therefore, to no one's surprise, there are vast gaps between the high estimates, made by the fishermen, and the low estimates, made by those who would protect the tuna from overfishing. From dock to cabinet ministry, there have been endless discussions about solving the problem at every level, but few protective measures have been taken, because doing so would require unprecedented domestic and international cooperation.

Fisheries management is a fine and noble goal, but there has to be something left to manage. During the 1960s, bluefin catches peaked at about 35,000 metric tons, but less than a decade later, overfishing sent the catch plummeting to less than half of that figure. A 1964 peak of 20,000 tons in the western Atlantic fell to 6,100 tons in 1978. The collapse of the New England tuna fishery has been comprehensively documented, most eloquently by Carl Safina in his 1997 *Song for the Blue Ocean*, but where the big fish were before they arrived off Georges Bank is still a mystery. The same is true of the massive schools of tuna that every year entered the bottleneck of the Straits of Gibraltar and swam into the Mediterranean, the functional equivalent of a gigantic fish trap. Somehow, the size, speed, and range of the great bluefins have kept much of their life history hidden from the prying eyes of researchers. Through great advances in tags and tagging techniques, we have been able to follow individual bluefins in the Atlantic and the Mediterranean. We are just beginning to get an idea of where they go and when.

How and where they are fished is also an issue. Unlike some other tuna fisheries, bluefin tuna in the Mediterranean are predominantly harvested by purse seine vessels. The good news is that this type of gear has relatively little bycatch. The bad news is that the illegal use of spotter planes makes it so easy to locate and capture schools of tuna that hardly any escape. Recent years have also witnessed tremendous modernization of the Mediterranean's purse seine fleet,

with larger, faster vessels outfitted with the latest in fish-finding technology. These vessels are so effective that traditional fishing grounds
in the western Mediterranean have been depleted and abandoned in
favor of high densities of spawning fish in the eastern Mediterranean.

At the heart of the problem is the rapid development of commercial tuna farming operations throughout the Mediterranean. Beginning as early as 1991, these tuna farms were not true aquaculture
operations that produce fish from spawning individuals. They are
more accurately termed "fattening operations," where tuna captured
by purse seine vessels are transferred to floating cages. Tuna are
caged anywhere from several months to several years, where they are
fed to increase their fat content and improve the color of the flesh in
order to better meet Japanese market standards. Nothing more and
nothing less than a tuna feedlot.

This is a problem, because roughly 10 to 25 kilograms of baitfish
are necessary to produce 1 kilogram of tuna. Therefore, the fattening
operations are grossly inefficient. In addition, the number of illegal,
unregulated, and/or unreported (IUU) catches has increased dramatically. Purse seine vessels no longer need to land their catch at port,
but instead transfer live tuna to cage operations directly at sea.
Indeed, even fish that are not destined for fattening are also directly
transferred to floating cages called "tuna hotels," where they are
slaughtered at sea and processed or blast-frozen. Some estimate that
up to 50% of the Mediterranean's total bluefin catch may be IUU.
Ultimately, a World Wildlife Fund (WWF) study reported that the
increase of IUU catches, exacerbated by the popularity of tuna farms,
may have generated a total catch in excess of 45,000 metric tons. This
catch is 40% above the 32,000 metric tons quota set by ICCAT, which
itself is 23% higher than the total quota recommended by scientists.
The harvest of Mediterranean bluefin tuna stock is 63% higher than
what the best science suggests.

As mentioned earlier, bluefin tunas come in three varieties: the
northern (*Thunnus thynnus*), which breeds in the Gulf of Mexico and
the Mediterranean and cruises the North Atlantic; the Pacific northern (*Thunnus orientalis*), which breeds in the waters of northern
Japan and crosses the North Pacific; and the southern (*Thunnus maccoyii*), which breeds in the waters north of Australia and south of
Indonesia and can be found throughout the Southern Ocean. All

three look very much alike, except that the northern version grows the largest—particularly in the waters of eastern Canada and New England. Because the three species do not mingle or interbreed, they are mostly differentiated by geography.

Pacific Bluefin Tuna

The species now known as *Thunnus orientalis* is the Pacific northern bluefin tuna. It's found primarily in the North Pacific from Japan to California (spawning in the vicinity of Japan), although specimens have also been taken off South Africa, western Australia, New Zealand, and the Galápagos Islands.

The three species of bluefin—southern, northern, and Pacific northern—have long been held to be separate. The true northern bluefin (*Thunnus thynnus*) does not visit the southern Pacific, so there is little chance of finding one off of Australia. As for the other two, the *visible* differentiating factors appear to be yellow versus blue caudal keels and yellow versus blue finlets.

Even though it breeds close to the islands of Japan, making it susceptible to a local fishery, the Pacific tuna population appears to be the only one of the three bluefin species that has not been severely overharvested. There is currently no management of bluefin in the north Pacific, a cause for worry given the status of the other populations. At present we know little about the movements of bluefin in the eastern Pacific, especially the larger animals. Based on the available information, we can conclude that bluefins appear to spawn only in waters off southern Japan, and that late in their first year, some individuals swim east. Data suggests that when the sardine population off of Japan diminishes, bluefin leave the area. Off the coast of Mexico and California, bluefin are most abundant in the summer and fall months, after which they seem to disappear.

Since 1952, the total catch for the whole Pacific Ocean has fluctuated between 10,000 and 35,000 tons, peaking around the 1980s, dropping off in the '90s, and climbing again at the beginning of the 21st century. By far the largest proportion was taken by Mexican purse seiners in the western Pacific, but there is also a Japanese longline fishery, as well as a purse-seine fishery that targets skipjack, yellowfin, and Pacific bluefins. The bluefins are not the most important product of this fishery by weight, but they are worth more because of the sashimi market. Unsurprisingly, the Japanese dominate this fishery, but the Taiwanese took nearly 3,000 tons in 1999.

Southern Bluefin Tuna

The southern bluefin tuna (*Thunnus maccoyii*) is a large, fast-swimming, pelagic fish found throughout the Southern Hemisphere mainly in waters between 30° and 50° South, but only rarely in the eastern Pacific. Some consider it a subspecies of the northern bluefin, which is technically known as *Thunnus thynnus*. The northern variety, found in all the temperate and tropical waters of the world—except the high southern latitudes—looks very much like the southern, but it gets much larger. (The International Game Fish Association (IGFA) record for a southern bluefin is 436 pounds; the record northern was a thousand pounds heavier.) Except for size, though, the difference in the two species of bluefin tunas is miniscule.

As early as the 1950s, the Japanese were catching *Thunnus maccoyii* in the northeast Indian Ocean. Southern bluefins proved to be so valuable that soon the Japanese expanded their operations to South and Western Australia. The tuna that are caught are frozen at very low temperatures (–60°C) and are either unloaded at intermediate ports and shipped to markets in Japan or are shipped directly to markets in Japan. From 1988 to 1995, a number of Japanese longliners (also catching yellowfin tuna, bigeye tuna, albacore, swordfish, and marlins) entered into a joint-venture agreement with Australian companies. But these agreements ended when the Australians switched over from pole-and-line fisheries to the purse seining (Robins and Caton, 1998). The Australian component of the fishery now uses purse seines to enclose a school of fish and then tows them to waters near the Australian mainland. There they are transferred to floating cages anchored to the ocean floor. The tuna are then fattened for several months and sold directly to Japanese markets as frozen or chilled fish. Because of the fishes' high fat content, premium prices can be obtained for *toro* in Japan. Australian tuna farmers boosted production from 140 tons in 1992 to more than 4,700 tons in 1998. The total value of the southern bluefin fishery is now estimated to be about AUS$1 billion.

Until recently, the only countries fishing the southern bluefin were Australia and Japan. The Australians used pole-and-line, purse seines, and trolling gear, but the Japanese used only longlines. In the 1950s, the annual catch of southern bluefin tuna (SBT to fisheries biologists) was 12,000 to 15,000 tons, and the fish was used mostly for canning. Heavy fishing pressure resulted in a significant decline in the numbers of mature fish, and the annual catch began to fall rapidly. It became apparent that the SBT stock was at a level where some kind of management and conservation were required. In 1985, Australia, Japan, and New Zealand, the main nations fishing southern bluefins at the time, began to apply strict quotas to their fishing fleets. In May 1993, the voluntary management arrangement between the three countries was formalized with the creation of the Convention for the Conservation of Southern Bluefin Tuna (CCSBT). Other fishing nations, such as Korea, Taiwan, and Indonesia, were active in SBT fishery, which reduced the effectiveness of the members' conservation and management measures. Of course, new counties trying to take advantage of the rich Japanese market caused the stocks to decline again. As a matter of policy, the CCSBT encouraged the membership of these countries. On October 17, 2001, the Republic of Korea joined the Commission, and Taiwan's membership became effective on August 30, 2002. Indonesia was accepted as a formal cooperating nonmember on August 2, 2004.

Not long after the formation of the CCSBT, the organization was called upon to adjudicate a conflict between the original signatories of the Convention, with Japan on one side and Australia and New Zealand on the other. Because the southern bluefin is a highly migratory species, it passes through the exclusive economic zones of several countries in the Southern Ocean. The Commission was formed because it was recognized that the stock was declining precipitously, and action was necessary by the countries that were actively fishing on the only population. Instead of cutting back, however, Japan began a no-limit "experimental" fishery in 1998 and took 1,400 tons over its assigned quota. In protest, Australia banned Japanese fishing boats from visiting Australian ports. (Not unlike "scientific research whaling," the Japanese experimental tuna fishery was nominally conducted for scientific purposes, but somehow, the meat ended up in fish markets and supermarkets.) This effectively shut down the lucrative arrangements between Japan and Australia for Japanese freezer ships to pick up the frozen tuna (farmed and wild-caught) that the Australians were consigning to Japanese markets. Australia and New Zealand requested an injunction under the International Tribunal for the Law of the Sea (ITLOS), and the tribunal suggested binding arbitration. An agreement was reached in May 2001 whereby Japanese ships were once again allowed into Australian ports and the Japanese agreed to substitute a limited scientific research program for their unrestricted "experimental" fishery.

Although management restrictions under the CCSBT have been in place for more than 10 years, the SBT biomass (total weight of fish) has continued to decline. The parental biomass is currently estimated at less than 10% of the 1960 level, well below what is considered a biologically safe level. Annual catches for countries operating outside the restrictions of the CCSBT, such as Korea and Indonesia, are probably on the order of 2,500 tons, and China is expanding its distant-water fishing fleet. According to the International Union for Conservation of Nature's (IUCN) Red List of Threatened Animals, the southern bluefin tuna is "critically endangered," which is defined as "facing an extremely high risk of extinction in the wild in the immediate future." In a 1997 TRAFFIC report on the southern bluefin tuna fishery, Elizabeth Hayes wrote, "The collapse of significant fisheries in the past several decades has indicated that it is possible to fish marine species to commercial extinction and that great economic suffering occurs as a result. If the warning signs are ignored, this possibility exists for SBT."[6]

In August 2006, an Australian investigation revealed that Japanese tuna boats, along with Taiwanese and Thai fishers, had been secretly taking more than twice the CCSBT quotas for the past 20 years and bringing the fish into Japan without reporting the actual catch. The discrepancies were first noticed by the Australian Tuna Boat Owners Association (ATBOA) when they saw "irregularities" in Japanese records of the fish caught in the Great Australian Bight. Japan had agreed to a 6,000-ton annual quota, but investigators learned that the country had been taking 12,000 to 20,000 tons every year for 20 years and hiding it.

The Japanese allowed only Japanese observers on their boats, so there was no one to report the excessive tonnage or the misrepresentation of the species. Some of the fish being delivered to Tokyo fish brokers as "bigeye tuna" were actually southern bluefins. Also, tens of thousands of tons of SBT were never entered in the Japanese public auction system, but were sold directly to retailers instead.

Following the revelations of Japanese overfishing, a CCSBT meeting was held in October 2006 at the Japanese tuna port of Miyazaki. Australian delegation leader Glenn Hurry announced that the 178,000 tons of SBT taken by the Japanese was actually worth $8 billion, not the $2 billion that had been previously estimated. The Australian delegation proposed that the Japanese annual quota, which was at 6,065 tons, be reduced to 3,000 tons. It is obvious that 10 years of flagrant disregard of quotas and regulations by the Japanese has been a major factor in the decline of southern bluefin stocks. It remains to be seen whether reduced quotas will enable the stock to recover. (Or if the Japanese intend to abide by the new quotas.)

Yellowfin Tuna

Yellowfins *(Thunnus albacares)* are probably prettier than bluefins and are more widely distributed, so more of them are caught commercially. With its extremely long, canary-yellow second dorsal and anal fins, the yellowfin is easily differentiated from other tunas. The pectoral fins, which also become yellow in adult fish, are very long, reaching to the base of the second dorsal. The finlets between the fins and the tail are also bright yellow. The most brilliantly colored of the tunas, the yellowfin is metallic blue or greenish-black above and pearl-white below; in younger fish, the lower flanks are crossed with interrupted vertical lines. Adult fish have a band of bright gold or iridescent blue (sometimes both) running along the flank. Spawning yellowfins have been observed to "flash" their colors, perhaps as a stimulant to the opposite sex. Conversely, dying tuna begin to lose their bright coloration and soon fade to shades of dull gray.

Spawning takes place twice a year and requires a water temperature of at least 79°F. At the Achotines Laboratory in Panama, efforts have been under way for several years to breed yellowfin tuna in captivity. Established in 1985 as part of the Inter-American Tropical Tuna Commission's (IATTC) Tuna-Billfish Program, the Achotines Lab is one of the few research facilities in the world designed to study the early life history of tropical tunas, particularly yellowfins. The laboratory is adjacent to Achotines Bay on the southeastern tip of the Azuero Peninsula on the Pacific side of the Republic of Panama, where the annual range of sea-surface temperature is approximately 21°C (70°F) to 29°C (84°F), ideal for spawning tuna. (The Azuero Peninsula is known to big-game fishermen as "the Tuna Coast" because of the yellowfin tuna, but also because it is the home of world-class blue, black, and striped marlins, as well as sailfish, dorado, and wahoo.) The continental shelf off Achotines Bay is quite narrow. The water reaches depths of over 600 feet less than 5 miles from shore, affording scientists ready access to oceanic waters where spawning of tunas occurs during every month of the year. Because little is known of the reproductive activities or early life history (egg, larval, and early-juvenile stages) of the various tunas, the IATTC established a research laboratory to focus on these aspects of tuna biology.

In 1992, IATTC scientists at Achotines began a joint project with Japan's Overseas Fisheries Cooperation Foundation to encourage breeding, spawning, and raising of tuna in captivity. From the program's inception in 1993 until its conclusion in 2001, several Japanese scientists were based at Achotines, working with IATTC personnel on the complex problems of breeding captive tuna. The tanks at Achotines held yellowfin tuna in virtually every stage of development, from floating eggs and inch-long larvae to 150-pound adults in the large tanks, which are 6 meters (20 feet) deep and 17 meters (45 feet) in diameter. Upon the Japanese departure in 2001, the facilities and equipment (much of which had been provided by Japan) became the property of the Republic of Panama and remained at the laboratory for use by IATTC scientists.

A captive population of 44 yellowfins first spawned in October 1996, which involved only two or three pairs of the largest fish. From the Achotines website: "Yellowfin tuna in the main broodstock tank have been spawning almost daily since October 1996, the only successful spawning of yellowfin in land-based tanks anywhere in the world. Spawning generally occurs from early afternoon to late evening." As Kurt Schaefer (2001) described it, "Each spawning event occurred around sunset, and was preceded by courtship behavior during the late afternoon. The courtship behavior included pairing of individuals, chasing, rapid color flashes exhibited by individual fish, and rapid horizontal or vertical swimming. During the following 3 months of 1996 spawning was continuous, with many of the fish exhibiting courtship behavior prior to each spawning event."[7] The numbers of fertilized eggs collected after each spawning event in the main broodstock tank range from several hundred to several million. The eggs are collected by several methods, including siphoning, dip-netting at the surface, and seining with a fine-mesh surface egg seine. Fertilized eggs are hatched in 300-liter (78-gallon) cylindrical incubation tanks.

Like many fish species, yellowfins are compulsive schoolers, but they often swim in mixed schools with skipjack, bigeye, and other tunas. Curiously, their association with dolphins has been observed only in the eastern tropical Pacific and not in the western Pacific, Atlantic, or Indian Oceans. But wherever yellowfins congregate, they are targeted by commercial fishers. Hundreds of thousands of tons are harvested annually, making yellowfin one of the most important of all commercially caught tunas. They are caught by longliners and pole-and-line bait boats, but the purse seiners figured out how to exploit the yellowfins' habit of aggregating under objects at the surface—particularly schools of dolphins. We don't know why they do this, but the habit has proven disastrous for millions of tuna (and dolphins). As tuna fishermen found their prey by spotting dolphins at the surface, and when they set their set their deep-water purse seines around the dolphins, they also caught the tuna, the object of the fishery in the first place. In addition to its desirability as a commercial species, *Thunnus albacres* is one of the world's most popular game fishes.

Yellowfins are found in every ocean (except the Mediterranean) in a wide swath between 45°N and 40°S. At least some of the stocks are migratory. Because of their size and strength, yellowfins are still highly regarded as game fish. Few other species can reach their size and put up such a fight. Therefore, they are among the primary objects of sport fishing clubs around the world. In *Fishing in Bermuda,* James Faiella wrote: "The yellowfin is considered the most prized of all tuna varieties both around Bermuda and elsewhere for their size, gameness, and the high quality of their flesh."

For example, Tuna Club members in Catalina, CA, caught a total of 6,532 tuna in 40 years. The best year was 1919, when 911 were taken. Tuna Club members could have caught 10 or a hundred times the number they caught over the years, and they wouldn't have come close to the numbers of yellowfins taken by commercial fishers in a given year. In just one part of one ocean, according to a 2002 report in *Pacific* magazine by Robert Keith-Reid:

> ...the annual yellowfin catch first exceeded 200,000 metric tons in 1980. By 1990 it had almost doubled to 380,000 metric tons. In the past four years it exceeded 420,000 metric tons with a peak of 480,000 metric tons... Tagging of yellowfin in the early 1990s, when catches were 10 to 20 percent below present levels, indicated that the stock was not being over-fished. But recent research shows that the stock has suffered a "significant" decline of about 35 percent since 1997. The decline is most evident in the western equatorial Pacific where the stock is estimated to be down by more than 50 percent since the mid 1990s. For the whole Western Pacific, the stock is estimated to be 30 percent below what it would have been had it not been fished.[8]

After skipjack, yellowfin is the second-heaviest-fished tuna. Like skipjack, it is canned and marketed as "light" tuna, but it is also an important component of sushi and sashimi. (The only tuna that can be labeled "white" is albacore.) When cooked, yellowfin meat is firm and mild-tasting and tends to be light yellowish-brown in color. In larger fish (20 to 30 pounds) the meat tends to become slightly darker and dryer. A report issued by the Japanese Fishing Authority (Anonymous, 2005) analyzed recent trends in tuna fishing in the Western and Central Pacific. In 2004, 1,447 longliners, 176 pole-and-line boats, and 54 purse seiners accounted for 31,717 tons of bigeye tuna, 41,406 tons of yellowfin, and 303,127 tons of skipjack. By an order of magnitude, skipjack is the predominant tuna species caught in the Pacific (and elsewhere), but yellowfin catches continue to rise. Most skipjack is canned, but more and more yellowfins are destined for Japanese restaurants, which are on the increase around the world. Charts with numbers usually cause the MEGO (My Eyes Glaze Over) syndrome, but I think the numbers tell a particularly important story about tuna fishing. Table 4.1 lists the number of catches of various tuna species in the Pacific. (Figures are in tons. I have included only a few years to show trends.)

TABLE 4.1 Catches of Various Tuna Species in the Pacific

Year	Yellowfin Tuna	Shipjack Tuna	Bigeye Tuna	Total
1975	332,098	423,713	108,730	864,451
1985	482,165	651,787	140,923	1,274,875
1995	619,031	1,201,004	190,055	2,010,090
2000	720,311	1,476,809	254,418	2,451,538
2003	866,707	1,549,025	210,647	2,626,379

Try to imagine what a million and a half tons of skipjack looks like. Or "only" three-quarters of a million tons of yellowfin. Recent analyses suggest that yellowfin is exploited to its optimum in the eastern Pacific Ocean and that no significant growth in volume will occur in the future in the western Pacific. In the Indian Ocean, exploitation leaves little room for a population increase. Although the yellowfin is not considered endangered, there is general concern that the increased catches of juvenile yellowfin (especially in the Atlantic, Indian, and western Pacific Oceans) will cause the stocks to suffer in the long term.

For the most part, the behavioral traits of wild animals have evolved to be beneficial to the species. Herding, flocking, or schooling, for instance, may be seen as stratagems to protect a given individual by offering too many choices to potential predators. Ultimately, of course, the predators evolved counterstrategies that enabled them to select one animal out of the school or herd and focus on that one to the exclusion of the others. Lions select one zebra out of the herd and chase only that one, ignoring other zebras galloping by—even those that cut in front of them. Longline fishing, where hundreds of miles of baited hooks are deployed, depends to a certain extent on the gregarious behavior of the target species. If tuna were not schooling fishes, not enough of them would take the baits deployed on the lines, and there would be no point in fishing for a given species in a particular place. The schooling yellowfins that so enraptured Zane Grey have another trait that ultimately have proven to be their undoing. They tend to aggregate near or under floating objects that can be as insignificant as a floating log, as large as a ship, or as active as a group of dolphins.

For reasons that are still unknown, yellowfins aggregate under schools of spotter and spinner dolphins in the eastern tropical Pacific, west of Central America and Mexico. In the 1960s, tuna fishermen out of San Diego learned that they could locate schools of yellowfin tuna by scanning the horizons for disturbances on the surface made by herds of leaping dolphins. In "setting on dolphins," a school of dolphins is rounded up like cattle by small outboard-motor speedboats. After the dolphins and tuna are encircled together, the net is closed ("pursed") at the bottom by a cable and rings. Then the net with the tuna and dolphins in it is brought aboard by a hydraulic power block. One set could net anywhere from 10 to 100 tons of tuna, a much more productive method of fishing than the old hook-and-line bait fishing. Production increased dramatically, but so did dolphin mortality. According to a 1986 study by N.C.H. Lo and Tim Smith, "the annual kill from 1959 to 1972 varied from 55,000 in 1959 to 534,000 in 1961. There were three distinct maxima of 534,000, 460,000, and 467,000, corresponding to peaks in the number of sets made on dolphins in 1961, 1965, and 1970. The total kill from 1959 to 1972 was estimated to be about 4.8 million."[9]

A great environmental outcry resulted in the passage of the Marine Mammal Protection Act in 1972, which made it a violation to harm any cetacean. But tuna fishermen lobbied for an exemption, and they continued to kill dolphins in staggering numbers. More than 300,000 died in 1972. Fishermen continued to set their nets on dolphins until they were sued in federal court by a consortium of conservation groups and forced to suspend their entire fishing operations. They were allowed to commence again only if they could abide by strict quotas imposed by the government, which were to be decreased annually to allow the fishermen to adjust to the new regulations. The first new quota, set in 1976, allowed the fishermen to kill 78,000 dolphins. The number was steadily reduced until it stood at 20,000 by 1981. In 1990, the StarKist Seafood Company (a subsidiary of the conglomerate H.J. Heinz) announced that it would no longer purchase tuna that had been caught with dolphins. StarKist began to label its cans of tuna "dolphin-safe." BumbleBee and Chicken of the Sea quickly followed suit. Because these three companies accounted for more than 80% of the tuna sold in the U.S., the dolphins were spared—for the moment, anyway.

In 1991, Mexico complained under the General Agreement on Tariffs and Trade (GATT) dispute settlement procedure. The dispute ended with the U.S. not being allowed to set an embargo on imports of tuna products from Mexico just because Mexican regulations on the way tuna was produced did not satisfy U.S. regulations. The report was never adopted, so Mexico and the U.S. held their own bilateral consultations aimed at reaching an agreement outside GATT. The outcome of the consultations was the Agreement on the International Dolphin Conservation Program (AIDCP), put into force in 1999. By the end of December 2002, the U.S. Department of Commerce ruled that encircling dolphins with nets a mile wide to catch tuna would not significantly harm them, through the implementation of the measures set forth by the AIDCP. Should all encircled dolphins be safely rescued from the nets, the tuna could be marketed as dolphin-safe. The previous definition of "dolphin-safe," introduced by the Earth Island Institute, excluded the labeling of "dolphin-safe" for any tuna caught by using the practice of encircling.

In 1994, President Bill Clinton signed into law the North American Free Trade Agreement (NAFTA), removing any restrictions on trade between the U.S., Canada, and Mexico. Under the terms of the MMPA of 1972, American fishermen could not fish in the eastern tropical Pacific without employing devices and procedures that would reduce the dolphin kill. But foreign fishers were not obligated to adhere to American restrictions and therefore could fish any way they wanted— including "setting on dolphins." The U.S. government concluded that circling dolphins in nets was harmless and threw open the door to allow Mexican fishers to sell tuna in the U.S. under a "dolphin-safe" label.

Further exploiting the inclination of tuna to aggregate, fishermen—particularly those in the South Pacific who fished for yellowfin and bigeye tuna—developed primitive devices that would attract the fish so that they could be caught. Indonesian and Philippine fishermen used floating rafts of bamboo or palm fronds, moored to the seafloor and weighted down with baskets of stones. The fish were speared, netted, or caught on hand lines. It was only a matter time before someone realized that attracting fish with one device and catching them with another was redundant, and "vertical longlining" was born. ("Horizontal longlining" is the traditional method of playing out mile after mile of lines and attracting the fish—and everything

else—to the baited hooks.) Combining the best features of fish aggregation devices (FADs) and longlines, this system consists of cables or
ropes supported at the surface by floats, moored to the bottom with
chains and anchors. Each suspended line is rigged with branch lines
that are festooned with baited hooks that are designed to attract
different-sized fish at different depths. The vertical longlines, therefore, are themselves FADs.

For the benefit of fishermen who want to try this new technique,
the Coastal Fisheries Programme of the Secretariat of the Pacific
Community (SPC) prepared a detailed manual, explaining everything
from rope-splicing and knot-tying to the selection of bait (and how to
catch it) for various targeted species. "Fish aggregating devices," reads
the introduction, "are floating rafts or buoys anchored in deep water
which, for reasons not yet fully understood, cause tuna and other types
of oceanic fish to gather around them... This fishing method, which
had now [1998] become known as vertical longlining, is still evolving,
with SPC continuing its work on streamlining the gear and increasing
the number of hooks that can be concentrated within a particular
area." The manual, titled "Vertical Longlining and Other Methods of
Fishing around Fish Aggregating Devices"[10] (Preston, Chapman, and
Watt, 1998), also details other methods of fishing around FADs. This
includes the Hawaiian night-fishing method called *ika shibi* ("squid-
tuna") because it was developed to catch the tuna that were attacking
the squid that the Hawaiians were trying to catch. In *ika shibi*, underwater lights are used to attract small squid, which in turn attract the
tuna, now the object of the fishery. The SPC report concludes:

> Vertical longline fishing around FADs can be a productive
> and potentially lucrative activity. It allows fishermen to target
> abundant resources of coastal tunas using small boats and
> simple, relatively inexpensive gear. Where cash markets for
> fish are well-developed, good-quality fresh tuna can com-
> mand premium prices. Provided they look after their catch
> properly, fishermen carrying out vertical longlining around
> FADs can target this market and make much greater profits
> than they could from many other styles of fishing.

Fish that are brought out of the water quickly suffocate, and
yellowfins caught by South Pacific fishers certainly could not be left

on deck to die in the sun. To help fishers solve this problem, the SPC published a booklet called "Onboard Handling of Sashimi-Grade Tuna." It succinctly explains how to gaff the tuna ("Never gaff the fish in the body, the throat, or the heart"), how to kill it ("stun the fish with a sharp blow to the top of the head, and then insert a spike into its brain"), how to bleed it ("When the tuna is struggling in the water... the blood attains a high organic waste (lactic acid) content and raises the temperature. Bleeding removes the organic waste and helps cool the fish's body"), how to clean it ("carefully rinse the fish inside and outside"), and how to chill and store it ("place it in a slurry of flake ice and sea water... protect the fish in a gauze sock or a plastic body bag... lower it gently into a refrigerated seawater tank."). The booklet concludes with this admonition: "No matter what methods of handling and presentation are requested by the buyers: always kill, bleed, and chill tuna that weigh over 25 kg as quickly as possible!"

Albacore

Identifiable by its winglike pectoral fins that reach beyond the anal fin, the albacore *(Thunnus alalunga)* is a medium-sized tuna that inhabits the temperate and subtropical waters of the world. They have a maximum life span of about 20 years, by which time they may reach 52 inches in length. (The present rod-and-reel record is 88 pounds.) Unlike some of the larger tunas, which are deepest in the region of the first dorsal fin, the albacore's greatest body depth is just forward of the second dorsal fin. Sport fishermen troll for albacore with feathered jigs, spoons, and lures or bait their hooks with mullet, sardines, squid, herring, anchovies, or any other available small fishes. Albacore is one of the world's most important food fishes and is the only tuna that can be labeled "white meat" on the can. It is commercially caught by trolling jigs behind a slow-moving boat, although other nations employ purse seines and longlines.

Albacore fishery is international, with fleets operating in most of the major oceans of the world. Albacore typically are caught between latitudes 10° and 45° both north and south of the equator, with most being taken on the high seas. The South Pacific albacore stock extends from the East Coast of Australia to the West Coast of South America. The longline fleet normally targets adult fish that are usually found in the surface mixed layer, but they have been caught as deep as 1,500 feet. *Thunnus alalunga* is a highly mobile species that moves throughout a very wide area of the South Pacific. While albacore travel in schools that generally are less dense than those of skipjack and juvenile yellowfin. Consequently, the commercial fishery is largely limited to longline or trolling.

According to a 2005 report by John Childers and Scott Aalbers of the National Marine Fisheries Service (NMFS) Southwest Fisheries Center at La Jolla, California, the U.S. troll-fishery in the North Pacific accounted for approximately 64,000 tons of albacore. This is approximately 20% of the total North Pacific catch of albacore; the Japanese account for another 73% of the total 320,000 tons, or 233,600 tons per year. The Japanese employ a pole-and-line fishery in the spring that targets two- to five-year-old fish off the Japanese coast eastward to the Emperor Seamount chain. There are also Japanese, Taiwanese, and South Korean longline fisheries, which harvest albacore in subtropical and temperate waters across much of the Pacific during the winter. Beginning in the early 1980s, Asian high-seas drift gillnet fisheries targeted two- to four-year-old albacore across much of the Pacific, but driftnets have supposedly been outlawed. There is a relatively small Canadian troll fishery for albacore during years when they appear in the waters off British Columbia.

The IUCN has not reassessed albacore in over 10 years. The last assessment (1996) was "data deficient," meaning that a population estimate is not possible. Assessments of the stocks of the North and South Atlantic from the same period showed them to be vulnerable and critically endangered, respectively, because of "actual or potential levels of exploitation." The North Pacific albacore population is considered a healthy stock at this time. It is considered an "eco-friendly" fishery in that there is very little bycatch and no impact on fishery habitat. Also, unlike some other tuna species, albacore do not swim with dolphins, so no albacore fishery is associated with dolphins. The NMFS considers the North Atlantic albacore population overfished, with overfishing still occurring, but the southern Atlantic stock is not considered overfished.

"Troll-caught" albacore are between 3 and 5 years old, harvested by trolling artificial lures with unbaited hooks behind a slow-moving boat. Commercial fishermen in North America have used this low-impact, environmentally responsible fishing technique to catch albacore for nearly a century. Albacore fishing fleets from other countries tend to use other fishing methods. Those who advocate the consumption of albacore maintain that younger troll-caught albacore contain more beneficial omega-3 fatty acids than older, larger albacore more commonly available on the market. Processing techniques also affect the omega-3 content of canned albacore. Most canned albacore sold by the big major brands comes from older, larger albacore, which is cooked twice during the canning process. Some fishermen now offer custom-canned troll-caught albacore, hand-packed and cooked just once to prevent the loss of omega-3s.

Regardless of where (or how) it is caught, most albacore ends up in cans in the U.S. In Japan, *shiro maguro* (literally, "white tuna") is uncommonly served as sushi or sashimi because the meat is so soft that it is difficult to handle. Moreover, albacore accumulates higher levels of mercury than other kinds of tuna, and some groups have urged testing and recall of canned albacore with high mercury levels. Longlined albacore are older fish and have accumulated more mercury than younger, troll-caught fish. The U.S. Food and Drug Administration (FDA) advises women of childbearing age and children to limit their consumption of albacore tuna (chunk white canned tuna) and tuna steaks to 6 ounces per week or less.

Bigeye Tuna

The large eyes of this species suggest that it lives and hunts at greater depths than other tunas. Bigeyes reach a maximum length of 7½; feet and can weigh 400 pounds. (The record is a 435-pounder caught off Peru.) Whereas the body of a bluefin is deepest around the middle of the first dorsal fin, the bigeye is deepest just forward of the second dorsal. (It is believed that the specific name *obesus* is derived from the depth of the body.) Bigeyes resemble yellowfins—they are both called *ahi* in Hawaii—but *Thunnus albacares* has yellow, scythe-like dorsal and pelvic fins, and *Thunnus obesus* has longer pectoral fins and a proportionately larger head. Like most of the large tunas, the bigeye is metallic blue-black above and silvery-white on its flanks and belly, with pale vertical striping.

Bigeyes are among the most commercially important tunas, especially in Pacific Rim countries such as Japan and Australia. They are usually caught on longlines, not in nets, and are sold fresh, not canned. The bright-red meat, higher in fat than that of other large tunas, is prized for sashimi and grilling. Bigeyes are found all over the world in tropical and subtropical waters, and they are popular big game fishes on both coasts of North America, in Hawaii, and in Australia. Among the countries catching bigeye tuna, Japan ranks first, followed by the Republic of Korea with much lower landings. The world catch increased from about 164,000 metric tons in 1974 to 201,000 tons in 1980, reaching a peak of 214,000 tons in 1987. In the Indian Ocean, the bigeye tuna fishery was dominated by Japanese fleets up to the end of the 1960s, but as operations of vessels from Korea became more important, they accounted for more than 60% of the catch in the late '70s. The most important fishing gear in the Pacific are longlines, which comprise some 400 "baskets" (consisting of five branch lines, each with a baited hook) extending up to 80 miles. Day and night operations are common throughout the year, but seasonal variations in apparent abundance are reflected in changes in fishing effort. In the 1970s, deep longlines employing between 10 and 15 branch lines per basket were introduced. This new type of gear is theoretically capable of fishing down to a 300-meter (984-foot) depth, as compared to the usual 170 meters (557 feet) reached by traditional longline gear. Catch rates for *T. obesus* increased for about three years and then declined to previous levels again, suggesting that only a portion of the bigeye resources were exploited. Bigeye tuna is exploited in increasing quantities as associated catch of the spring and summer pole-and-line fishery in the northwestern Pacific, and of the purse-seine fishery in the eastern Pacific, both directed primarily at skipjack and yellowfin tuna. In Japan, its meat is highly priced and processed into sashimi in substitution for bluefin tuna. The catch reported for 1996 to the Food and Agriculture Organization of the United Nations (FAO) was 328,067 tons, of which 101,591 tons were taken by Japan, 64,498 tons by Taiwan, and 28,418 tons by Korea.

Bigeye tuna meat is reddish-pink in color, and, like yellowfin, it begins to discolor when exposed to air. For this reason, bigeye is usually not loined or filleted until shortly before use. Larger bigeyes typically have a higher fat content than the smaller ones, but even a fish as small as 25 to 30 pounds may be rich in fat. Bigeye tuna is one of the preferred species in the preparation of sashimi. With a high fat content, bigeye is also among the most desirable species for grilling.

The Environmental Protection Agency (EPA) has issued a health advisory for longline-caught bigeye tuna because of high levels of mercury. The IUCN considers the bigeye tuna a "vulnerable" species.

Skipjack

The small skipjack tuna *(Katsuwonus pelamis)*, also known as ocean bonito and striped tuna, is the most heavily-fished of all tuna and is one of the world's most important food fishes. Skipjacks are found worldwide in tropical and subtropical waters, often aggregating in schools that may number as many as 50,000. In the Atlantic, they frequently associate with blackfin tuna *(Thunnus atlanticus)*, and in the Pacific and Indian Oceans, they school with the yellowfin *(Thunnus albacares)*. In the eastern tropical Pacific, all three species are fished by "setting on dolphins." Skipjacks reach a length of 3 feet, but most are smaller. The world record-holder weighed 41 pounds and was caught off Mauritius in the Indian Ocean. In the Atlantic, skipjacks frequently associate with blackfin tuna *(Thunnus atlanticus)*, and in the Pacific and Indian Oceans, they school with yellowfins *(Thunnus albacares)*. The skipjack is a popular game fish, and it is the mainstay of California tuna fishery. It is of tremendous commercial importance in Japan, Hawaii, and the Caribbean, where it is marketed frozen, salted, and fresh. When canned, it is known as "light-meat" tuna.

Because yellowfin and skipjack aggregate, they are often caught together. Catches of both species are increasing. In 2002, the total catch of skipjack was 2,076,000 tons, amounting to 51% of the total tuna catch. Yellowfins amounted to another 32%, at 1,321,000 tons.[11] In general, the outlook for world production of skipjack and yellowfin tuna is mixed. For yellowfin, most of the fisheries, with the possible exception of the eastern Indian Ocean, are probably fully exploited. For skipjack, catches can possibly be increased in the Pacific, but probably not much, if any, in the Atlantic and Indian Oceans. In the eastern Atlantic, the catches by the surface fleets targeting yellowfin and skipjack have reached the upper sustainable limit of yellowfin and probably are near that limit for skipjack. This tendency became obvious in the early 1980s and caused many purse-seine vessels from the Atlantic to transfer their operations to the western Indian Ocean (ICCAT, 1999).

The western Pacific supports the largest tuna fishery in the world, producing about 60% of the world's skipjack and 35% of the world's yellowfin. Analyses conducted by scientists of the SPC, based mostly on data from tagging experiments, suggest that the skipjack stocks of the region can support an increase in catch. However, for this increase to become reality, the stocks of currently underexploited skipjack must be identified, there must be a demand for the raw material, and they must be vulnerable to fishing gear. Increasing fishing effort may lead to increased catches of skipjack. However, in the western Pacific, as in the eastern Pacific, skipjack are often caught together with small yellowfin and bigeye. Therefore, the problem lies in ensuring that the increase is in catches of skipjack only, not those of yellowfin and bigeye.[12]

Almost 50 years ago, the NMFS built the world's first research facility designed to maintain tunas in captivity at Kewalo Basin in Honolulu. Local fishers would bring in adult yellowtail and skipjack tuna, and they would be maintained in large tanks. Studies were conducted on visual acuity, sound sensitivity, olfaction, energetics, thermoregulation, geomagnetic sensitivity, and the spawning and rearing of tuna eggs. High-quality, coral-filtered seawater is used in several 20,000-gallon pools to hold tuna and other pelagic fishes. Skipjack captured at sea were installed in tanks at the Kewalo lab. They spawned about eight hours after capture, but the eggs did not survive.[13]

Commercial Tuna Fishing

Fishing with traps is perhaps the oldest known type of "commercial" fishing—that is, catching large numbers of fish to feed more than the fisherman and his family. The Phoenicians, who lived along the shores of the eastern Mediterranean some 30 centuries ago, are believed to have built traps that consisted of palm-tree branches stuck in the sand. They were used to guide the tuna into shallow water, where they were beaten to death with clubs or stabbed with spears (Sara, 1980). Almost completely enclosed by Europe and Asia Minor to the north and Africa to the south, the Mediterranean is open to the North Atlantic through the Straits of Gibraltar on the west and to the Black Sea by the narrow passage known as the Bosporus. The average depth of the Mediterranean is 4,900 feet, but extensive areas of the seafloor are below 6,800 feet. The deepest recorded point is 17,275 feet (about 3.27 miles) in the Hellenic Trough, west of the Peloponnesus. It is 2,400 miles from the Straits of Gibraltar to the shore of Lebanon, and the longest north-south distance (from Trieste to the shore of Libya) is about 1,000 miles. The Mediterranean's 1.45 million square miles constitute the largest fish trap in the world; it was easy for the fish to get in, but very hard for them to get out.

For thousands of years, fish trappers have taken advantage of the enclosed nature of the Mediterranean. Improved and modified over time, the individual traps consist of a complex of nets that are held up by means of floats and are anchored to the bottom with weights. They form a series of one-way passages that funnel tuna into a final chamber, where they can be killed. Sara's summary history of trap fishing in the Mediterranean identifies areas around Spain, the Balearic Islands, Corsica, Sardinia, Italy, Sicily, the Adriatic, Greece, and Turkey where trap fishing for tuna has been practiced for thousands of years. The surface circulation of the Mediterranean essentially runs counterclockwise. It moves eastward along the coast of North Africa, passing through the narrow Strait of Sicily and circling back in the northern quadrant, toward the Strait of Gibraltar and the open Atlantic. Because migrating tuna tend to swim close to the surface, they follow this circulation pattern until their journey is rudely interrupted by fishermen who lay traps for them. (By the 20th century, fishermen would catch fish off North Africa as well, but that is part of the tuna-farming story, which comes later.)

Tuna fishing was once one of Sicily's most important and profitable industries. Until the first decades of the 20th century, coconut-fiber nets over a mile in length were deployed by the hundreds. But diminishing numbers of tuna and market laws that have made this fishing technique more capital-intensive have left only about ten *tonnare* (tuna fisheries) in the Mediterranean. Only Bonagia and Favignana are left in Sicily. What was once a source of pride (not to mention the primary source of income) for entire communities has turned into a tourist attraction. It provides a few makeshift jobs for the unemployed in a social context poor of prospects and is kept alive by the obstinate will of the remaining *tonnaroti*. The canneries in Sicily are closed; almost all the tuna caught in Favignana is shipped to Japan. Like everyone else, the Japanese fish buyers await the annual *mattanza* (tuna killing).

Other than the trap fishers, the earliest commercial fishers probably speared their prey, or worked from a canoe or dory with a baited hook on the end of a line. A variation of this method is employed today in tropical Pacific and Atlantic waters to catch the smaller tuna species, such as albacore and skipjack. Dories are not used. Instead, the fishermen stand at the rail of a fishing boat, attracting schools of tuna by "chumming," and using bamboo poles with unbarbed, unbaited hooks. The tuna are yanked out of the water by the large crew of fishermen, thrown over their heads onto the deck, killed, and stored below decks in freezers. Some technically advanced countries have replaced the fishermen with "jigging machines" that perform the same function, thus decreasing labor costs.

The Greeks did not have a word for longlining, one of the most efficient of all fishing techniques. Longlining consists of a single line that may be 100 miles long (the distance from New York to Philadelphia), supported along its length by floats. The lines are hung with thousands of hooks baited with live or frozen baitfish and are deployed in an area where a particular species is being sought. Hanging from the longlines are as many as 3,000 hooks on "branch lines" that are dangled into the water and that can be adjusted to fish at depths ranging from 180 to 500 feet. It can take up to 8 hours to set the net and 12 to retrieve it. The gear is passive, in that it captures whatever fish happen to take the bait. The target species takes the bait, but so does every other kind of fish in the area. When tuna are the object of the fishery, sharks, billfishes, and any other fishes that are caught are often discarded, because it's too much trouble to separate them. In 1995, an estimated 1,500 shy albatrosses (*Diomeda cauta*), out of a breeding population of 8,000, were caught in longlines and killed. Probably the most heinous use of longlines is in sub-Antarctic waters. Fishers of the Patagonian toothfish (*Dissostichus eleginoides*) scour the waters for their target species but kill hundreds of thousands of other fishes, whales, seals, dolphins, and as many as 150,000 seabirds annually. Longlining accounts for about 30% of the world catch, including most of the billfishes taken commercially. The largest longline fleets are those of Japan, followed by those of Taiwan, China, and South Korea.

When Japan developed monofilament fibers that could be used in open-ocean driftnetting in the mid-1970s, it introduced the most durable and destructive method of fishing ever devised. Large-scale, high-seas driftnets were first used in the North Pacific by fleets from Japan, Taiwan, and South Korea. Free from a connection with any boat, driftnets are set with floats at the top and weights at the bottom so that they drift passively in the water and trap anything that swims into them. Traditionally, these were small nets used in coastal waters to catch dense schooling fish such as herring. But with the introduction of light synthetic netting, driftnet fishing underwent a major change. The nets could now be used on the high seas, where they are very effective at catching wide-ranging species such as tuna and squid.

Early in fishery, big tuna were caught on hook and line, with chum being thrown in to excite the voracious fish into biting at anything and everything in the water. Fishermen stationed along the rails with heavy rods and unbaited, barbless hooks yanked the heavy fish over their shoulders, hoping to have them land on deck—which they often didn't.

In the western North Atlantic, the purse seine and the longline changed tuna fishery so much that by 1964, the combined landings from these two fisheries had skyrocketed to 20,000 tons. As it became apparent that some sort of conservation measures were necessary to protect the great fish from overfishing, ICCAT was born. For control purposes, the Commission considered the Atlantic tuna as two stocks, separated by 45°W in the North Atlantic, with a dogleg around the bulge of South America to 25°W in the South Atlantic. Until the 1980s, most commercial tuna fishermen avoided taking the really big fish—bluefins can reach 1,500 pounds—because they were too difficult to handle. But when the Japanese sushi market opened its bottomless maw, the larger fish became the specific target of fishery. Prices skyrocketed, and it was almost impossible to convince people *not* to fish for tuna.

For more than two decades, ICCAT considered the biomass that existed in the mid-1970s to be the maximum sustainable yield (MSY) level for the western Atlantic bluefin tuna stock. But since 1975, the population has been allowed to decline by an additional 88%. According to ICCAT's latest stock assessment, the biomass of this stock had declined to only 12% of that needed to produce the MSY. Thus, in just four decades, the population was driven from a healthy level (over three times the MSY level) to a level just above extinction. This occurred because of unrestrained fishing sanctioned by ICCAT on the world's most valuable fish. The population is being held at this precarious level by continued overfishing allowed by ICCAT, ostensibly to provide scientific monitoring information on the bluefin's status. In reality, it is unnecessary to kill any remaining bluefin until they can recover, because the abundance of each year's class could be assessed using aircraft and other nonlethal means, such as tagging. But this would eliminate the large profits continuing to be made by a few fishers who have considerable political influence.

The tuna of the eastern zone, which are caught by Europeans, are managed under a strict annual quota set by the European Union. Those of the western Atlantic, targeted by American fishermen, have been managed under strict catch quotas since 1995. (Neither of these quotas includes farmed tuna.) Nevertheless, in both areas, the stocks of bluefin tuna have fallen dramatically: there has been an 80% decline in the eastern (European) stock over the past 20 years, and a 50% drop in the western Atlantic population.

Because of the prices they can fetch, bluefins have been overfished, and their North Atlantic breeding populations are estimated to have declined about 90% in the last 20 years. As with all fish populations, exact counts are impossible. Therefore, vast gaps exist between the high estimates, made (to no one's surprise) by the fishermen, and the low estimates, made by those who would protect the tuna from overfishing. From dock to cabinet ministry, endless discussions have taken place at every level about solving the problem. But few protective measures have been taken, because doing so would require unprecedented domestic and international cooperation.

ICCAT is not based in Washington (its headquarters are in Madrid), but it might as well be. The commission is made up of 22 member countries on both sides of the Atlantic, plus Japan, which is, of course, a major fisher, importer, and consumer of Atlantic tuna. Under pressure from the powerful commercial fishing interests, ICCAT has consistently supported the fishers at the expense of the fish, while paying only the faintest lip service to recreational fishers. Even as the Atlantic tuna populations plummeted, and the fish were listed as endangered, ICCAT allowed the harvest of *Thunnus thynnus* at levels that endangered the species even further.

ICCAT's charter explicitly states that tuna stocks should be managed for maximum sustainable yield (MSY). This approach seeks to maximize the annual harvest by holding the population at approximately 50% of the predetermined environmental carrying capacity. At this level, the population should reproduce at its maximum rate so that the recruitment of new fish to the population is maximized each year. As long as the population is not reduced below the MSY level, the theory goes, fishermen can harvest the annual surplus indefinitely. But bluefin tuna populations rise and fall for a variety of environmental reasons, and trying to factor in the MSY only contributes to the chaotic nature of the population assessments. Because the MSY may never be determined with any sort of accuracy, quotas can swing wildly from year to year and impact the population in ways that fishery biologists do not yet understand. ICCAT began keeping records in 1976. But, as Myers and Worm pointed out in 2003, over the past 50 years, Japanese and other longline fleets around the world have reduced the populations of large predatory fishes (sharks, tuna, billfishes) by 90%, leaving the remaining 10% for today's fishers. Add to that ICCAT's dedication to maximizing the total allowable catch (TAC) for all commercial tuna fishers, no matter where they are based or where they fish, and you can begin to understand why North Atlantic tuna populations are at an all-time low. And why Japanese consumption of bluefin tuna is at an all-time high. Low population added to intensified fishing effort only leads to disaster, as is happening in the Mediterranean.

Obviously, a robust population requires the addition of new animals, which means that the spawning stocks of the tuna must be protected—or at least not killed off. ICCAT failed to protect the spawning stocks of Atlantic bluefin for many years, and population levels have fallen far below the level required to sustain MSY. Between 1970 and 1993, the recruitment of young fish into the adult population fell from over 300,000 per year to only 50,000 or fewer (Safina, 1993). In 1975, stock size estimates for spawning fishes (those over 320 pounds or 145 kg) were at only 25% of levels estimated in 1960. By 1990, spawning stock was at only 7% of the 1960 level. Furthermore, ICCAT still operates under the assumption that there are two distinct stocks of northern Atlantic bluefin: one that spawns in the Gulf of Mexico and migrates north along the coast of North America, and another stock that spawns in the Mediterranean and migrates along coastal Europe and northern Africa. The western stock has declined precipitously over recent decades, and the catch from the western stock is highly regulated by ICCAT and the U.S. National Marine Fisheries Service (see Figure 4.4).

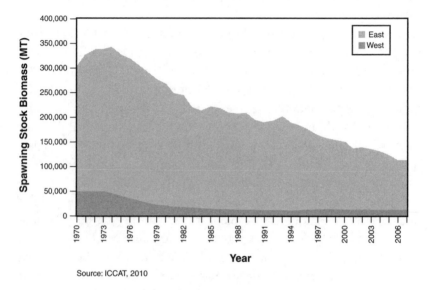

Source: ICCAT, 2010

Figure 4.4   Atlantic bluefin tuna stock size

Source: Tag-A-Giant

Tagging studies confirmed that some subadults or adults hatched in the Gulf of Mexico found their way to the Mediterranean, but tag returns were very limited. Eastern fishermen tend not to report the capture of tagged western fish in the Mediterranean because they fear it would cause the imposition of restrictive quotas. Even today, European ICCAT representatives are reluctant to redefine bluefin stock structure because they don't want to consider restrictive quotas on eastern fishermen. This reluctance, coupled with the introduction of tuna ranches in the Mediterranean, have resulted in such a massive crash of the eastern Atlantic and Mediterranean bluefin tuna populations that the WWF has called for an immediate closure of all Mediterranean tuna fisheries.[14]

By 1987, the Japanese squid fleet had expanded to 1,200 boats, each deploying up to 30 miles of nets every night during a seven-month fishing season. Some of the nets were 40 miles long. Japanese and Taiwanese boats driftnetting for albacore kill not only the tuna, but tens of thousands of other animals as well. In 1989, conservationist guerilla Sam La Budde made a film called *Stripmining the Seas*, which showed driftnets being hauled aboard and drowned dolphins being kicked overboard. The film was seen by many people, including members of the U.S. Congress. Objections to driftnetting kept piling up. In 1989, the United Nations adopted a resolution to reduce driftnet fleets and ban driftnetting in the South Pacific. Japan and Taiwan were the major culprits. A 1989 report showed that the Japanese squid fleet alone was responsible for the death of a million blue sharks, 240,000 seabirds, and 22,000 dolphins. Over worldwide objections, the Taiwanese continued to deploy their "curtains of death," and they are still being used by pirate driftnetters. A net that has been cut loose or has broken loose does not quit working. It keeps killing fishes, dolphins, and sea turtles even when there is no one to haul in the net to harvest or release the prisoners. Known as "ghost nets," these gigantic net walls keep on fishing long after the mother ship has departed.

The Mediterranean has been the scene of intense driftnet fishing, even though it supposedly has been outlawed. Prohibitions have had little effect, however, and driftnets are still being set by the fishers of various Mediterranean countries, particularly Greece and Italy. In the summer of 2006, two conservation organizations, Greenpeace and Oceana, deployed vessels to document and film the illegal driftnetters at work. The Greenpeace flagship *Rainbow Warrior* spent three weeks confronting (and filming) rogue fishing boats in the Mediterranean. Sofia Tsenikili of Greenpeace Greece said, "If people are horrified by the images of whales being harpooned in the Southern Ocean, they'd be equally repulsed by the thousands of dolphins and other creatures that are being entangled and killed by fishermen using huge illegal driftnets each season in the Mediterranean." Oceana, a network of marine conservationists, has also documented the use of illegal driftnets by Italian fishers in the Mediterranean. The *Oceana Ranger* sailed through 1,500 miles of the Ligurian and Tyrrhenian Seas, observing numerous vessels "capturing species like swordfish or albacore tuna with driftnets that are totally banned. We have also witnessed how these catches are unloaded in ports without any type of control...and after being loaded into trucks, they are 'laundered' through irregular supply chains." The illegal fishers were reported to the Italian Coast Guard, but it is unlikely that anyone can stop driftnetting—it is just too lucrative.

When the stocks of western North Atlantic codfish crashed 10 years ago, fishing for cod was banned to allow them to recover. But as reported by Bundy et al. in 2000, the population dynamics have been so drastically altered that cod may never reappear in their former numbers. Not only cod, but also virtually all high-quality table fish, such as tuna, haddock, and flounder, have fallen to about 16% of what their numbers were in 1990.

Endnotes

[1] Hori, T. 1996. *Tuna and the Japanese*. Japan External Trade Organization.

[2] Brill, R.W. and P.G. Bushnell. 2001. The cardiovascular system of tunas. In B.A. Block and E.D. Stevens, eds. *Tuna: Physiology, Ecology, and Evolution*. 79-120. Academic Press.

[3] Fromentin, J.M. and J.E. Powers. 2005. Atlantic bluefin tuna: population dynamics, ecology, fisheries and management. *Fish and Fisheries* 6(4):281-298.

[4] Bigelow, H.B. and W.C. Schroeder. 1953. Fishes of the Gulf of Maine. *U.S. Fish Wildl. Serv. Fish. Bull.* 74:1-577.

[5] Seabrook, J. 1994. Death of a giant: stalking the disappearing bluefin tuna. *Harper's* 288(1729):48-56.

[6] Hayes, E.A. 1997. *A Review of the Southern Bluefin Tuna Fishery: Implications for Ecologically Sustainable Management*. TRAFFIC Oceania.

[7] Schaefer, K.M. 2001. Reproductive biology of tunas. In B.A. Block and E.D. Stevens, eds. *Tuna: Physiology, Ecology, and Evolution*. 225-270. Academic Press.

[8] Reid, T.R. 1995. Tsukiji: The great Tokyo fish market. *National Geographic* 188(5):38-55.

[9] Smith, T.D., ed. 1979. Report of the status of porpoise stocks workshop (August 27-31, 1979, La Jolla, California). *NMFS Southwest Fisheries Center Administrative Report LJ-79-41*. 62.

[10] Preston, G.L., L.B. Chapman, and P.G. Watt. 1998. *Vertical Longlining and Other Methods of Fishing Around Fish Aggregating Devices (FADs): A Manual for Fishermen*. Secretariat of the Pacific Commission.

[11] de Leiva, J.I. and J. Majkowski. 2005. *Tuna resources*. FAO. Rome.

[12] Hampton, J., A. Lewis and P. Williams. 2002. *The Western and Central Pacific Tuna Fishery: 2000 Overview and Status of Stocks*. Tuna Fisheries Assessment Report/Secretariat of the Pacific Community. Oceanic Fisheries Programme Report No. 3:59.

[13] Schaefer, K.M. 2001. Reproductive biology of tunas. In B.A. Block and E.D. Stevens, eds. *Tuna: Physiology, Ecology, and Evolution*. 225-270. Academic Press.

[14] Bregazzi, R.M. 2006. *The Plunder of Bluefin Tuna in the Mediterranean and East Atlantic in 2004 and 2005: Uncovering the Real Story*. World Wide Fund for Nature.

5

Tsukiji Fish Market

The Tsukiji Market in Tokyo is the largest wholesale fish market in the world. More than 2,000 tons of seafood is auctioned off every day between 5 a.m. and 2 p.m. at 1,667 stalls, with over 50,000 fisherman, traders, and restaurant owners participating in the action. The market covers 556 acres mostly occupied with buying and selling stalls, or "pits" as on the floor of the New York Mercantile Exchange (NYMEX). Tsukiji officially opened in 1935. In its first full year of operation, the market handled 183,000 metric tons of seafood valued at ¥45 million, more than $20 million in 1936 dollars or roughly $313 million by today's standards.[1]

The market has its own docks on the Sumida River, which opens into Tokyo Bay, so some of the produce comes straight from the sea. Refrigerated trucks arrive from all over Japan starting at midnight. By 5 a.m., the pallets have been forklifted from the trucks and delivered to the stalls, and almost everything has been arranged in displays that visibly demonstrate the Japanese penchant for design and packaging.

The Tsukiji market is often included on the schedule of tourists, who want to get there before everything is sold. Some of the boxes (there are a lot of Styrofoam boxes here) contain species that even amateurs would recognize. There are fish that look like red snappers; the little skinny ones are probably some kind of sardine (or anchovy); if it looks like an eel, it probably is an eel (Whoa! I didn't know people ate *moray* eels); and many more-or-less recognizable varieties of salmon, bass, groupers, jacks, carp, perch, mackerel, and triggerfish (Do people really eat triggerfish?). Even an ichthyologist would be hard-pressed to identify all the kinds of fishes; Japanese ichthyologists often come to Tsukiji to look for new species. There are elongated, silvery fish with tooth-filled mouths; purple fish with big lips;

tiny silver things that look as if they belong in a home aquarium; black fish, yellow fish, red fish, blue fish, striped fish, spotted fish, dried fish, smoked fish, salted fish, long fish, short fish, fat fish, skinny fish. There are flatfishes with both eyes on the same side of the head: halibut, flounder, sole, plaice, turbot. A veritable zoo of fishes: sea horses, squirrelfish, cowfish, roosterfish, goatfish, goosefish, rabbitfish, wolffish. And dolphinfish, sailfish, spearfish, swordfish, cutlassfish, scabbardfish. And the deadly *fugu*, a puffer fish that can kill you if it's not prepared by a master chef. Not all the fish are dead; many healthy, live fish are swimming in tanks. They will be selected by wholesalers and delivered to restaurants as quickly as possible—freshness being the key. There are trays of carefully packed salmon roe and tuna roe; fishes for sale before they would have been born; and here is the roe of sea urchins (*uni*), a delicacy that commands a particularly high price.

Other types of marine life and seafood are also traded at the market: clams, mussels, periwinkles, and mollusks in shells that look as if they belong in a shell collector's cabinet. Tiny squid, little squid, big squid, cooked octopuses, uncooked octopuses, bright-red octopuses, little brown octopuses; cuttlefishes of all sizes and colors; tiny crabs, little crabs, big crabs, giant crabs (the so-called spider crabs of the Bering Sea). Jellyfish, lobster, shrimp, prawns, crayfish, sea urchins, sea cucumbers, sea anemones, and many varieties of seaweed. If it ever lived in the ocean, it can be found at Tsukiji. And even if it *never* lived in the ocean—even if it never lived *anywhere*—it can also be found here. All this seafood does not originate in local waters. Every kind of commercial fishery sends its products to Japan. Tsukiji is the final destination for Scottish and Norwegian salmon, Alaskan pollack and king crab, aquacultured shrimp from the Gulf of Mexico and Thailand, octopus from West Africa and the Mediterranean, and squid from the Japanese distant-water fisheries in the Falkland Islands and Baja California. Minke whales were killed in the Antarctic. The tuna have come from New England and also from ranches in Tunisia, Morocco, Spain, Italy, Malta, Greece, Croatia, Turkey, Mexico, and South Australia.

In the stalls, are tuna of every kind, ranging in size from the little bullet tunas through the larger bonitos, albacore, and skipjack. Most of the fishes are displayed in booths, but the star of the show, the main reason for the tourists, is not to be found in a common booth. The bluefin tuna, known as *maguro*, will be found only in special rooms—large open spaces the size of a high school gymnasium without the bleachers. Harsh sodium lights glare overhead; the fish here will be examined very carefully. The temperature is kept at a level where the frozen fish will not thaw. Everybody wears a coat and rubber boots, and most of the workers wear hats and gloves. You can see their breath, and you can see a mist rising off the ranks of frozen tuna. (Most of this tuna, which will be marketed as *fresh*, starts its journey to a restaurant aboard a fishing boat, where it was flash-frozen soon after it was caught.) Potential buyers, identifiable by the yellow plastic government licenses clipped to their baseball caps, walk carefully among the arrangement of frosted, tailless tuna. The removal of the tail fin, which takes place immediately after the fish is caught, makes the fish much easier to handle and ship. Each fish also has a half-moon-shaped hole where the gills used to be; the breathing apparatus decomposes during shipment. The fish are grouped according to size and ocean of origin: the 200-pounders from the Indian Ocean are together, the 500- to 600-pounders from New England or the fish farms of Australia lie side by side, and so on. Each fish has a number on it, and as the buyer examines the fish, he makes notes on a little pad. The auctioneer rings a handbell to signal that his auction is about to begin. He watches the buyers who bid on each fish with subtle hand signals; his singsong calls continue until each fish in the lot is sold.

Originally, the Cape Cod fishermen would bring their harpooned tuna to the dock at Sandwich, Yarmouth, or Barnstable, where a local dealer would pay them by the pound. They got anywhere from $2 to $30 a pound, but a 400-pound tuna at $2 a pound is worth $800, and $12,000 at $30 a pound. Payment varied from fish to fish, and from season to season, but these giant tuna were worth so much money at the dock that the fishermen could afford to pay a spotter pilot $100 for each fish they harpooned. The dealers on the dock would then sell the tuna to Japanese buyers, who paid much more per pound. By the 1992 season, they were selling $18,000 fish to the Japanese. It didn't take the New Englanders long to realize that they could circumvent part of this multilevel system. They banded together to form a cooperative called Cape Quality Bluefin (CQB) and negotiated their own deals with Japan. For the 1990 season, CQB handled 100,000 pounds of tuna and grossed $2,153,000. At the docks in Massachusetts and Maine, technicians from Tsukiji instruct the fishermen on the proper techniques for handling and packing tuna for export. When some of the CQB fishermen went to Japan to observe the Tsukiji auctions, they saw a 350-pound fish sell for $42,000, or $120 a pound.

Years of experience enable the buyers at Tsukiji to examine the fish with an eye (and nose) toward identifying the richest, reddest meat with the highest fat content. Near the base of what would have been the tail, a slice of flesh has been half-mooned back, revealing the bright red color of the meat. The buyer can cut off a sliver, hold it up to the light, smell it, and taste it. After all, it is precisely the taste and "mouth feel" that determine the quality and price of the *maguro*. He will also rub the sliver between his thumb and forefinger to test the fat content. The tuna are auctioned one at a time. The auction may appear casual to an outsider, but every hand gesture is recorded, and the auctioneer's assistant writes down everything. As each fish is sold, it is marked in red with the buyer's name. Many of the tuna are sold right there to local merchants. The carcass will be delivered, often by handcart, to a booth in the market, where it will be butchered by a man wielding something that looks an awful lot like a samurai sword. The frozen carcasses are sectioned by a man working a table saw. By noon, most everything has been sold. The great number of trucks belonging to wholesalers, fish companies, and restaurants have taken to the streets of Tokyo to begin the final distribution process.

A giant bluefin, hatched from a tiny egg in the Gulf of Mexico, grew to full size in the North Atlantic. It may have crossed the Atlantic several times. Its life was ended by a harpooner out of Barnstable, Massachusetts, and the fish was gutted on the dock, sold to a Japanese buyer, trucked to Logan Airport, and airlifted to Narita in Tokyo. From there it traveled by refrigerated truck to Tsukiji, and with many other frozen tuna carcasses, it was unloaded and taken to the auction sheds so that buyers could ascertain its quality and bid on it. Along the way, it passed through the hands of several distributors, all of whom made a small profit. Cut into small pieces, it was sold to a Tokyo restaurateur, who had it prepared as sashimi. A two-ounce portion will sell for about $75.

Tuna Farming

In a remote bay on the south shore of Nova Scotia, 25 miles west of Halifax, some fishermen conceived the idea of trapping big bluefin tuna in mackerel traps and fattening them for sale. It was originally tried in 1937, but there was no market for what was then known as "horse mackerel,"[2] so the experiment failed (Butler, 1977). By the mid-1970s, however, the skyrocketing Japanese sashimi market changed everything for the trap fishermen of St. Margaret's Bay. In 1975, the first impoundment nets (the equivalent of an open-water fish tank with sides of netting) were constructed, about 500 feet across and 50 feet deep. When they arrived, the tuna had just migrated north from their spawning area in the Gulf of Mexico and were emaciated and of little commercial value. So they were fattened on two feedings a day of herring and mackerel culls, squid, and whiting.

At St. Margaret's, it was Japanese technicians who built the original eight holding pens; even at this early date, the Japanese had recognized the efficacy of shipping bluefin tuna directly to Tokyo. By 1976, the Canadians were shipping 300 frozen bluefins a year to Japan, each one wrapped in protective paper, and packed in ice in an individual wooden "coffin" to keep the temperature as low as possible. They were transported by refrigerated truck to JFK International Airport in New York and then air-freighted to Tokyo. Business was so good that the following year, Janel Fisheries doubled the number of impoundment nets at St. Margaret's and shipped three-quarters of a million pounds of dressed tuna to Japan at a freight rate of a dollar a pound[3] (Butler, 1982). St. Margaret's Bay fishermen have been selling "farmed" bluefin to Japan since the 1970s. Because the Canadian tuna are fed on mackerel, a very oily fish, the fat content of these fish makes them particularly desirable at the Tokyo auctions. In 1978, only three years after this lucrative business had begun, the large tuna became scarce, and in 1981, only 116 fish were trapped in St. Margaret's Bay. Janel never closed the operation. The trap net tuna fishery of St. Margaret's continues to this day, a low-profile precursor of the larger, more intensive, and more efficient tuna ranches of Japan, Australia, and the Mediterranean that have come to dominate the news recently.

Aquaculture—raising food fishes from eggs to edible sizes—is not a sport, but it is not fishing, either. It is raising "domesticated" animals for food, just as pigs, chickens, and cows are raised. Catching wild fish and fattening them in pens is something altogether different. It is not exactly fishing, and it is not exactly mariculture. It is, as it were, another kettle of fish. It is changing everything we thought we knew about fishing, and unfortunately, everything we thought we knew about preserving marine resources for the future.

When a loophole big enough to drive a factory ship through was discovered in the regulations governing Mediterranean bluefin tuna fishing, it could have signaled the extinction of the Mediterranean's bluefin population within a few years. Although there are strict quotas on the number of fish that can be caught in nets or by harpoons (*spadare*), no regulations whatsoever are applied to the practice of post-harvesting, which means catching wild tuna and keeping them in pens before they are slaughtered. In 2001 there were post-harvesting "farms" in the waters off Spain, Italy, Malta, and Croatia, accounting for some 11,000 tons of tuna caught, as compared to a total of 24,000 tons caught throughout the Mediterranean by direct fishing. More than 90% of the post-harvested tuna went to Japan, and the appetite of the Japanese for tuna belly meat is insatiable. "If nothing is done," says Paolo Guglielmi, of the World Wildlife Fund's Mediterranean Programme Office, "wild bluefin tuna will completely disappear from the Mediterranean, perhaps with no possibility of rebuilding stocks."[4]

Post-harvesting—now known as tuna ranching—has completely reshaped fishing in the Mediterranean, and the fish are much the worse for it. Not only are the tuna threatened, but the fish caught to feed them while they are in the pens are also being fished to destruction. Almost all the countries that fish for tuna in the Mediterranean are switching over to this "feedlot" technology. In each country, the purse-seine catches have declined, and the total catch has increased. The entire catch of the Croatian tuna fleet (increased from 19 boats in 1999 to 30 in 2000) consists of undersized fish destined for the pens. According to a WWF report, "In the Mediterranean, tuna farming started just a few years ago, but estimated production in 2001 gives an indication of the huge development of this activity in the region. In fact, production in the Mediterranean is likely to make up more than half of the world total and is almost exclusively destined for the Japanese market." Given the eagerness with which Mediterranean nations sell their fish to Japan, it is not a little surprising to learn that Japan maintains a 35-vessel longline fleet in the western Mediterranean, targeting large, prespawning tuna. Perhaps they believe they can avoid the cost of the middleman. In a further attempt to avoid European markups, Japan has now introduced its own tuna farms, with pens in 18 Mediterranean locations.

Even though post-harvesting is classified as "aquaculture," the fish are all wild-caught, just as if they had been harpooned or purse-seined. True aquaculture requires that the fish be raised from eggs, not simply moved from one place to another to be fattened. But even though the Australian system (now practiced in the Mediterranean) does not qualify under this strict definition, it still demonstrates all the ills that besiege legitimate aquaculture, such as that practiced with Atlantic salmon, as we shall see. Like salmon, tuna are carnivorous and must be fed large quantities of small fishes, which themselves may be threatened by overcollecting. This kind of "farming" therefore does not relieve commercial fishing pressure—it increases it. Waste from the pens is another problem, as is their location—close enough to shore and urban centers to disrupt and often pollute the littoral zone. And because tuna farming falls between the definition of a fishery and true aquaculture, it is completely unregulated on a world scale.

The first commercial tuna-farming operation in the Mediterranean was in 1979, at Ceuta, Spanish Morocco, across the Strait of Gibraltar from European Spain. Lean tuna were caught in *almadrabas*—huge fish traps that consist of miles of nets suspended from buoys and anchored to the seafloor—as they tried to leave the Mediterranean after the June and July spawning season. Only 200 tons (only?) were caught, and the product was sold at a premium price to the sashimi market in Japan. With some modifications, what began in Ceuta was the beginning of what would become a major industry throughout the Mediterranean. In the future, tuna fishermen wouldn't wait to trap the tuna in *almadrabas*; they would catch the tuna in purse seines and tow them to the fattening pens.

After its rise and fall as the heart of South Australia's tuna fishery, Port Lincoln is once again at the epicenter of a thriving fishery, this time without fishing rods. The tuna are placed in holding pens about 5 miles off the shores of Boston Bay and are fattened for months on tons of dead pilchard.

The Australian tuna-ranching industry has prospered wildly since its inception in 1991. In 2005, the southern bluefin tuna harvest reached 9,000 tons, the biggest to date. The fishery is worth AUS$280 million a year. There are now 15 southern bluefin tuna ranches in South Australia, located primarily in two areas just east of Port Lincoln: Boston Bay and Rabbit Island. Environmental groups have been lobbying for quotas, arguing that the very stock is threatened. But the tuna-ranching industry claims that a reduction in the catch would put people out of work, and besides, the status of the stock is fine. The total export value of the industry grew from $45 million in 1994 to $252 million in 2001—an increase of 56% in just eight short years.

In 2002, a "new kind of mariculture" was taking place off the Pacific coast of Baja California. Mexican fishermen net young bluefins and tow them to special enclosures in Puerto Escondido, near Ensenada, where the fish are kept in circular pens and fed live sardines three times a day for six to eight months. When they reach a weight of about 190 pounds, they are killed and frozen, mostly to feed Japan's appetite for fatty tuna. On average, these tuna were sold at roughly $45 per pound. There are now a dozen offshore fish farms in Mexican waters, and North American and Japanese investors are looking to get in on the sashimi bonanza.

The first Mexican farm, off Cedros Island on the Pacific side of the Baja Peninsula, was opened in 1997. It managed to produce only 64 tons of tuna in its first three years of operation. Two more farms were opened in 1998 and 1999, at Salsipuedes and Todos Santos Bay (off Ensenada). Eight more were sighted in Bahia La Paz, just north of the city of the same name. As of 2005, Baja California had 22 tuna ranches, producing more than 5,000 tons of tuna. Over the past few years, Japanese fish buyers have paid tuna farmers more than US$50 million, securing almost the entire harvest. A report by tuna industry expert and market analyst Roberto Mielgo Bregazzi states the following:

Donshui, a subsidiary of [the] Japanese conglomerate Mitsubishi, is investing 150 million dollars in building fish farms for tuna in La Paz, Baja California Sur. Mitsubishi, one of the world's most diversified transnationals, is the world's largest tuna trader... Mitsubishi is partnering with local entrepreneur Mateo Arjona, in order to invest 18 million dollars building 22 large pens to hold yellowfin tuna ranching near san Juan de la Costa. Waters in the bay of La Paz are considered the best in the world for tuna ranching.[5]

Although the weather and waters in Mexico might be ideal for tuna ranching, no fishing operation is foolproof, and there will always be natural hazards to threaten the fish and fishermen. Weather anomalies such as El Niño and other storms can wreak havoc with a ranching operation, and occasional red tides (algal blooms) can kill all the fish in a pen. In March 2003, a cage full of southern bluefins being towed from the Great Australian Bight to Port Lincoln collapsed. The netting entangled the fish, preventing them from swimming. Because tuna need to keep moving in order to breathe, many of them drowned. Although the Australian Tuna Boat Owners Association said the loss was minimal, other observers put the death toll at close to 5,000 fish. The large quantities of baitfish used to feed the tuna attract sea lions, and sometimes they get into the pens and attack the tuna. In November 2003, an 18-foot-long great white shark got into the tuna pen at Coronado Island (Mexico), and although it was shot numerous times, it refused to die. A study by Hubbs-Sea World Research Institute of San Diego (funded by Chevron) will determine the feasibility of establishing a "tuna ranch" in the Santa Barbara Channel, to be affixed to an old Chevron oil-drilling platform. But the same problems attendant upon "traditional" aquaculture are present in tuna farming. Salmon and tuna are carnivores (more accurately, *piscivores*) and require smaller fish to eat, so growing these fish in pens requires more, rather than less, fishing in the wild. A number of ecological threats have been shown to derive from penned fish, including concentrated fecal matter and rotting food released into the surrounding waters; genetically altered fish escaping and breeding with wild fish; and, probably most frightening of all, diseases spread from captive fish into the wild population.

On June 7, 2005, the Bush Administration submitted to Congress for consideration the National Offshore Aquaculture Act, which would grant the Secretary of Commerce the authority to issue permits for tuna ranching in federal ocean waters. The bill was introduced by Senators Ted Stevens of Alaska (a state that prohibits aquaculture) and Daniel Inouye of Hawaii. If passed, the bill would allow aquaculture (including fish farming) anywhere from 3 to 200 miles off American shores. The Hawaii state legislature has already passed legislation that allows tuna ranching in the waters of the western Hawaiian islands. (Sometimes referred to as the Leeward Islands, the western Hawaiian Islands consist of a chain stretching some 1,300 miles to the west of Kauai, consisting of Nihoa, Necker, French Frigate Shoals, Gardner Pinnacles, Maro Reef, Laysan, Lisianski, Pearl and Hermes Reef, Midway, and Kure Atoll.) But instead of 1,300 miles west of Kauai, the original plan called for the Ahi Nui Tuna Farming Company to catch juvenile bigeye and yellowfin tuna and fatten them in an 18-pen tuna ranch to be developed 2,200 *feet* from the western shore of the Big Island. (*Ahi nui* means "big yellowfin tuna" in Hawaiian.) Community opposition resulted in the tuna farm's being moved 20 miles offshore. With the legislation pending, there are plans to test a tuna ranch off Santa Barbara, California, at the site of the Chevron oil company's obsolete Platform Grace. This region has already seen its share of ecological disasters. On January 28, 1969, at Unocal's Platform A, 3 miles off the coast of Santa Barbara, a drilling operation resulted in an uncontrolled flow of oil from a deep reservoir through oil-bearing sands. Some 3.2 million gallons (79,000 barrels) were released into the Pacific Ocean. Three days after the spill began, winds and currents drove the oil ashore, contaminating more than 100 miles of shoreline. By the fourth day, it had spread to the Channel Islands of Santa Rosa, Catalina, and Anacapa. Eventually, the spill covered more than 800 square miles and reached all the way to the Mexican border. Marine and terrestrial plants were destroyed; marine mammals, seabirds, fishes, and invertebrates were oil-soaked and killed. Bills were introduced in the California and federal legislatures to create oil-well-free zones. In 1972, the National Marine Sanctuaries Act was passed, leading to the establishment of the Channel Islands National Marine Sanctuary in 1980.

Now the Japanese have entered the tuna-ranching sweepstakes. Japanese ranchers favor smaller tuna because they can compete with fishermen, who get a better price for a smaller fish if they sell them directly at the fish market, rather than selling them to a tuna farmer. Still, the Japanese Fisheries Agency now estimates that of the 21,500 tons of tuna imported in 2005, 90% of the total (19,500 tons) was *chikuyuo*—ranch-fattened fish. Originally, the idea was that sashimi-quality tuna was supposed to be *fresh*, but there is no way to ship unfrozen fish from Greece to Japan, so fresh has been replaced by frozen. The fish are transferred from fishing boats or tuna ranches to large freezer ships, known as reefers, which then sail to Japan. The largest of these reefers has a cargo capacity of 4,500 tons. (A portion of the vast number of tuna carcasses seen every day at the Tsukiji market have arrived in reefers from Malta, Vietnam, Panama, or other distant ports.) Also, illegal tuna fisheries around the world (commonly known as IUU for "illegal, unreported, and unregulated") kill an almost incomprehensible number of the target species, plus countless sharks, seabirds, marine mammals, and other fishes.

The increase in tuna ranches in Mexico and the Mediterranean has put a crimp in the one-time dominance of the Australians. If a surplus of "product" is supplied to Japan from the Mediterranean tuna farms, the market will crash, and the income that supports the heavily capitalized Port Lincoln ranches will disappear. (Attempts are being made to stir up interest in bluefin tuna in the huge—and untapped—Chinese market.) But the greatest threat to the Australian tuna-farming industry is the declining stocks of the tuna themselves. In 1984, quotas were introduced into tuna fishery because the catches were declining dramatically. By 1988, the Australian tuna quota was cut from 14,500 tons to 6,250. When it was discovered that the southern bluefins migrated from Indonesia and western Australia to South Australia, Western Australian fishery was completely curtailed to allow the fish to get to South Australia.

Tuna ranching has become a worldwide industry—and a worldwide threat to the tuna populations. In the Mediterranean, where giant bluefins used to be herded into pens to be killed for local consumption in the *mattanza*, juvenile tuna are now purse-seined and towed to pens for fattening. Harvesting tuna before they are old enough to breed is a guaranteed path toward population collapse. In June 2006, Greenpeace called for the immediate closure of the Mediterranean bluefin tuna fishery, claiming that the population was on the brink of collapse. The Greenpeace vessel *Esperanza* observed tuna farms and fisheries around the Balearic Islands, in the waters north of Egypt and south of Turkey, and talked to the captains of the fishing vessels. Greenpeace concluded that "45,000 tons of bluefin tuna may have been caught each year in 2004 and 2005, despite the fact that only 32,000 tons can be caught legally." The organization found that bluefin tuna fishery was out of control in Europe and that ICCAT was incapable of enforcing regulations on the fishery. The WWF issued a report titled "The Plunder of Bluefin Tuna in the Mediterranean and East Atlantic in 2004 and 2005: Uncovering the Real Story" on June 30, 2006. It called for an immediate closure of the eastern Atlantic and Mediterranean tuna fisheries, because fleets from the European Union (EU), particularly France, Libya, and Turkey, "are greatly exceeding their fishing quotas and deliberately failing to report much of their massive catches...." (Unreported catches are slaughtered and processed at sea before being shipped to the lucrative Japanese market.) Roberto Mielgo Bregazzi, author of the WWF report, said, "Atlantic bluefin tuna stocks risk imminent commercial collapse. In the race to catch shrinking tuna stocks, industrial fleets are switching from traditional fishing grounds to the last refuges in the eastern Mediterranean and Libyan waters."

Inside the harbor at Cartagena, Spain, in September 2006, Greenpeace activists created a symbolic "tuna graveyard" with crosses and a banner saying "R.I.P. Bluefin Tuna 1996–2006," commemorating the decade during which tuna ranching had been taking place there. The environmental organization called for the immediate closure of the Mediterranean bluefin tuna fishery until it could be properly managed. Greenpeace also requested the adoption of urgent measures, including the establishment of a network of marine reserves to protect 40% of the Mediterranean Sea and regenerate its fish stocks. "Tuna ranches like this one are the cowboys of an industry that is directly responsible for wiping out the bluefin tuna from the Mediterranean Sea," said Greenpeace Spain's Sebastián Losada aboard the Greenpeace flagship, *Rainbow Warrior*. "A few greedy commercial interests, subsidized by the EU, are employing pirate fishing fleets and fattening tuna to fatten their own wallets," said Losada. "They are depriving hundreds of fishermen from trying to make a legitimate living from the bluefin tuna."

Faced with an imminent crash in Mediterranean tuna populations, ICCAT, at its November 2006 meeting in Dubrovnik, Croatia, adopted a weak EU plan. It included a catch quota of 29,500 tons in 2007 compared to the 15,000 tons recommended by ICCAT's own scientists. The plan also allowed fishing during the peak spawning season, which is the worst possible decision for a depleted stock. According to a recent WWF report, actual catches of bluefin tuna in the Mediterranean are more that 50% over the quota set by ICCAT. This illegal activity has meant that artisanal fishermen are catching 80% less tuna compared to the 1990s. Stocks in the oldest fishing grounds of the Balearic Islands have collapsed, and six farms in Spain closed this year due to lack of tuna. EU fishing fleets are responsible for the bulk of illegal catches of bluefin tuna in the Mediterranean.

Countries *currently* farming tuna, and those *considering* farming tuna, do so almost exclusively for the Japanese market. Open-water tuna fisheries are in decline, but ranching has been a godsend to the fishermen. Countries now engaged in tuna ranching are Australia, Cape Verde, Croatia, Cyprus, Greece, Indonesia, Italy, Japan, Libya, Malta, Mexico, Oman, Panama, the Philippines, Portugal, Spain, Tunisia, and Turkey. Note that of these 18 countries, half are on (or in) the Mediterranean. (Countries considering tuna ranching include the U.S., Costa Rica, and Malaysia.)

It is interesting—but unsurprising—to note that many international tuna ranching companies are capitalized by Japanese investments or have Japanese citizens as advisors or board members. The Sicilian tuna ranch operated by New Eurofish of Castellemare del Golfo was incorporated by local businessman Guglielmo Maggio and Mitsui & Co., Ltd. of Japan. On the north coast of Bali, southeast Asia's largest tuna-ranching center is a joint venture between Japanese and Indonesian investors. Malta Fishfarming Ltd. and Melitta Tuna Ltd. are subsidized by Takayama Seafood, which invested US$157,000 in the project in the form of tuna futures.

In Costa Rica, in July 2006, the company Granjas Atuneras de Golfito S.A., established by foreign interests from Spain, Venezuela, and Peru, proposed a yellowfin tuna farm off the Pacific coast at Dulce Gulf. The operators claimed that in addition to raising wild-caught yellowfins, they would be breeding them. The plan was opposed by a consortium of diverse groups, including fishermen, chambers of tourism, the indigenous Guayami community, development associations, businesses, scientists, senators, and conservation organizations. Once the groups began investigating, they found that multiple national laws had been violated and that the proposed project would put the entire ecosystem and economy of the Dulce Gulf at risk.

Tuna farming creates not only ecological problems, but also problems that have to do with the very nature of the fish itself. Until the early 1990s, there was a market in Japan for the prime, very expensive, sashimi-quality meat that came from the wild-caught fat northern and southern bluefins. And there was a secondary market for the lower-quality meat that was served in nonsashimi restaurants and sold in supermarkets. "However," wrote Miyabe et al. in their 2003 review of Mediterranean tuna farming, "[northern] bluefin and southern bluefin of smaller size that had been accepted only at the lower-quality markets before, now fattened by farming and available in abundance, started to constitute a middle category, filling the gap between the two extremes."[6] Farm-fattened fish are now a source of lower-priced *toro*, which can be sold in sushi bars and supermarkets. A glut of lower-priced tuna meat made open-ocean bluefins even more desirable, which encourages heavier fishing pressure on the pelagic populations. Tuna have the misfortune to be at or near the top of the list of "most popular food fishes," so it is more than a little painful to realize that *bluefin tuna* is literally being eaten out of existence. At the dock and in restaurants, prices for these fish rise as their numbers diminish. This might sound like nothing more than a traditional supply-and-demand equation, but the difference between fishing and manufacturing is that once fish are gone, you cannot make any more.

Because the number of wild-caught tuna is declining and the number of ranch-fattened tuna is limited by the fecundity of wild fish (and how many are caught before they can reproduce), it would appear that the only way to continue to appease the insatiable (and discriminating) sashimi god is to figure out a way to breed bluefin tuna in captivity.

Tuna Frenzy

Rumor has it that Tokyo has 7,000 sushi restaurants. They range from simple stalls at the Tsukiji fish market (where *toro* is too expensive to serve) to elaborate restaurants that appeal to tourists, people on expense accounts, and wealthy Japanese businessmen. New York City has had modest sushi parlors for years, but recently, spectacular Japanese restaurants seem to be opening everywhere. The first of the *nouveau japonais* restaurants was *Nobu*, opened in 1994 by restaurateur Drew Nieporent and featuring the culinary creations of Nobu Matsuhisa. Trained in Japan, Matsuhisa opened his first restaurant (called Matsuhisa) on La Cienega Boulevard in Los Angeles in 1987, but his was not traditional Japanese cuisine. The fusion menu blends Japanese dishes with Argentine and Peruvian ingredients and eschews sushi and sashimi. Particularly popular with movie stars, Matsuhisa charges at least $80 per person, and you can easily spend $250 on dinner for two.

There are now Nobu restaurants in London (opened 1997), Las Vegas (1999), Milan (2000), Miami Beach (2001), and Tokyo. Opened in 1998 in the upscale Aoyama district, Nobu Tokyo offers the same "fusion" menu as the other restaurants, with nontraditional dishes such as black cod with miso and squid in light garlic sauce. New York has three Nobus. Although none of them serves unadorned raw fish, all three serve yellowtail (*hamachi*) and tuna (*toro*), two of the fish that are farm-raised:

- Yellowtail tartar with caviar: $21
- *Toro* tartar with caviar: $30
- Yellowtail sashimi with jalapeño: $17

Many new Japanese restaurants do serve sashimi, however, such as Matsuri on West 16th Street in Manhattan. In a spectacular, soaring space decorated with glowing, giant paper lanterns, the menu is typical Japanese, with tempura, teriyaki, grilled fish, and meats, but also a generous selection of sushi and sashimi.

Although other cities claim the title, the centers of haute cuisine in the U.S. are Los Angeles and New York. It is no coincidence that the Japanese chef who is currently the most brilliant star in the restaurant firmament opened his first restaurant in L.A. and followed it with one in New York. Masayoshi Takayama operated Ginza Sushiko in Beverly Hills and in 2004 opened Masa in the new Time-Warner Center at Columbus Circle. With a prix fixe of $350 (excluding tax, tips, and beverages), Masa immediately became the most expensive restaurant in a city known for pricey dining. Lunch or dinner for two can easily exceed $1,000. The *toro*, Masa's *pièce de résistance*, is likely to have been bought at an auction at Tsukiji. But because many of the prime northern bluefins come from New England, it is possible that Masa's exalted pricing incorporates a *toro* trip from New England to Japan and back again.

Because wild bluefins can be caught off the coasts of New England, it seems unnecessary to fly New England tuna to Japan and then back to the U.S. Of course, some of the top-quality bluefins caught in the Atlantic are purchased by Japanese buyers and auctioned off at Tsukiji, but many New England bluefins make a much shorter trip: New England waters, Massachusetts dock, New York fish market, New York Japanese restaurant.

The bluefin, of course, is the *ne plus ultra* of the tuna "industry." Young bluefins have lighter-colored flesh and are less strongly flavored, but as they grow into adulthood, their flesh turns dark red, and their flavor becomes more pronounced. The bluefin is generally the variety of choice for fresh-tuna connoisseurs. It has more fat, and thus more flavor, than the other varieties. (Even though they are genetically distinct, there is no visible difference between the northern and southern bluefin tuna to sashimi lovers.) At maturity, the flesh is dark red, sometimes even wine-colored, with an appearance very similar to raw beef. (Fresh tuna is usually sold already skinned, because the skin is extremely tough.) Because it is served raw, only the freshest and highest-quality fish is used for sashimi. It is usually served with condiments such as shredded daikon (Japanese radish), gingerroot, wasabi, and soy sauce.

Although tuna are found in all major bodies of water (except the polar seas), the majority of the tuna supply comes from the Pacific Ocean, which accounts for 2.3 million tons, or about 66% of the total world catch. The rest of the commercial tuna sold around the world comes from the Indian Ocean (20.7%), the Atlantic Ocean (12.5%), and the Mediterranean and Black Seas (0.8%). Yuichiro Harada, a senior managing director of the Organization for the Promotion of Responsible Tuna Fisheries (OPRT), set up by Japanese fishermen, reports that the number of tuna fishing boats is decreasing in Japan. Rising fuel costs are forcing financially weak fishing firms out of business. In the meantime, the consumption of tuna is increasing in the U.S., Europe, Taiwan, and China. Americans now consume 100,000 tons of tuna as sashimi a year. Taiwan is a major supplier of bigeye tuna to Japan, with catches by Taiwanese boats accounting for some 20% of Japan's tuna consumption of about 450,000 tons a year. While skipjack and albacore provide the "light-" or "white-meat" tuna consumed in such great quantities in salads and sandwiches, three species (bluefin, yellowfin, and bigeye) are made of the red meat that is favored for sashimi. And although restaurants often claim that their *toro* comes from only New England bluefins flown to Japan, red tuna meat is just as likely to come from the southern bluefins of Australia, or "farmed" bluefins from the Mediterranean or Mexico.

Tuna are fished in over 70 countries worldwide and are marketed fresh, frozen, and canned. Only about 1% of tuna comes to the market to be sold fresh. The rest goes to the cannery, because canned tuna is America's most popular fish. Tuna has been fished from the warm, temperate regions of the Mediterranean, and the Pacific, Atlantic, and Indian Oceans since ancient times. Depending on the species, weights average from 10 to 600 pounds per fish. The majority of the commercial tuna harvest comes from California. The average annual consumption of tuna in America is 3.6 pounds per person, most of which is canned.

The death of the tuna, of course, is the life of the tuna business, and the life of the tuna business is canned tuna, mostly skipjack and albacore. When the fish are unloaded from the vessel, they are thawed in running water or sprays of water. The fish are then quickly gilled, gutted, headed, and finally frozen. After cutting, the tunas are loaded into trays and taken to the precooker. After precooking and cooling, the cleaners remove the skin from the fish and separate the loins from the skeleton. After cutting the loins into solid pack or chunks, according to their firmness, the last step, canning, is a totally automated process. Canned tuna products are packed in oil, brine, springwater, or sauce. Once the cans are sealed, they are cooked a second time ("retort cooking") for 2 to 4 hours. After the retort cooking, the cans are cooled, labeled, and finally packed into cardboard boxes for distribution.

From the earliest days of the California tuna industry, when San Diego had the world's largest tuna fleet, there were canneries close to the docks. Like Monterey, where the fishery was for sardines, San Diego also had a "Cannery Row." With the increased fishing activity in the far Western Pacific and the closure in the early 1980s of both San Diego tuna canneries, fewer and fewer boats need to come to San Diego. Instead, they are using canneries and getting their repairs and provisions at such places as American Samoa and Puerto Rico. The Chicken of the Sea plant in Los Angeles, the last major tuna cannery in the continental U.S., moved its operations to American Samoa. The original company was founded in 1914 when Frank Van Camp and his son bought the California Tuna Canning Company and changed the name to the Van Camp Seafood Company. In 1963, Van Camp Seafood was purchased by Ralston Purina. When it was purchased in 1997 by the investment group Tri-Union Seafoods, the company name was changed to Chicken of the Sea International. The investment group sold the company in 2000 to Thai Union International, now the sole owner. In 2001, Thai Union closed the Chicken of the Sea cannery in San Pedro (Los Angeles harbor). In American Samoa, the canneries are the largest private employers in the territory.

High labor costs were responsible for the closure of the mainland American tuna canneries. (In American Samoa, U.S. federal tax laws apply, but minimum-wage laws do not.) For the most part, the canneries employ people at less than what would be considered a minimum wage in developed countries. The operations were often relocated to areas closer to the fisheries to avoid the additional costs of shipping tuna around the world. There are canneries in the Philippines, American Samoa, Puerto Rico, Fiji, Thailand, Japan, Indonesia, Taiwan, and Port Lincoln, South Australia.

There are many varieties and grades of canned tuna to choose from. Solid or fancy pack contains large pieces of tuna and is usually albacore. Only albacore tuna may be labeled and sold as "white tuna." Many pay the higher price for white tuna because it has a milder flavor and lighter color. Flaked tuna is broken apart and used in salads where the tuna is mashed and mixed. You can eat tuna raw, cooked, broiled, smoked, grilled, on a roll, as a burger, as a fishcake, as a dip, in a melt, in a salad, in a sandwich, in a pita, in a potpie, in a casserole, as a sauce (vitello tonnato), in a wrap, with mayonnaise, with noodles, with rice, with olives, with onions, with capers, with relish, with wasabi, with pesto, with soy sauce, with risotto, with fettuccine, with spaghetti, with macaroni, with tarragon, with chickpeas, with cheese, with artichokes, and in combinations that are waiting to be invented.

U.S. processors use either domestic or imported raw (fresh, chilled, or frozen) tuna as raw material to produce different varieties of canned and pouched tuna. It is distinguished by the type of meat (white or light), the packing medium (water or oil), and the form. In the U.S., most canned tuna is available as either "solid" or "chunk." According to the Food and Drug Administration (FDA), which sets strict definitions for how canned tuna is marketed, the difference between "solid" and "chunk" is as follows: The source of most chunk light meat is skipjack, although other species of tuna can be added. Albacore, which is the only tuna species that can be called "white," is packed almost exclusively in water in solid form.

The U.S. Tuna Foundation (USTF), a lobbying organization based in Washington, D.C., was established in 1976 to represent the interests of the U.S. canned tuna industry, including the U.S. distant-water fishing fleets and the "big three" canned tuna brands: StarKist, Bumble Bee, and Chicken of the Sea International. On its website, the USTF provides this look at the market for canned tuna in this country:

- Japan and the U.S. are the largest consumers of tuna, using about 36% and 31%, respectively, of the world's catch.
- Canned tuna is the second most popular seafood product in the U.S. after shrimp.
- In the U.S., Americans eat about one billion pounds of canned or pouched tuna a year. Only coffee and sugar exceed canned tuna in sales per foot of shelf space in the grocery store.
- Of Americans who eat canned tuna, the vast majority—83%— eat it for lunch. In fact, canned tuna is the only regularly consumed seafood at lunch.

- Over one-half of canned tuna (52%) is used in sandwiches. Another 22% is used in salads, 15.5% is used in casseroles/ helpers, and 7.5% is used in base dishes.

- Households with children under 18 are about twice as likely to have tuna sandwiches available than households without children.

- Light meat accounts for 75% to 80% of annual domestic canned tuna consumption; albacore or white meat makes up the balance.

- Chunk light meat in water is the most popular form of canned tuna, although a demand remains for oil-packed canned light meat tuna.

Some species, such as yellowfins, albacore, and skipjack, are being removed from the ocean in quantities that would drive less-prolific species toward extinction. The less-numerous southern and northern bluefins have been fished so heavily that they are considered endangered. People are trying to make vegetarians out of captive tuna—a fate worse than, or at least comparable to, death. Look at the North Atlantic, for instance. ICCAT recommendations have been published since the mid-1970s, and the results have been a bonanza for the fishermen and an unmitigated disaster for the fish. As long ago as 1975, the director of the National Marine Fisheries Service, in consultation with the U.S. Fish and Wildlife Service, published a proposal to list the bluefin tuna as threatened under the Endangered Species Act. But the proposal was withdrawn when the Atlantic Tunas Convention Act gave the U.S. authority to implement ICCAT's management recommendations. Big mistake. For decades, ICCAT recognized two distinct populations of North Atlantic bluefins, the western and the eastern. The western population breeds in the Gulf of Mexico, and the eastern in the Mediterranean, and it was assumed that never the twain shall meet. Wrong again. Tagging experiments showed that the stocks intermingled, so harvesting fish from one stock affects the other. And although the quota for the western Atlantic stock (the Gulf of Mexico breeders) was reduced to 2,700 tons, the quota for the eastern stock was kept at around 50,000 tons. That's 50,000 *tons*, not 50,000 tunas. Fifty thousand tons is 10 million pounds, and that's a lot of tuna to take out of the North Atlantic every year.

Conserving the Tuna

Hundreds of thousands of tons of bluefin tuna—which translates into billions of fish—are caught every year, by fishers in the Mediterranean, the North Atlantic, the central and southern Pacific, and the Indian Ocean. The tuna of the western North Atlantic were purse-seined intensively in the 1960s for canning, but by the 1970s, commercial fishers targeted larger fish for the Japanese market. In 1981, ICCAT declared the Atlantic bluefin seriously depleted and tried to set a quota "as near to zero as feasible." Within two years, political pressure by the fishermen's lobby rejected this idea, and the quota for 1983 was 2,600 metric tons—a far cry from zero. Continued fishing pressure drove the breeding population to an all-time low, and conservation groups began a futile campaign to save the tuna. In 1992, ICCAT halved the western North Atlantic quota, but when the population was found to have "stabilized," industry lobbyists pounced. ICCAT rescinded the 50% cut and increased the quota again. The spawning population is now at 10% of what it was when ICCAT was formed in 1966, and the 2005 IUCN *Red Data Book* lists the Western Atlantic bluefin tuna as "Critically Endangered."

A WWF report published in September 2006 indicates that Armageddon for the Mediterranean tuna is nearly at hand. The report, written by Roberto Mielgo Bregazzi and presented at the Brussels meeting of the European Parliament's Fishing Committee on September 13, reveals that almost no tuna are left in the western Mediterranean, at one time among the most productive of all tuna-fishing grounds. Bregazzi writes: "Today there is consensus that in a context of sustained increase of fishing and farming overcapacity, all the attempts to achieve a real regional management of this key Mediterranean fish resource have resulted in a complete failure. It is not an overstatement to say that the fishery—itself amongst the oldest in the world—faces a high risk of collapse."[7] In the area around the Balearic Islands, the 1995 bluefin tuna catch was more than 14,000 tons; by 2006 the total catch had fallen to 2,270 tons. The tuna farms, which would be filling their pens by September, have managed to achieve only a 75% capacity, and six Spanish tuna ranches have ceased operations. The latest findings support the earlier warnings by

WWF that huge illegal catches might portend the decimation of the Mediterranean populations and, inevitably, the collapse of the species. At the 2006 ICCAT meeting in Madrid, having learned that the French tuna fleet had illegally exceeded its quota by more than 3,000 tons, an international consortium of scientists said that the bluefin tuna will be lost forever if no action is taken to restrain the French and other Mediterranean fishers.

The collapse of the tuna stocks is exacerbated by the wholesale quantities of tuna that are not recorded or are not included in a particular nation's total because they are transferred from fishing boats to reefer freezing vessels and are shipped directly to Japan. This IUU (illegal, unreported, and unregulated) fishing—primarily by French, Libyan, and Turkish fleets—accounted for some 25,000 tons of tuna in 2004 and 47,965 tons in 2005. Aside from stopping and prosecuting IUU fishers, the WWF report calls on ICCAT "to adopt a real long-term recovery plan for the East Atlantic stock of BFT which should include a set of effective management measures... but in the meantime, given the virtual unregulated nature of the fishery and the strong likeliness of a near collapse, *WWF calls for the immediate and complete closure of the fishery."* (Emphasis in the original.) Given the ineffectuality (or unwillingness) of ICCAT to control its member nations (not to mention IUU fishers), the closure of the Mediterranean fishery seems highly unlikely. The tuna-ranching operations offered only an interim solution, and not a particularly good one at that. As many tuna were caught for the fattening pens as were caught in the purse-seine fishery. Besides, a significant number died before they reached a saleable size. As long as the Japanese are prepared to pay for sashimi-grade tuna, there will be fishermen to catch them— and the Japanese market shows no signs of abating. If the bluefins of the Mediterranean disappear, where will the sashimi come from?

Tuna ranchers in the Mediterranean, South Australia, and Baja California are capturing half-grown bluefins (the Aussies are capturing half-grown *southern* bluefins) and towing them in nets to offshore pens. There they are fed and fattened until they are the right size to be killed, frozen, and shipped to Japan. It is becoming clear that tuna farming itself might signal the end of an industry, because the process of scooping up all the tuna leads irrevocably (and obviously) to the end of the fishery.

Although it is usually known as tuna *ranching*, the capture of tuna and their transfer to fattening pens is certainly another form of fish *farming*, or aquaculture. But because the procedures differ from most fish-farming operations—most salmon, carp, and tilapia are raised from eggs—tuna farming is usually not included in general discussions of aquaculture. The feeding of captive tuna is perhaps the most serious problem facing ranchers around the world. In the Monterey Bay Aquarium's Outer Bay tank, the bluefin and yellowfin tunas are fed sardines, smelt, squid, and a "gelatin diet," which consists of gelatin-like cubes infused with vitamin and mineral supplements. This is not feeding for the market, and it is actually better if the tuna do not overeat. Early in the history of the Outer Bay exhibit, tuna in holding tanks were dying of congestive heart failure because they were not getting enough exercise, so they were put on a "low-fat" diet.

According to Bregazzi (2005), "about 45,000 tons of baitfish, secured both locally and overseas, were used in 2000–2001. About 60 tons of southern bluefin tuna were also successfully fed a manufactured pellet. An average-size southern bluefin tuna increases in weight by 10 to 20 kilograms (22 to 44 pounds) during the ranching process," which usually lasts for 3 to 7 months. In the 1999–2000 season, Australian tuna ranches produced 7,780 tons of ranched SBT, valued at over $2 million. By 2003 the total was 8,308 tons, and the 15 SBT ranchers in Australia were looking forward to a 9,000-ton year. The tuna ranchers of Australia, however, do not foresee a constantly increasing harvest and a concurrent rise in gross income.[8]

As Australia heads for 9,000 tons, European ranches in the Mediterranean will nearly double the Australian production, and Mexico is approaching 4,000 tons. Europe and Mexico will ship 19,000 tons of frozen northern bluefin tuna to Japan, while Australia, the only country farming southern bluefins, will ship 9,000. Because northern bluefins grow larger than their southern counterparts, the shipments from the Mediterranean and Mexico are favored in Japan—another problem for the Aussies. In 2004, the South Australian government shut down the pilchard fishery, the main source of food for the tuna ranches, because too many dolphins were being killed. The $300 million tuna-ranching industry was facing an unprecedented crisis: not enough fish to feed the tuna.

In 1981, when J.H. Ryther wrote "Mariculture, Ocean Ranching, and Other Culture-Based Fisheries," small-scale culture of marine creatures was considered the only possibility. It was not feasible to contemplate farming anything on a large scale. At that time, Pacific salmon fry were raised in hatcheries and released back into the wild to compensate for the loss of wild salmon whose natural spawning beds had been eliminated by dams and other obstructions. According to Ryther, the worldwide mariculture total for 1975 was 3 million tons, of which the largest proportion was 0.2 million tons of milkfish in the Philippines, Indonesia, and Taiwan; 0.1 million tons of salmon raised in nets; and 0.2 million tons of ocean-ranched salmon in the U.S., Japan, and the USSR.[9] Today, by a substantial margin, China leads the world in aquaculture, and most of the fish farmed in China are carp, used for regional consumption in low-income households. In other parts of the world, farmed tilapia, milkfish, and channel catfish have replaced depleted ocean fish such as cod, hake, haddock, and pollack. The worldwide landings for the "capture fisheries" (those in which wild fish are caught at sea) have leveled off at around 85 to 95 million metric tons per year, with most stocks being recognized as fully fished or overfished. Ten years ago, the figure for aquaculture was 10 million tons, but by 2000, it had nearly tripled (Naylor et al., 2000), and the FAO reported that the total for 2003 was 42.3 million tons. Global aquaculture now accounts for roughly 40% of all fish consumed by humans.

The tremendous increase in fish farming in recent years has been offered as a possible solution to the problems of worldwide overfishing, but aquaculture has its own problems. In some cases, aquaculture be contributing to, rather than solving, the overfishing problem. The species most prominently farmed around the world are carp, salmon, trout, shrimp, tilapia, milkfish, catfish, crayfish, oysters, hybrid striped bass, giant clams, and various shellfish. Of these, shrimp and salmon make up only 5% of the farmed fish by weight, but almost one-fifth by value. Farming is the predominant production method for salmon, and aquaculture accounts for 25% of world shrimp production—a tenfold increase from the mid-1970s.[10]

Marguerite Holloway (2002) said that aquaculture is "a $52 billion-a-year global enterprise involving more than 220 species of fish and shellfish that is growing faster than any other food industry."[11] By 2005, the total for world aquaculture production, including aquatic plants, amounted to 60 billion tons.

Each species of farmed fish has its own requirements, and it is impossible to generalize about the benefits or detriments of fish farming as a whole. Carnivorous species, such as salmon and shrimp, require food, which is usually provided in the form of fish meal, made from ground-up fish. The cost of providing food for farmed salmon often exceeds the price that the salmon can command. Moreover, in this case, farming contributes to overfishing, because the small fish— such as Peruvian anchovies—are harvested almost exclusively for fish meal. (Not only fishes eat fish meal, of course; most processed fish meal is fed to chickens and pigs.) To feed the carnivores, fishermen are fishing for fish to feed to fish.

The top 10 seafoods consumed in the U.S., in terms of kilograms per capita, are tuna, shrimp, pollack, salmon, catfish, cod, clams, crab, flatfish, and scallops. Farmed seafood, particularly salmon, shrimp, and catfish, saw an enormous change from 1987 to 2000, with salmon rising 265% during that period. Obviously this huge increase was a function of the exponential increase in salmon farming and, to a lesser extent, the much-publicized health benefits derived from eating salmon. Note that tuna, the most popular seafood in the U.S., is not farmed—at least not in the traditional sense. Bluefins are being ranched, which is not exactly farming, but the fishers of albacore, skipjack, and yellowfin are susceptible to all the ecological variables listed here, with the addition of one more: overfishing.

Wild Atlantic salmon are born in a multitude of rivers in countries with access to the North Atlantic. The far-flung salmon countries include Canada, the U.S., Iceland, Norway, and Russia in the north; the United Kingdom, Ireland, and the Baltic countries in the middle of the range; and France and northern Spain on the southern margin. The young salmon leave their freshwater home and migrate thousands of miles to feed in the rich marine environment of the North Atlantic off Greenland and the Faeroes. After a year or more in these feeding grounds, the fish undertake their most impressive return migration to the rivers of their birth, where they spawn and complete the cycle. From time immemorial, the cycle of spawning, ocean feed-ing, and return migrations went on as if the resource were a perma-nent feature of the natural world, until the 1950s and 1960s, when developments occurred that began to threaten the fish dramatically. The sea feeding grounds, long a mystery, were located, and interna-tional exploitation of the fish began at an alarming rate. New types of gear, such as the nylon monofilament net, were introduced with dis-astrous results, as unregulated ocean fishing fleets began to devastate the stocks of fish while at sea. By the mid-1970s, up to 2,700 tons of salmon were being taken annually from their ocean feeding grounds, and following this massive loss of stock, salmon numbers began to fall precipitously.

The total weight of farmed salmon in 2002 was 1,084,740,000 tons. Farmed salmon are fed meal and oils from wild-caught fish. Each pound of salmon produced requires at least 3 pounds of wild-caught fish, challenging the presumption that fish farming necessarily reduces commercial fishing pressure. In fact, a net loss of protein in the marine ecosystem as a whole occurs when wild catch is converted into meal for aquaculture consumption. Pens full of salmon produce large amounts of waste—both excrement and unconsumed feed. This may result in water quality conditions (such as high nutrients and low oxygen) that are unfavorable for both farmed fish and the natural ecosystem. It is also suspected that nutrients released from salmon farms stimulate micro-algal blooms, but proof of this is lacking because little research has been done. The densely packed condition in pens promotes disease, a common problem in most salmon farms. Furthermore, there have been documented disease transfers from farmed salmon to wild populations, and the potential effects are seri-ous. Although antibiotics are used to treat some diseases, there are concerns about the effects of antibiotic-resistant bacteria on human health. There has been an emphasis on developing vaccines to pre-vent specific diseases, which reduces the need for antibiotics.

While populations of North Atlantic wild salmon plummet, more than 100 local populations in the eastern Pacific have disappeared. Salmon are extinct in 40% of the rivers where they once spawned along the North American Pacific coast. The potential for interactions with farmed fish and transmission of disease from farmed to wild salmon are especially threatening in the context of these declines.

Governments typically encourage aquaculture because it is viewed as economic development, but this often leads to the intensive, large-scale farming methods most often associated with environmental damage. Because the costs of this damage are not borne by the industry, nor is the value of ecosystem services factored into the cost of production, the industry feels no pressure to operate in environmentally sound ways. The increase in worldwide salmon consumption is coupled not to fishing, but to farming.

Tuna and salmon are both fish that people like to eat, but although farmed salmon sales have skyrocketed in the U.S., there has not been a comparable increase in the sale of "ranched" tuna. (The Japanese obviously have no compunctions about eating tuna fattened in pens, and it doesn't matter if the pens are in Australia, Mexico, or the Mediterranean.) Farmed salmon filets are available year round, but the bluefin tuna supply is uneven, and the price varies with the season. According to the 2006 WWF report "Costco Wholesale recorded fresh-farmed filet sales of over 14 million kilograms in 2002 while fresh tuna sales were 354,545 kg—2.5% of farmed salmon sales," albacore and skipjack—the "white-meat" and "light-meat" tunas—overwhelmingly dominate the canned tuna market. However, bluefin and yellowfin tuna are still uncommon menu items, likely to be served in upscale "white tablecloth" restaurants, where signature dishes such as "sesame seared tuna" can command hefty prices. Yellowfin "steaks" are often seen in specialty stores, but even though they are still wholesome, they turn brown quickly and do not sell well. And as much as supermarkets would like to offer some form of fresh tuna, so far it has proven to be more than a little impractical because of the high prices and the variation in pricing that depends on a daily evaluation of the fish coming in. Nevertheless, after Japan and the EU, the U.S. is the third-largest export destination for Mediterranean wild and ranched bluefin tuna. This statistic is based on the increase in high-quality sushi and sashimi restaurants in the northeast, California, and Florida. Now if only we could *breed* tuna, like cows or pigs....

In his 2005 article "When Will We Tame the Oceans?," John Marra, a biological oceanographer at Columbia University's Lamont-Doherty Earth Observatory, wrote that "Fishing in the ocean is no longer sustainable. Worldwide, we have failed to manage the ocean's fisheries—in a few decades, there may be no fisheries left to manage."

He acknowledged that "fish farming can harm the environment in many ways; indeed, some mariculture operations have caused whole-scale destruction of coastal ecosystems... marine farming can pollute in many ways that are aesthetically, chemically and genetically destructive... crowding in aquaculture enclosures or ponds can easily amplify disease and cause it to spread more quickly than it would in the wild... the mariculture of carnivorous species puts additional pressure on fisheries to provide ever-larger quantities of wild fish for feed, exacerbating the decline of wild fish populations...."[12]

Marra's recommendation was large-scale domestication of the ocean. Move the mariculture systems farther offshore to the waters of the outer continental shelves, and deploy much larger fish pens (closed-net structures containing as much as 100,000 cubic meters of water), which could be floated below the surface and towed from one destination to another, feeding the fish along the way. Another suggestion concerns "herding" of tuna at sea, based on the inclination of certain tunas to aggregate under an object that is significantly different from their surroundings. This propensity has already been exploited by tuna fishermen in the design and implementation of fish-aggregating devices (FADs). A FAD can be something as simple as a towed log or platform or as innovative as a fire hose directed behind the boat to create a disturbance on the surface.

Marra says that taming the sea will mean the disappearance of commercial fishermen, and "the bulk of the fish we eat will come from more limited varieties. In such a future we will have to accept an ocean with fish that can be cultured, and we will have to accept less freedom of the seas..." The common goal should be to maintain the ocean as a sustainable source of food, both economically and ecologically. As on land, sustainability of the ocean's food supply for the world's population means domestication of the seas. It is only a matter of time before fisheries around the world crash. Some of the vanishing species—particularly cod, salmon, and tuna—were once the exemplars of plenitude. If the wild-capture fisheries are in decline—because the target species are in decline—it seems self-evident that the only recourse available to a fish-eating world is mariculture. Farmed fish—all of which is destined for human consumption—for 2004 totaled 50 million tons. Most capture fisheries are operating at full or nearly full capacity, which means that the world total will not go up. As the fisheries decimate the wild populations, the world total is more likely to go down. It is incumbent upon fisheries managers and governments to solve the problems associated with aquaculture and to figure out how to replace the decreasing wild populations with farmed fish for a fish-hungry world.

If there aren't enough little fish to feed the big fish, we simply must find something else for the big fish to eat. In "Dollars Without Sense," his prescient discussion of big-money tuna ranching, Canadian environmental biologist John Volpe identified one of the major problems with tuna ranching: It takes 3 kg of wild fish to produce 1 kg of farmed salmon (a 3:1 ratio). For farmed cod the ratio is 5:1. The ratio reaches 20:1 for ranched tuna, in part because tuna are warm-blooded, an energy-intensive physiological state for a cold-water fish. The farms around Port Lincoln alone consume more than 20,000 kg of pilchard, sardine, herring, and anchovy per day. Clearly the consumption of 20 units of edible fish to make one unit of product is no one's idea of a conservation strategy.

But a "conservation strategy" is probably the furthest thing from the minds (or the business plans) of the Port Lincoln ranchers. It is all about money. (Port Lincoln is said to be home to the highest number of millionaires per capita in the Southern Hemisphere.) It is possible that greed will signal the downfall of the tuna-ranching business. As Mediterranean ranches flood the markets with sashimi-grade tuna, Japanese prices continue to drop, but ranching costs do not.

We all know that Japan is an island nation, poor in natural resources, and greatly dependent on the sea for protein, but that does not logically lead to the conclusion that it should catch every swimming thing and serve it up for sale in the Tsukiji fish market. At one time, Japanese whalers hunted various whale species for food in the nearshore waters of Japan, but this subsistence whaling was replaced by commercial enterprise. It was not until the conclusion of World War II that General Douglas MacArthur reintroduced whaling to Japan as a means of feeding the starving populace. Well into the 1980s, the Japanese continued large-scale whaling, not for food, but for commerce. With an increasing armada of catcher boats and factory ships, they included in their hunting grounds great swaths of the northeastern Pacific and the Antarctic. The early Japanese whalers provided food for the people, but by the middle of the 20th century, hardly anybody ate whale meat. The Japanese whaling industry claimed that it had to remain in business for subsistence reasons. However, the International Whaling Commission's 1983 implementation of a moratorium on commercial whaling was probably greeted with a sigh of relief by the thousands of Japanese schoolchildren who had been fed the whale meat that nobody else wanted to eat. As of 2006, the Japanese had hijacked the International Whaling Commission so that the fate of the moratorium hung by a thread. It is more than a little likely that commercial whaling will resume in the next couple of years.

The wild codfish is commercially extinct in the western North Atlantic. Although they will probably never be able to replicate the previous abundance, the Norwegians have started a program to farm cod commercially. To date, the program is small enough that the problem of an adequate food supply hasn't come up. But the Norwegians estimated that they would be harvesting 30,000 tons of farmed cod by 2008, and finding enough fish to feed them will present a very serious challenge. At the Aquaculture Protein Center in Norway, they are experimenting with fish meal made of various combinations of soybeans, corn, rapeseed, sunflower seeds, flaxseeds, and wheat gluten. To date, experimental formulas that have provided the proper nutrients are too expensive. Besides, it has not been satisfactorily demonstrated that a vegetarian fish tastes the same as a carnivorous one. And somehow, a vegetarian diet tends to reduce the amount of omega-3 fatty acids in the flesh. But this shortcoming can probably be met in humans by supplements.

Experiments are under way in Australia to feed farmed tuna on pellets made of vitamin-fortified grain, and these have met with some small success. Some researchers have suggested feeding the fish vegetables until about three weeks before they are killed, and then feed them a more "natural" diet just before they die.

But what can be accomplished in South Australia may not be possible in Croatia, Cyprus, Libya, Tunisia, or Turkey. The Aussies are fishing the main population of southern bluefins. But all those Mediterranean countries are in competition for the breeding stock of northern bluefins, and they might find that environmental safeguards or studies cut into their profits. Some environmental events are beyond the reach of traditional regulatory agencies. When the Israelis bombed Lebanon in July 2006, a power station in Jiyyeh, only 80 feet from the sea, was blown up. Tens of thousands of tons of heavy fuel oil gushed into the eastern Mediterranean, and uncontrolled fires burned the rest of the oil. Early reports estimated the spill at 10,000 tons, but it could have been as much as 35,000 tons—close to the 40,000 tons that spilled into Prince William Sound in Alaska in 1989, when the 987-foot-long supertanker *Exxon Valdez* ran aground. This was generally considered the worst oil spill in history. A month after the bombing, the oil began to sink, covering the bottom with a 4-inch-thick blanket of sludge. As the first large "oil spill" in the Mediterranean, the Jiyyeh event will have massive detrimental effects on the marine life of the region—including the bluefin tuna that breed there.

The price commanded by a bluefin tuna makes it possibly the most commercially valuable marine finfish in the world on a per-pound basis. Despite an alphabet soup of regulatory commissions—IATTC, ICCAT, CCSBT, NOAA, NMFS, ATBOA, SARDI, ATRT, UNCLOS—tuna fishing continues unabated, and the wild populations of northern and southern bluefin tuna have been reduced to critical levels. Tuna ranches exacerbate the problem by catching tuna before they breed. But this might be worse for the population than catching large numbers of adults. As the tuna populations continue to fall, the Japanese demand for *toro* will increase; fewer tuna will mean higher prices, and higher prices will mean intensified fishing. Intensified fishing will, of course, result in fewer tuna. (Of course, all bets would be off if the Japanese somehow relaxed their demand for *maguro*, but that seems as likely as Americans giving up hamburgers.)

The factors that influence the Japanese market price for bluefins are freshness, fat content, color, and shape. But the fisheries pay no attention to these considerations, and they are governed by regulations that are based only on population estimates. If the highest-quality fish are selected from North American landings for sale in Japan, the overall profit goes up. Tuna fishery is rife with IUU fishers, who ignore quotas, restrictions, boundaries, and any other rules and regulations that might threaten their catch. The Japanese market is only too eager to absorb thousands of tons of bluefin tuna, regardless of where or how it is caught. (Japanese SBT fishermen have contrived to circumvent even their own restrictions, bringing in thousands of tons of illegal tuna every year and then falsifying their records.) It would be good for the tuna and, in the end, good for the consumer if tuna fishing were not practiced in such a remorseless manner. But a modification beneficial to the tuna would entail nothing less than a modification of the fundamentals of human nature, and I don't see that happening in the near future.

In the Clean Seas annual report for 2006, the Hagen Stehr CEO wrote a manifesto for his tuna-breeding project:

- Worldwide, wild fish resources are diminishing steadily—in some cases, rapidly.
- Worldwide, consumption of seafood is steadily increasing—in many cases, dramatically.
- Catches of tuna are declining again in the Mediterranean due to overfishing, pollutants, and health concerns. Scientists believe the resource is doomed and will collapse in the foreseeable future.
- The Mexican tuna harvest is unreliable because of environmental factors and overfishing. The tonnage harvested is continuing to decline.
- In the Southern Hemisphere, overfishing of the SBT resource is being vigorously addressed by Pacific governments, harvests are being severely restrained, and market prices are being driven up.

Clean Seas Aquaculture Growout Pty. Ltd. is a publicly traded company, founded by Hagen Stehr in 1969 and now owned and managed by the Stehr Group in Port Lincoln. The Australian government provided a grant of $4.1 million to assist in the commercialization of SBT breeding. Clean Seas is so sure of success in breeding southern bluefins that it made a public offering of 18 million shares in the company, according to the October 2005 prospectus. It has already successfully raised captive-bred yellowtail kingfish (*Seriola lalandi*) and mulloway (*Argyrosomus hololepidotus*), which are now in significant commercial production. In part, Hagen Stehr's "Chairman's Letter" in the prospectus reads as follows:

Over the past 6 years Clean Seas parent, the Stehr Group, has been actively working towards breeding SBT and has made significant advances in several areas including broodstock management, on-shore fish transfer, fish husbandry practices, and the pelletized feeding of juvenile SBT... The next step for Clean Seas is the propagation of our own broodstock facility at Arno Bay. Fertilized SBT eggs to be produced in the new facility will be transferred to our existing hatchery facility for the controlled production of SBT fingerlings by adaptation of proven protocols for the other species being propagated. The directors believe that over the next three years this should lead to the establishment of an exciting and long term commercially viable SBT business.

It appears that investing in Clean Seas would have been a good idea. In October 2006, southern bluefin broodstock were airlifted from their pens to a 3-million-liter (790,000-gallon) tank designed to replicate the optimum conditions for spawning.

Unless tuna can be raised as if they were domesticated animals, the world populations will continue to decline, eventually reaching the point of no return. In November 2006, 14 marine biologists published a major study in the journal *Science*, in which they said that unless things change dramatically, in 50 years, nothing will be left to fish from the oceans. The study, innocuously called "Impacts of Biodiversity Losses on Ocean Ecosystem Services," points out that as of 2003, 29% of all ocean fisheries were in a state of collapse. As Ransom Myers and Boris Worm pointed out in 2003, 90% of the big fishes are already gone, and we are fishing on the remaining 10%. Of course, not only fishing has contributed to this sorry state of affairs. Worsening water quality, toxic algal blooms, dead zones, invasive exotic species, and the disappearance of animals and plants that filter pollutants from the water have all played a role. Notice that all these calamities are anthropogenic—caused by man. *Homo sapiens* is by far the greatest threat to environmental stability (especially if you throw global warming into the mix), but also its only hope. The solution to the problem of overfishing is painfully obvious—don't fish so heavily—but this is very difficult to implement. If we can't keep the tuna fishermen from catching all the tuna, it is our responsibility to somehow ensure that the tuna will survive and prosper far from the longlines and nets.

Endnotes

[1] Theodore Bestor's history of Tsukiji (The Fish Market at the Center of the World).

[2] Butler, M.J.A. 1977. The trap (mackerel) and impoundment (bluefin) fishery in St. Margaret's Bay, Nova Scotia: its development. *Col. Vol. Sci. Pap. ICCAT* 6(2):237-241.

[3] Butler, M.J.A. Plight of the bluefin tuna. *National Geographic* 162(2):220-39.

[4] Tudela, S. 2002a. Tuna farming in the Mediterranean: the 'coup de grace' to a dwindling population? *World Wildlife Fund Mediterranean Program Office*, Rome.

[5] Bregazzi, R.M. 2004. *The Tuna Ranching Intelligence Unit*—September 2004. Advanced Tuna Ranching Technologies. Madrid.

[6] Miyabe, N. 2003. Description of the Japanese longline fishery and its fishery statistics in the Mediterranean Sea during recent years. *Col. Vol. Sci. Pap. ICCAT* 55(1):131-137.

[7] Bregazzi, R.M. 2006. The Plunder of Bluefin Tuna in the Mediterranean and East Atlantic in 2004 and 2005: Uncovering the Real Story. World Wide Fund for Nature.

[8] Bregazzi, R.M. 2005. *The Tuna Ranching Intelligence Unit*—Special November 2005 ICCAT Sevilla-Spain Meeting Edition. Advanced Tuna Ranching Technologies. Madrid.

[9] Ryther, J.H. 1981. Mariculture, ocean ranching, and other culture-based fisheries. *BioScience* 31(3):223-230.

[10] Naylor, R.L., R.J. Goldburg, H. Mooney, M.C.M. Beveridge, J. Clay, C. Folke, N. Kautsky, J. Lubchenko, J. Primavera, and M. Williams. 1998. Nature's subsidies to shrimp and salmon farming. *Science* 282:883-884.

[11] Holloway, M. 2002. Blue revolution [Fish farming]. *Discover* 23(9):57-63.

[12] Marra, J. 2005. When will we tame the oceans? *Nature* 436:175-176.

6

Fishing for Maguro

The worldwide bluefin tuna fishery is directed almost exclusively toward the insatiable Japanese sashimi market. Whether they are caught in the North Atlantic, the Mediterranean, or Australia, the large tuna are destined for the Tsukiji Fish Market in Tokyo, where a daily auction takes place, often for prices in excess of $100,000 per fish. Although scientists have been trying for years, tuna cannot be farmed in the traditional fashion (fish grown from eggs). But they can be ranched, where juvenile tuna are trapped in nets and towed to pens where they are fattened until they are large enough to be killed for the sashimi market. These tuna ranches can be found off almost every country on the Mediterranean, and in Australia, Costa Rica, Malaysia, Japan, Mexico, and Panama as well.

In his 1995 book *Giant Bluefin*, Douglas Whynott summarized the early history of commercial tuna fishing as the fish morphed from large, undesirable "horse mackerel" into the most valuable fish in the world:

> Since 1958 in Cape Cod Bay a small seiner called the *Silver Mink*, captained by Manny Phillips, had been netting 500 to 600 tons of school bluefin per season... He was giving fish away. He was selling school bluefin for five cents a pound to a cannery in Maine... Another fisherman, Frank Cyganowski, in his first year as a seiner captain, making his first set off Martha's Vineyard, hauled in sixteen tons of sixty-pound bluefin. The fish were sold to Cape Cod Tuna, the cannery in Eastport, Maine, for five cents a pound, and so Frank Cyganowski's first set was worth $1,600...

From 1962 to 1970, a fleet of two dozen Canadian seiners made yearly catches of from 6,000 to 10,000 metric tons of tuna... In 1956 Japanese longline trawlers began to fish in the Atlantic Ocean, first in equatorial waters, later expanding into tropical and temperate waters in both hemispheres. Japanese longliners typically set lines fifty miles long with two thousand hooks per line. By the peak year of 1965, a fleet of several hundred boats was setting 100 million hooks. At first they targeted yellowfin and albacore tuna, and the catches were landed at ports in the Atlantic, but in the 1970s, with increased demand for tuna, target species changed to northern and southern bluefin and to bigeye tuna, which inhabit colder waters.[1]

In his 2001 discussion of tuna conservation, Carl Safina wrote, "Because the prices surrounding them run so high, bluefins are depleted everywhere they swim."[2] When the Japanese learned that giant tuna could be caught off eastern Canada and New England, the bluefin market exploded. Prior to the arrival of the Japanese purse seiner *Kuroshio Maru 37* in 1971, the large, red-meat bluefin tuna were worth only a few pennies a pound—if you could find a buyer. When fishermen brought fish to *Kuroshio Maru 37*, they received 10 cents a pound, but they didn't know that Frank Cyganowski was receiving another 21 cents a pound, thus becoming the first Japanese/New England middleman. The next year, Nichoro Gyogyo K.K. sent *Kuroshio Maru 32*, another purse seiner with a large cargo capacity, prepared to pay the fishermen $1 a pound. Fish that had brought $40 two years earlier were now worth $1,000. Soon the price of a single "giant" shot up to tens of thousands of dollars. When Atlantic coast fishermen found that they could earn a year's pay in an afternoon, the uncontrolled slaughter of what Barbara Block called "the cocaine of the sea" began.

By 1990, Japan was consuming 800,000 tons (1,600,000,000 pounds) of tuna per year, of which 74% (690,000 tons) was caught by the Japanese tuna fleet, and the remainder by foreign fishers. As of 2001, wrote Carroll, Anderson, and Martínez-Garmendia, "More than 45 countries now compete to supply bluefin tuna to Japan. From 1994 to 1997, the main sources of fresh bluefin tuna exports to Japan were Canada, the U.S., and the Mediterranean region. In 1997, Japanese bluefin tuna imports of fresh U.S. product accounted for about 15% of all imports. However, the U.S. share was greater during the summer months, when it comprised more than 25% of total Japanese imports."[3] The enormous Japanese sushi and sashimi markets are supplied by what is essentially a consortium of tuna fishermen from around the world, all eager to cash in. Large Atlantic wild bluefins are caught off New England, Maritime Canada, New Jersey, and North Carolina, and their (smaller) Pacific counterparts are fished off California, Japan, and Hawaii. The southern bluefins (SBT) can be caught off Australia and New Zealand, and nationals from any and every country participate in the international bluefin sweepstakes. With everybody and his uncle chasing after the remaining bluefins, it is not particularly surprising that these big fish have become scarce. But because greed and gluttony always trump caution and care, a system of creating more giant tuna was developed that appeared at first to solve the problem of scarcity. But the tuna farmers proved to be just as venal and careless as the open-water fishermen, and they managed to overfish the very fishery they had created. Now the tuna ranches are running out of fish too.

The Japanese will tell you that bluefin tuna are plentiful throughout the world's oceans and that their fisheries (and their purchases) are hardly making a dent in the populations—which are on the rise anyway. ICCAT publishes report after report about catch statistics, management, and fishing gear, but it appears to be little more than a lobbying organization for tuna fishermen and has no way of reducing fishing pressure. But ask conservation organizations such as Greenpeace or WWF, and you will hear that the bluefin tuna is in very serious trouble. No population of animal, no matter how widespread and fecund, can withstand such massive inroads into its numbers. And the practice of tuna ranching, which removes large numbers of potential breeders from the population, will surely have unexpected consequences.

It was always assumed—at least by fishermen—that as a particular fish species grew scarce, they would simply find another place to fish for it. Or if a particular species declined, they would find another species. As Myers and Worm put it in a follow-up to their 2003 report, "Although fishing pressure on large marine predators, such as sharks, tuna, billfish, large groundfish, etc., is high, it has long been assumed that these species are largely extinction-proof. The main reasons for this idea were the seemingly inexhaustible abundance of marine life, the remoteness of many marine habitats, and the extreme high fecundity of marine fish populations."[4] This rosy attitude has proven to be disastrously flawed. If you remove most of the fish of a given species from the ocean, there may not be enough left to regenerate the species. Gone are the days when cod fishermen on the Grand Banks—once the world's richest neighborhood for *Gadus morhua*—could lower a basket on a rope and bring it up filled with wriggling cod. The cod fisheries of New England and Maritime Canada can no longer sustain any level of commercial fishing.

Once known as horse mackerel and used mostly for bait or pet food, bluefin tuna has been elevated to the very pinnacle of menu desirability, eaten in various countries and cooked (or not) in various ways. Always the most fashionable and expensive item on the Japanese menu, *maguro* is the red, fatty belly meat of the bluefin tuna, always served raw. You can order it in expensive Japanese restaurants in New York, Los Angeles, Paris, London, Rome—and at practically every restaurant that isn't a noodle shop or a McDonald's in Tokyo. Outside of Japan, bluefin tuna is also served grilled, as carpaccio (raw, thin-sliced), or even as tuna filet mignon. But even if the fish was caught off Cape Cod and served in Boston, it is identified as *maguro* because of the pervasive Japanese influence. Fish is healthy food. Something about omega-3 fatty acids is supposed to make you live longer or reduce your cholesterol. On the other hand, for many people, red meat has become a potentially unhealthy alternative. Therefore, Japanese restaurants, where the overwhelming emphasis is on fish, are more popular than ever. (A few Japanese restaurants specialize in beef, but interestingly, "Kobe beef" from specially fed and massaged cows resembles red-meat tuna.) Thirty years ago, the idea of eating raw fish was repulsive to most Westerners, but nowadays they gobble it up in restaurants in New York, London, and Paris. Japanese cuisine has revolutionized how Westerners think about fish, and Japanese fishermen have revolutionized how the world thinks about tuna.

Theodore Bestor, Professor of Japanese Studies at Harvard (and author of *Tsukiji: The Fishmarket at the Center of the World*), points out that sushi has become a global phenomenon: "Japanese culture and the place of tuna within its demanding culinary tradition is constantly shaped and reshaped by the flow of cultural images that now travel around the globe in all directions simultaneously, bumping into each other in airports, fishing ports, bistros, and bodegas everywhere.

In the newly rewired circuitry of global cultural and economic affairs, Japan is the core, and the Atlantic seaboard, the Adriatic, and the Australian coast are all distant peripheries."[5] Japanese food is in vogue in urban Asia, and demand for sashimi and sushi products is on the rise. This has created opportunities for selling sashimi-grade tuna, particularly in cities such as Shanghai, Guandong, Beijing, Hong Kong, Taipei, Singapore, Kuala Lumpur, Bangkok, and Ho Chi Minh City. Many holiday resorts in the Asian Far East have also added sashimi tuna to their buffet lunch and dinner menus. Fresh tuna loins treated with carbon monoxide (to promote color retention) that are used for sashimi and sushi products are exported to Hong Kong and Taiwan regularly. Supermarkets in Singapore and Malaysia have introduced fresh tuna loins in the seafood section. Fresh sashimi is also an item offered in many upmarket hotels and restaurants in the Asian Far East. China, housing the largest population in the world, is potentially a big market for sashimi as well as canned tuna. Nowadays, Chinese tuna fleets operating in the Pacific Ocean are selling part of their catches on the mainland. In 2005, the leading Japanese conglomerate Nissho Iwai launched a promotional campaign for sashimi tuna in China.

The rising global popularity of sashimi will surely be the downfall of the bluefin tuna. The all-out onslaught on the species, whether wild-caught or raised in pens, will end badly for everybody, including fishermen, fish dealers, restaurateurs, and consumers. It goes without saying that it will end badly for the tuna. If tuna become scarce—and how could they not?—the price will go up, which will encourage intensified fishing effort, which will, of course, reduce the populations even more. This is the lesson so painfully learned with codfish. As the fish became scarcer, the cod fishermen whose lives and livelihoods depended on this fish tried to increase their catches. After all, they had to make payments on the boat, pay off the mortgage, send their kids to school, feed their families—and besides, this was the only job they knew. Western Atlantic codfish stocks declined to the point where the U.S. and Canadian governments were forced to close down the fishery permanently, which put the cod fishermen out of business whether or not they agreed with the scientists.

The cod fishermen of Norway, however, are becoming codfish farmers, and on an increasingly larger scale. According to Paul

Greenberg's 2006 article, "In 2002, the Ministry of Fisheries established the Tromso cod breeding facility, at a cost of $18 million. The
Tromso-based seafood export council has started a 'Cod TV' cable
channel, and a network of government agencies, farmers, and
researchers has come together as 'Sats pa Torsk!' ('Go for cod!')."[6]
Norwegian cod scientists figured out how to keep juvenile cod from
eating their penmates, how to slow their sexual maturation, how to
change their diet from uncultivatable zooplankton to cultivatable
rotifers, and how to make industrial production economically feasible. They just haven't done it yet. Fishermen of New England and
Maritime Canada no longer seek cod in their waters, because there
aren't enough to support a fishery (and the governments have shut
down the fisheries anyway). But the Norwegians are banking on their
ability to breed cod in sufficient quantities to establish cod as viable
food fishes once again. The future of the Atlantic cod—and of the
Norwegians who would eat *lutefisk* (cod cured in lye)—swims now in
pens, not in the open ocean.

One has only to pay a visit to the Tsukiji market to realize that the
Japanese approach to marine life is somewhat different from that of
most Westerners. As a seagirt island nation with little in the way of
natural food resources, Japan is largely dependent on the sea to provide the major source of its protein, whether in the form of fish, shellfish, cephalopods, lobster, shrimp, jellyfish, sea cucumbers, seaweed,
shark meat, or whale meat. After World War II, with the Japanese
economy in tatters, General Douglas MacArthur arranged for the
delivery of tankers that could be converted into factory ships so that
the Japanese could hunt whales to feed their starving people. From
that time onward, the Japanese slaughtered whales in numbers that
defied both imagination and logic. Faced with international restrictions, they ignored them. As they paid lip service to the quotas at
International Whaling Commission (IWC) meetings, they killed
every kind of whale anyway and then lied about what they had done.
In Matsuda's history of the tuna fishery, he says, "The tuna industry is
the symbol of Japanese fisheries,"[7] and indeed it is, but perhaps not in
the way he intended. As with the whales, the Japanese killed as many
tuna as they could (and, in the case of southern bluefins, lied blatantly
about the catch statistics). But because they maintain the market for
large tunas, they encourage every other fishing nation to participate

in this free-for-all. Their takeover of the IWC in 2006 changed the rules (and came close to abolishing the moratorium on commercial whaling that had been passed in 1983). In the same way, their tremendous influence in ICCAT virtually guarantees that bluefin tuna will continue to be caught in numbers that will fulfill the bottomless lust for sashimi and, as an unfortunate by-product, drive tuna closer and closer to extinction.

No elaborate cooking techniques, no fancy sauces, no exotic accompaniments. Just a piece of red, raw fish on a plate that commands prices higher than traditionally expensive items such as beluga caviar and white truffles. Caviar and truffles are rare and often require esoteric methods of collection (black-market sturgeon for caviar and rooting pigs for truffles). But as one can see at Tsukiji every day, bluefin tunas arrive by the hundreds. They may be becoming rare, but they are certainly not in short supply. Buyers sample the meat to find the best-quality *toro*, which can be sold for astronomical prices at Tokyo (or New York) restaurants. Bluefin tuna *toro* may be the modern-day equivalent of the Dutch "Tulipmania" of the 17th century, where buyers of particularly rare hybrids would mortgage their houses, sell the family jewels, or otherwise contrive to raise enough money to buy a single tulip bulb. When the bubble burst, many people went bankrupt as the perceived value of the bulbs plummeted to nothing. Will modern consumers ever come to realize that, however succulent, a piece of fish is just a piece of fish, and that the current tunamania may be driving the tuna out of existence?

Once upon a time, the North American passenger pigeon was the most numerous bird on Earth. In the Eastern U.S., they numbered in the billions, outnumbering all other species of North American birds combined. In 1800, early American naturalist Alexander Wilson witnessed a flock between Kentucky and Indiana that he estimated at a mile in width and 240 miles long. Wilson estimated that this flock contained 2.2 billion birds—and later he said that was an underestimate. Larger and more graceful than the common street pigeon, *Ectopistes migratorius* was a soft gray on its head and back and rufous-pink on the breast, fading to white on the underparts. The bill was black, the feet red, and the eyes orange. Their flocks darkened the skies and extended for miles. Their nesting sites covered hundreds of square miles of forest, with dozens of birds in each tree. As the forests were cleared and converted into farmland, the pigeons' habitat began to disappear, but by far the major contributor to the decline was man. Many passenger pigeons were shot for food, but untold millions were shot for sport. In one competition, a participant had to kill 30,000 birds just to be considered for a prize. Thousands of hunters slaughtered millions of birds, which were sold and shipped out by railroad cars at a price of 15 to 25 cents a dozen.[8] The last legitimate sighting of a wild passenger pigeon was in 1900 in Ohio. This bird was shot, and its remains are in the Ohio State Museum. A few individuals lingered on in captivity into the early years of the 20th century. By 1909, the Cincinnati Zoological Gardens had the three remaining birds, two males and a female. By 1910, only "Martha" was left, named after George Washington's wife. Martha died in a cage at the Cincinnati Zoo on September 1, 1914.

Conclusion

There is no real utility for the tuna fish other than its place on a sushi menu. Perhaps canned albacore is more a staple of Western diets, but even that is a stretch. The fish doesn't cure cancer, it doesn't generate BTUs, and it cannot be used in microchips. Bluefin and other types of tuna are delicious when served with brown rice, crunchy tempura flakes, and spicy sauce. As ridiculous as it sounds, it seems that this is enough to drive our society to over-exploit the tuna population, especially the Pacific bluefin. "Investing" in tuna is not meant to suggest that I condone overfishing. I also don't recommend jumping on the next flight to Tokyo, buying a harpoon gun, and striking it rich. But the facts are the facts: Bluefin tuna are going extinct. As mentioned, the tuna ranchers of Port Lincoln, Australia benefit greatly from higher tuna prices. Because they are essentially setting the market on the fish, I see no evidence that would suggest a decrease in the amount of catch that is being pulled from the water each year. The demand is simply there. Large Japanese and Australian corporations have been preparing for an inevitable rise in the price of tuna.

As mentioned, Chevron Corporation is funding the Sea World Research Institute in its feasibility studies on tuna ranching in Mexico and is allowing one of its mid-ocean oil drilling platforms to be used as part of the facility. Mitsubishi International is reportedly deep-freezing Atlantic and Mediterranean bluefin tuna for several years so that it can sell its inventories in the future, when prices will be substantially higher. Japanese sources report that Mitsubishi controls nearly 40% of the tuna imports in Japan, which is the epicenter of the fish market.

For an outside investor, gaining exposure to the seafood market is difficult—which is true in any niche over-the-counter (OTC) market. Some of the big trades currently being made are in a type of tuna futures contract, or quota contract. These instruments were described briefly earlier, but essentially they work similar to a carbon credit. For example, XYZ Fishing Corporation may use only 70% of its allotted catch quota in a given year, whereas ABC Fishing Corporation projects that it will be 30% over its allotted catch quota. ABC Fishing would then purchase the excess quota from XYZ at some premium to where the underlying fish is priced in the market. In Australia, this is a booming business. As time progresses and it becomes more and more difficult to fish bluefin tuna, these quota contracts will be worth more than gold.

This book is meant for investors who are creative and want to seek opportunities off the beaten path. When ideas need to be stripped down to a few equity names, it always becomes difficult to convey the real story of why that opportunity exists. In the case of tuna, the real arbitrage exists in these tuna quota rights, or actually working with companies that breed and farm the bluefin. This is not an easy answer, but that is the fun of seeking out opportunity. There are equities in the market such as Clean Seas Tuna Ltd. (ASX: CSS), the Australian company founded by Hagen Stehr, and Shanghai Kai-cung Marine International Co. Ltd. (SHA:600097). I do not have any view on these equities, and neither I nor the coauthors own these shares. I believe, however, that these equities do little justice to the opportunity at large. Over the next few years, possibly a more liquid futures contract will be released so that restaurant chains can hedge against soaring tuna prices. Until then, investors must get creative building some exposure to seafood prices.

Endnotes

[1] Whynott, D. 1995. *Giant Bluefin*. North Point Press.

[2] Safina, C., A. Rosenberg, R.A. Myers, T.J. Quinn, and J.S. Collie. 2005. U.S. ocean fish recovery: staying the course. *Science* 309: 707-708.

[3] Carroll, M.T., J.L. Anderson, and J. Martínez-Garmendia. 2001. Pricing U.S. North Atlantic bluefin tuna and implications for management. *Agribusiness* 17(2): 243-254.

[4] Myers, R.A. and B. Worm. 2003. Rapid worldwide depletion of predatory fish communities. *Nature* 423:280-283.

[5] Bestor, T.C. 2000. How sushi went global. *Foreign Policy* 121:54-63.

[6] Greenberg, P. 2006a. Green to the gills. *New York Times Magazine* June 18. www.nytimes.com/2006/06/18/magazine/18fish.html?pagewanted=7&_r=1.

[7] Matsuda, Y. 1998. History of the Japanese tuna fisheries and a Japanese perspective on Atlantic bluefin tuna. *Col. Vol. Sci. Pap. ICCAT* 50(2):733-751.

[8] Matthiessen, P. 1959. *Wildlife in America*. Viking.

Part III

Blue Gold

"If there is magic on this planet, it is contained in water."
—Loren Eiseley, *The Immense Journey*, 1957

"Water is life's mater and matrix, mother and medium. There is no life without water."
—Albert Szent-Gyorgyi, Hungarian biochemist and winner of the 1937 Nobel Prize in Physiology or Medicine

In virtually every nation on Earth, at least some of that country's citizens can stand on the ocean's shore and gaze into the seeming infinity of eternal water. Even landlocked nations often have seas and lakes large enough to provide this vista. Romanians, Bulgarians, and Ukrainians look across the Black Sea; Turkmen, Kazakhs, and Azerbaijanis view each other across the Caspian; Ugandans can look across Lake Victoria and see, on the far shore, the dim outline of Tanzania or Kenya. In addition, rivers flow, or at least muddle, through every nation, even Saharan nations such as Algeria, Libya, and Chad. But as you will see, the availability of potable (drinkable) water, essential to human survival, is not afforded to all those who seek and see these endless vistas.

Oceans, lakes, and rivers have beckoned explorers, adventurers, and migrants from time immemorial. Water has provided ease of transportation, the ability to move large objects great distances, energy, personal mobility, and the answer to the question of what lay beyond that seemingly endless horizon. But the essentiality of water is even greater than all that—something far more elemental.

We evolved from water. Every organism on Earth first developed in the oceans, and 80% of the planet's denizens reside there still. Humans are among the survivors who left that water world and via intellect, brutality, and/or luck exist on land today.

Spencer Wells, an American geneticist and anthropologist, used DNA markers to postulate quite convincingly that our human ancestors, our own "Adam" and "Eve," originated in Africa. They were able to migrate across the whole of the coastal Middle East and Southwest and Southeast Asia and then on to Australia, Indonesia, and the Philippines only because of the life-giving oceans. Roughly 40,000 years ago, man was more prey than predator. By staying close to the coast, man could avoid both the predators of the sea and, for the most part, the predators of the land. Collecting potable water where freshwater rivers ran into the sea, as almost all ultimately do, the fecund oceans and rivers always provided ample water and food—seabirds, fish, clams, oysters, and other shellfish.

Mankind has come a long way since these early explorations and migrations. But one thing has not changed: We still need our daily quota of disease-free water, or we will die. Today, we use water to generate energy, as with hydroelectric power; we enable commerce and global development by using it to transport massive quantities of goods in the cheapest way possible; we irrigate our fields and crops, providing food, none of which can grow without water; we bathe in it and clean our clothes and dishes in it; and, of course, we sustain our own biological survival with it. Many developed nations (most of which developed *because of* the availability of rivers, lakes, and streams for sustenance, food, and transportation) have a clear advantage over other regions and nations on this water planet. Some less-developed nations have water, but not the means to keep it disease-free. Others have endless miles of ocean coastline but cannot drink a drop of that water. Both of these problems can be addressed today—for a price. It is for these two categories of nations that the future is most secure—and these nations may well control the future of mankind. Not necessarily those with oil, although they may barter it for water or use their profits to create potable water. Not those with coal, or wind, or endless sun. Those with water.

Part III discusses the distribution, science, geopolitics, and investment possibilities of water. Answers to important questions will be posed:

- Who has water?
- Who doesn't?

For those who don't, to what lengths will they go to get it? What might one nation be willing to do if another nation inhibits its access to water?

Will science and technology provide inexpensive desalination for areas that border the world's great saltwater oceans? Even if they do, where does that leave the 44 landlocked nations with no access to the world's oceans? Do they have enough fresh water in lakes and rivers to ensure their inhabitants' survival? And how secure are those sources? Who controls the headwaters of those rivers?

Can we take the precious little freshwater we have and make it pure enough to ensure the survival of an ever-expanding world population? In short, is there enough water to keep alive the 6.9 billion people the U.S. Census Bureau estimates are on the planet today, let alone the 8.3 billion the United Nations forecasts as its *medium* variant projection in just 20 years?

Will water be used as a political carrot or stick to control another nation's domestic and foreign policy? (If you think oil is a club in the wrong hands, imagine the power of life and death you hold over another for the one substance he or she cannot live without for more than three days.)

What sectors, industries, and companies rely on water the most? Which are the most vulnerable to water shortages?

What sectors, industries, and companies might benefit the most from ensuring access to potable water? Today waterborne pathogens kill more children than any other factor. Watching a child being lowered into a mud hole 40 feet below ground to scrape "water" and mud into a goatskin bag is not the future of mankind. Yet, for many, it is the present. Huge opportunity exists for scientists and commercial enterprises that can provide water free of pathogens that kill rather than give life.

We came from water. We cannot exist without water. From water comes food to nourish us and comes rain, freshwater lakes, rivers, springs, and aquifers. Water is the one substance we need for our very existence that has no replacement on Earth. All foods can be substituted with some other food. While some cultures may prefer rice, and others wheat, and still others corn or soybeans, to the human body it's all the same. Around the world, people wear different clothing made of different fibers and live in shelters composed of different materials. Oil and coal can be replaced with other sources of energy. But water is the one thing we can neither replace nor substitute.

Water is life.

7

Water: Who Has It, and Who Doesn't

"All the water that will ever be is, right now."
—*National Geographic, October 1993*

"Between earth and earth's atmosphere, the amount of water remains constant; there is never a drop more, never a drop less.
"This is a story of circular infinity, of a planet birthing itself."
—*Linda Hogan, Northern Lights, Autumn 1990*

Before we address the issue of which regions and nations have the most affordable and accessible water resources, let's take a look at what the entire world must divvy up. The information comes from *Water in Crisis: A Guide to the World's Fresh Water Resources* (Oxford University Press, 1993), in the chapter "World Fresh Water Resources."

Although more than 70% of the Earth's surface is covered by water, 97.5% of that is salt water, as shown in Figure 7.1. Salt water will kill you if you drink it without diluting it with freshwater. (The next chapter talks more about the science of water.) That leaves just 2.5% of Earth's water resources as "potentially" available to support human, animal, and plant life.

Except. Except that 69% of that 2.5% is unavailable because it is frozen in the ice caps of Antarctica, Greenland, and the far-north Arctic islands. Another 30% of this 2.5% potentially drinkable water is locked in the ground, either as economically unrecoverable water in the soil itself or as deep aquifers inaccessible for human use. Even if

The World's Water

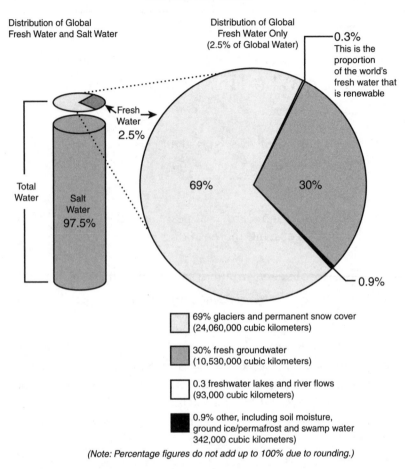

69% glaciers and permanent snow cover
(24,060,000 cubic kilometers)

30% fresh groundwater
(10,530,000 cubic kilometers)

0.3 freshwater lakes and river flows
(93,000 cubic kilometers)

0.9% other, including soil moisture,
ground ice/permafrost and swamp water
342,000 cubic kilometers)

(Note: Percentage figures do not add up to 100% due to rounding.)

Source: Igor Shiklomanov, "World Fresh Water Resources" in Peter H. Gleick, ed.,
Water in Crisis: A Guide to the World's Fresh Water Resources, 1993

Figure 7.1   The world's water

Source: *Water in Crisis: A Guide to the World's Fresh Water Resources* (Oxford University Press, 1993)

we count all this water because, at some price, we may be able to filter water from soil or tap the deeper aquifers we haven't already begun to plunder, we must remember that it took eons to store water as glacier or aquifer. Both of these sources are nonrenewable and currently are noneconomic and not feasible to recover. However, creating new mouths to feed is eminently "renewable." We must accept the hard fact that just three-tenths of 1% of the water we see is available for the world's 6.9 billion (and growing) population. Only the water found in lakes, streams, rivers, reservoirs, and underground sources that are shallow enough to be tapped at an affordable cost is regularly renewed by The Water Cycle and therefore available on a sustainable basis.

Is this remaining three-tenths of 1% distributed equally across nations and regions? Not on your life—and "your life" is precisely what is at stake.

Where Is the Water?

The amount of water on the surface of the Earth, and in the atmosphere that protects us, is relatively constant. It exists as humidity—basically, water droplets too small for gravity, the sun, wind, and other atmospheric conditions to coalesce into rain or snow. It exists as saltwater oceans, freshwater lakes, glaciers, rivers, ice, rain, and snow. The amount extant is recycled by plants and animals in an endless chain of evaporation, transpiration, condensation, and precipitation. So it would seem the problem is merely capturing what is available and using it as wisely as possible.

That is what happens over most of the world today. Every year farmers on the Indian subcontinent and all across Southeast Asia eagerly await the coming of the monsoons. At their most virulent, they may bring flooding, death, and destruction. But without those blessed rains, there would be no rice. Without those rains, there would be no dilution of the man-made, animal-made, and man-caused concentration of sewage and chemicals that renders the groundwater undrinkable. And without those rains, often collected in open cisterns, there would be no water in the dry season.

That is why the coming of the monsoons is a time of trepidation but, overshadowing this trepidation, also a time of great joy. I was a defense attaché in Myanmar (Burma) for three month-long tours in the 1990s. Every year, with the first big fat black clouds releasing water in March and April, the entire Burmese nation enjoys a Water Festival. Deprived, rationed, or self-rationed for so many months, with the first rains every inhabitant takes to the streets and throws pails of water at passing bicyclists, cars, and pedestrians or engages in squirt-gun shenanigans. Or they simply stand, arms akimbo and smile wide, as the cooling drops of rain pelt their bodies.

There are only three problems with this delightful scenario and reliance on the ever-dependable cycle of drought and monsoon:

- The supply of water may be constant, but with more and more people covering every square meter of this overburdened planet, the demand has gone into the stratosphere. An increasing number of nations simply have too many mouths to feed and thirsts to quench for the current level of potable water to sustain.

- As the eminent American biologist Dr. Garrett Hardin presciently observed, "We can never do merely one thing." We may rejoice that the world's standard of living is, in the aggregate, improving. We see nations once consigned to the Third World now either "emerging" or "developing." Certainly, from a social perspective, that is desirable. But "we can never do merely one thing." As individuals improve their economic condition, they don't first want tickets to the opera. They don't even lust after a motor scooter first. What they want is more protein in their diets. That typically means transitioning from a cereal-based diet (rice, corn, wheat) to a diet with more animal protein. If 1.3 billion Chinese are going from eating half a chicken over seven days to enjoying a whole chicken and maybe a little pork as well, that means way more grains are being used for animal consumption. And that means more water is being used to grow more grains to provide less, albeit higher-quality, protein.

- I said earlier that the amount of water on the surface of the Earth, and in the atmosphere that protects us, is relatively constant. And I discussed inaccessible groundwater and inaccessible large aquifers. But some aquifers are closer to the surface and have been discovered and exploited via wells that pump this stored water to the surface. These aquifers are saturated subsurface rock that we think of as lakes or pools of water that have accumulated as some rain and snowmelt are pulled by gravity down into the ground rather than drained away via a river or stream. Nature has provided these pools of water—if only we will use them sparingly and wisely. Thus far, we have not done so. We need not look to the developing world to see this. Americans have only to consider Las Vegas, with its tens of thousands of irrigated green lawns and open swimming pools. About seven-eights of the water Vegas uses comes from the Colorado River. But the large population increase and tourist flow has forced residents to also tap, for the other one-eighth, a large aquifer that is now being drained at such a rapid pace that it may be dry in less than 40 years—even if the population and tourism quit growing.

Because of these three mitigating factors/problems, those who actually have abundant water are clearly to be envied, and possibly viewed more favorably for their investment possibilities. Water could be used to secure the health and success of a population, used as a geopolitical weapon ("You cut off my supply of natural gas, I cut off your supply of water."), or sold directly to less-fortunate neighbors. Whatever the case, nations with water increasingly will be in the economic, geopolitical, and investment catbird seat.

A country might trade, say, oil for water (via desalination, for instance). Or it might give concessions to its upstream neighbors whose mountainous snows and rivers supply its own parched plots of earth (think Turkey and Iraq, or Sudan and Egypt). Or a country could simply plunder another nation to get at its precious water (as may have been the case with Tibet, from whose high plateaus most of the water for China and Southeast Asia is sourced). Regardless, every nation gets at least some of what it wants, and others approach close to all of what they need—for now, anyway.

The supply of water is finite but huge. The supply of potable water is finite and sustainable at today's current population—barely. With 384,000 new mouths to feed and thirsts to quench every day, it is no longer sustainable. Danger exists and, as in every crisis, opportunity as well. Technologies exist to make nonpotable water drinkable. The issue isn't whether it's possible to render seawater or wastewater drinkable. The issue is one of affordability and accessibility.

A nation rich in internal renewable water resources per capita may spend its treasures and talents on other technologies, enhancements, and productivities. A nation poor in internal renewable water resources per capita may expend its treasures and talents on mere survival.

So who has the water?

The UN now standardizes the use of certain terms to be able to answer that question. Total Actual Renewable Water Resources (TARWR) is a standardized index that reflects the water resources theoretically available from all sources within a nation. It basically adds all internally generated surface water annual runoff and ground-water recharge derived from rain, fog, and snow, as well as any external flow entering from other nations that contributes to both surface water and groundwater. Then the index subtracts a factor to correct for the same water that comes from surface and groundwater system interactions and any flow volume required by treaty to leave the country. The result is expressed in cubic kilometers of water.

The map shown in Figure 7.2 indicates that China, Indonesia, and India all seem to be in pretty good shape. In fact, in terms of the absolute amount of TARWR, Indonesia is #5 with 2,838 km^3, China is #6 with 2,830 km^3, and India is #9 in the world with 1,880 km^3. They are behind Brazil, #1 with 8,233 km^3; Russia, #2 with 4,508 km^3; the U.S., #3 with 3,051 km^3; and Canada, #4 with 2,902 km^3. India is slightly behind Colombia and Peru. These nine countries account for some 60% of the world's freshwater supply.

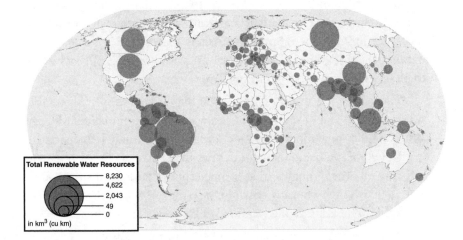

Figure 7.2   Total renewable water

Source: ChartsBin.com

Ay, there's the rub. This map refers only to supply, not demand. It shows which nations are blessed with water resources, but it fails to note how many thirsty voices are crying out for water in that nation. If you instead look at the situation on a per capita basis, for some nations—again, with major investment implications—the numbers are turned on their heads. Figure 7.3 is a more accurate rendering of nations with water to spare, those in the middle, and those in dire straits.

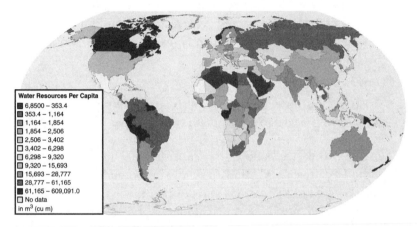

Figure 7.3   Total renewable water resources per capita by country

Source: ChartsBin.com

The ballyhooed BRIC nations of India and China, thanks to their massive populations, must devote significant effort to ensure their population's survival by buying water rights, desalinating ocean water, bartering for water, or taking it by military action. Neighbors Russia and the nations of Southeast Asia have ample amounts above those needed to satisfy their populations. In this more appropriate analysis, the UN says that roughly 1,000 cubic meters per person per year is more than enough. Below that, water is "a potentially serious constraint, and a major problem in drought years...when even slight variations can render whole communities unable to cope and create disaster conditions." The countries in the middle have more than enough but are not as blessed. The countries at the bottom must desalinate, spend, barter, or attack to get enough. Here are the top nations in descending order of water per person:

- French Guiana and Iceland are the undisputed leaders, with, respectively, 609,091 and 539,683 cubic meters (m^3) per person.

- Suriname and Guyana, two sparsely populated rain forest nations next to French Guiana in South America, are next, also with six-digit amounts per capita.
- Canada has 87,285 m^3.
- Norway has 80,134 m^3.
- New Zealand has 77,305 m^3.
- Virtually the entire rest of South America is blessed with both the Andes Mountains and the Amazon rain forest, where almost all nations have less than Norway but more than the last two entries on this list.
- Russia has 31,883 m^3.
- Australia has huge deserts but also favorable rains and mountains, giving it 23,346 cubic meters of water per person per year.

The U.S., while well above the "subsistence" threshold of 1,000 m^3 that the UN uses, at 9,789 m^3 is solidly in the middle of the pack and at the low end of the nations at the top of the list. Given the cost of desalination and, heaven forbid, shipping water long distances, the U.S. is fortunate that it has a special relationship with its primary trading partner, ally, and neighbor to the north that most other nations do not enjoy. (By the way, that UN subsistence level is defined as the minimum to sustain life and ensure agricultural production in countries with climates that require irrigation for agriculture. So it refers not just to water consumed as water but also to the amount of water necessary to grow food to ensure subsistence.)

So which nations need to begin planning *today* to secure future water sources and/or build desalination plants and/or clean up their polluted water supplies? As you would suspect, typically these are the most populous nations engaged in a headlong rush to industrialize (the resulting pollution further reduces their potable water supplies) and desert nations closer to the equator cursed with scant rain and snow. They include the countries listed in Table 7.1. It was taken from the current CIA World Factbook, which ranks all countries' water availability in cubic kilometers per 100,000 people. This table lists only the lowest 20.

TABLE 7.1   World Rank by Water Availability Per 100,000 Population

Rank	Country	Cubic Kilometers
150	Rwanda	0.05
151	Algeria	0.04
152	St. Kitts and Nevis	0.04
153	Burundi	0.04
154	Tunisia	0.04
155	Barbados	0.04
156	Djibouti	0.03
157	Oman	0.03
158	Israel	0.02
159	Malta	0.02
160	Yemen	0.02
161	Bahrain	0.01
162	Maldives	0.01
163	Jordan	0.01
164	Singapore	0.01
165	Libya	0.009
166	Saudi Arabia	0.009
167	Qatar	0.007
168	United Arab Emirates	0.004
169	Kuwait	0.0007

Source: CIA World Factbook

For comparison, given the CIA's different methodology, Iceland has 53.4 km^3 per 100,000 people, and the U.S. has 0.99^3 km for every 100,000 residents.

This leads to Figure 7.4—nations dependent on others for much of their water supply. This need not necessarily lead to conflict, of course. For example, South America has plenty of water for all. It obtains water from other nations simply because the Andean/Amazon watersheds border so many other countries. And many Mideast nations, thanks to desalination (or the fact that their neighbors have even less water to provide, pilfer, or plunder than they do), are not dependent on other nations. Still, this provides an interesting geopolitical perspective and rounds out the idea of not just who has water and who doesn't, but who is dependent on the good intentions of the people upstream.

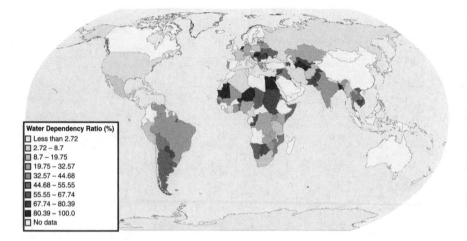

Figure 7.4   Total renewable water dependency ratio

Source: ChartsBin.com

For the record, 38 countries depend on other nations for over 50% of their renewable water resources: Argentina, Azerbaijan, Bahrain, Bangladesh, Benin, Bolivia, Botswana, Cambodia, Chad, Congo, Djibouti, Egypt, Eritrea, Gambia, Iraq, Israel, Kuwait, Latvia, Mauritania, Mozambique, Namibia, Netherlands, Niger, Pakistan, Paraguay, Portugal, Republic of Moldova, Romania, Senegal, Somalia, Sudan, Syrian Arab Republic, Turkmenistan, Ukraine, Uruguay, Uzbekistan, Vietnam, and Yugoslavia.

What all this taken together illustrates is that for now and into the near future—say, 2025 or 2030—the developed countries of North America and Europe, including Russia, will not see any serious threat to their water supply. Declining or stable populations are and will remain well aligned with available water resources.

However, North Africa, the Middle East, South Africa, China, India, probably Iran and Afghanistan, and possibly Pakistan, may face severe water shortages due to physical scarcity of water, a high level of pollutants in the freshwater supply, and overpopulation.

Even water-rich South America and Sub-Saharan Africa may face water supply issues by 2025. In their case, however, the issues are more likely to be overpopulation and the difficulty of providing pure, disease-free water.

The wildcard, of course, in this "Who has water and who doesn't?" conundrum is unconventional water sources. I have relied primarily on the UN Food and Agriculture Organization of the United Nations (FAO) and the CIA World Factbook in researching the numbers in this chapter. Neither of them yet takes into account the use of nonconventional water sources such as the production of freshwater by desalination of brackish or salt water or the reuse of urban or industrial wastewaters (with or without treatment)—mostly in agriculture, but increasingly for industrial and even domestic uses. And yet these two areas are where we will have to concentrate our efforts going forward. The Hydrologic Cycle (also called The Water Cycle) ensures that no less water is available to us in the future—but no more either. It is fixed. And that leads to the geopolitical implications of water.

I spent many years in the U.S. intelligence community. Most analysts therein dwell on matters military, economic, political, cultural, and social, not biological. But I suggest that far more emphasis be placed on the economics and politics of water, whether for national defense, geopolitical positioning, economic necessity, or investment opportunity. We'll return to this topic in greater detail and discuss the investment implications a bit later. But to place this subject in the most rational context, first we must make sure that we understand something of the science of water.

8

Mimicking the Water Cycle: Making Water Potable

"Irrigation of the land with seawater desalinated by fusion power is ancient. It's called rain."
—*Michael McClary*

"Filthy water cannot be washed."
—*African proverb*

"In every glass of water we drink, some of the water has already passed through fishes, trees, bacteria, worms in the soil, and many other organisms, including people.... Living systems cleanse water and make it fit, among other things, for human consumption."
—*Elliot A. Norse, in R.J. Hoage, ed.,* Animal Extinctions, *1985*

We have seen the various forms the water on the Earth takes—as seawater, glaciers, groundwater, aquifers, humidity, in living creatures, and as renewable freshwater as rain, lakes, rivers, streams, and so on. And we have seen which nations and regions enjoy the highest concentrations of this last category of renewable freshwater—Total Actual Renewable Water Resources (TARWR). Now let's look at how that water cycles from each region and back into it or others—typically, having been filtered by Nature and once again fit for consumption.

I swear Figure 8.1 is the same illustration I first saw in my fifth-grade physical geography class. Because The Water Cycle hasn't changed in a few thousand millennia, I guess the intervening years of my life are but an eyeblink in time, and this diagram is still as valid today as it was back then. It illustrates rather well the process of water passing "through fishes, trees, bacteria, worms in the soil, and many other organisms, including people." Then it transpires or evaporates into the atmosphere, where it is stored until it again rejoins the Earth as rain, snow, fog drip, or Seattle mist.

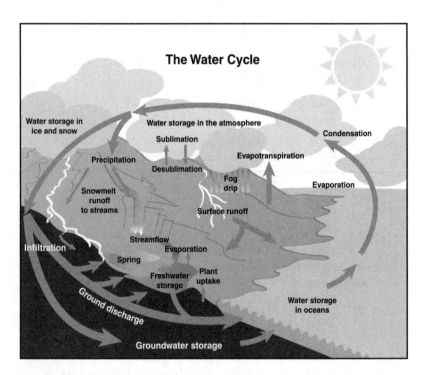

Figure 8.1   The Water Cycle[1]

Source: U.S. Geological Survey

The Water Cycle has no beginning and no end. It doesn't "start" as rain, and then "become" a river, and then "ascend" as transpiration. It's a cycle, without beginning or end, that defines the movement of water on the surface of, underground, and above the Earth itself, constantly moving and constantly changing from liquid (water) to gas (water vapor) to a solid (ice) and back again.

Since I live in the high country in the Sierra Nevada, I'll start, arbitrarily, at that point in the cycle. As snow gently falls in the

Sierra, it accumulates and is stored during the winter as snow. Where the sun or water touches it, it refreezes, some as ice. Most people, if they think about snow and ice at all, know that snow melts. Eventually. Really, it does. (Those of us in rural mountain areas with lots of sunshine think about melting snow favorably, if not often. Those living in cities think of snow often and unkindly, as some disgusting, sooty, freezing mass to be gotten through until spring.) Here in the mountains, the melting snow forms creeks that become streams that become rivers for spring kayaking and wonderful hiking and rock-hopping. But this is only one way snow takes a different form by becoming water again. The other way is via sublimation (which has nothing to do with hiding your true feelings about snow).

Sublimation is the process in which snow turns to vapor without passing through the liquid stage first. Out West, we have Chinooks—dry warm winds in midwinter that sort of zap the snow and turn it into its gaseous form without passing through liquid. It's typically very dry here in the Sierras. Our winter humidity ranges around 20% to 30%. That's one reason why we don't mind winter so much. Even though the temperature is low, the sun is shining on our faces, and it isn't a "wet" cold. Living at just under 7,000 feet, the combination of lower air pressure at this altitude, bright sunshine, and dry winds creates the right environment for Chinooks. People in the Rockies think they have a monopoly on them, but we steal a little of their thunder, or at least terminology, for our own version.

Whatever you call them, these winds are basically straight from the Pacific (when they are wet, we call them "Honolulu Expresses"). Some of the moisture gets wrung out as the wind passes over the Sierras, and the rest as the wind tries to get over the Rockies. Once these winds come down from the mountains onto the high plains (Reno and Denver are both mile-high cities), they can actually become quite mellow—as warm as 60 or 70°F with a relative humidity of 15%, 10%, or less. Here you are in midwinter and suddenly, for a short respite, anyway, you are peeling off layers of winter clothing. The air in these winds is so devoid of moisture that when it hits a snowpack, the frozen water evaporates, rather than melting.

Melting not only fills our streams, rivers, and high-country lakes but also contributes hugely to the supply of groundwater and refreshes who knows how many aquifers. In the springtime, I begin to water my smaller plants, but my big trees and well-established mature bushes I never worry about. I know that their taproots are reaching down to find that water moving at a snail's pace from the 9,000-foot peaks around me to the 6,223 feet that roughly defines the natural rim at Lake Tahoe. Since I live between those two elevations, I figure the snowmelt I can see above the surface is only part of the story. The rest is slowly moving through my taproots on its way to fill Tahoe another 6 feet or so for the summer.

The story is the same elsewhere in the country, although other areas may receive more or all of their precipitation as rain rather than snow. In either case, the effect is the same. The cycle of water coming back to Earth is continual. Some of it is stored, and much of it is used. But it never stops moving in any case. As humans, animals, and plants breathe, we release some of that water we drank, or water that the plants picked up from the groundwater, as water vapor. When the sun heats water, it's called evaporation; when plants are heated by the sun and release moisture, it's called transpiration.

If you don't believe plants release huge amounts of moisture into the atmosphere, just put a plastic bag around a plant that's in direct sunlight. As it heats up, you'll see the plant perspiring—OK, "transpiring"—as the bag begins to collect water vapor on the inside. Or you can just believe the U.S. Geological Survey website, which says that a single acre of corn gives off about 3,000 to 4,000 gallons of water each day!

All of this respired, perspired, and transpired moist air joins that which has evaporated from the land, lakes, and seas in the bright sunlight. It rises into the atmosphere, where cooler temperatures cause it to condense into clouds. Air currents move clouds around the sky, where cloud particles smack into each other or join to form bigger clouds. Sooner or later, all that smacking or becoming heavier by joining cause the water to fall from the sky as rain or snow all over again.

Of course, as I alluded to in mentioning snow melting into the ground and moving as groundwater through the dirt and rock underneath rather than into streams and rivers, a lot of precipitation soaks into the ground as "infiltration." Some infiltrates deep into the ground to (slowly) attempt to replenish the aquifers that store huge amounts of freshwater for long periods of time and that we humans are now emptying as if there were no tomorrow. On the other hand, some infiltration stays close to the land surface and can seep back into surface-water bodies (and the ocean) as groundwater discharge. (Or it can be sucked up by big trees, which then transpire it back into the atmosphere.)

Because we humans are so blasé about stealing the water from these aquifers without concern for future generations, I think an illustration (see Figure 8.2) and explanation are in order.

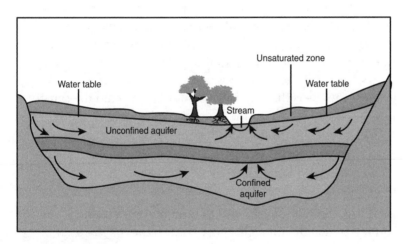

Figure 8.2   Aquifers

Source: U.S. Geological Survey

To quote the USGS website:[2]

Natural refilling of deep aquifers is a slow process because groundwater moves slowly through the unsaturated zone and the aquifer.

Large amounts of water are stored in the ground. The water is still moving, possibly very slowly, and it is still part of The Water Cycle. Most of the water in the ground comes from precipitation that infiltrates downward from the land surface. The upper layer of the soil is the unsaturated zone, where water is present in varying amounts that change over time, but does not saturate the soil.

Below this layer is the saturated zone, where all of the pores, cracks, and spaces between rock particles are saturated with water. The term groundwater is used to describe this area. Another term for groundwater is "aquifer," although this term is usually used to describe water-bearing formations capable of yielding enough water to supply peoples' uses. Aquifers are a huge storehouse of Earth's water, and people all over the world depend on groundwater in their daily lives.

The top of the surface where groundwater occurs is called the water table. In the diagram, you can see how the ground below the water table is saturated with water (the saturated zone). Aquifers are replenished by the seepage of precipitation that falls on the land, but there are many geologic, meteorologic, topographic, and human factors that determine the extent and rate to which aquifers are refilled with water. Rocks have different porosity and permeability characteristics, which means that water does not move around the same way in all rocks. Thus, the characteristics of groundwater recharge vary all over the world.

To access freshwater, people have to drill wells deep enough to tap into an aquifer. The well might have to be dozens or thousands of feet deep....

In an aquifer, the soil and rock is saturated with water. If the aquifer is shallow enough and permeable enough to allow water to move through it at a rapid-enough rate, then people can drill wells into it and withdraw water. The level of the water table can naturally change over time due to changes in weather cycles and precipitation patterns, streamflow and geologic changes, and even human-induced changes, such as the increase in impervious surfaces, such as roads and paved areas, on the landscape.

The pumping of wells can have a great deal of influence on water levels below ground, especially in the vicinity of the well.... Depending on geologic and hydrologic conditions of the aquifer, the impact on the level of the water table can be short-lived or last for decades, and the water level can fall a small amount or many hundreds of feet. Excessive pumping can lower the water table so much that the wells no longer supply water—they can "go dry."

Whether the water in The Water Cycle is visible, as in lakes, streams, or oceans, or invisible, as in groundwater, there is no getting around this simple truth that should guide us in our wise use of water: *The cycle of water and the cycle of life are inextricably intertwined; indeed, they may as well be one and the same.*

So much for how the finite amount of water in the world cycles and recycles itself endlessly and forever, cleaning and purifying as it goes. If mankind will not stop making babies to fill every plot of available earth, we need to do something that shortcuts but imitates what Mother Nature does every day. That is, we need to find ways to purify putrid or fetid or disease-carrying water and wastewater in seconds rather than years, decades, and eons. We also need to figure out how to "evaporate" just the nonsalty part of seawater and make it a life-giver rather than a killer when ingested.

It's ironic that the one substance that has no replacement on Earth is also the one substance that, in its less-pure forms, kills more human beings than any other every single year. Waterborne pathogens exist in such diverse forms and colossal numbers because *everything* we recognize as life needs water to live—humans, animals, fruits, vegetables, everything. And to survive, these pathogens must find a host and a means of sustenance themselves. Perhaps that is why 80% of infectious diseases are waterborne and only 20% are airborne or caused by animal-to-human or human-to-human contact.

There is a reason why people around the world, regardless of their level of education or sophistication in the field of pathogenic microorganisms, learned to drink water that was malted (as in beer), fermented (as in wine), or boiled (as in tea, coffee, mate, and other herbal drinks). To this day, those of us who have served tours of duty in the Middle East know that the culture calls for many bladder-distending cups of tea to provide and return hospitality and thanks. Like most religious or cultural food and beverage rules, this tradition flowed from a survival instinct long before it served as a sign of welcome and repose.

Today, there are numerous ways to ensure clean water, free from most, if not all, pathogens. But such methods may be impractical in the developing world. As any good backpacker knows, with the tools we have available in developed nations and the knowledge we've gained on the subject, we can ensure the best outcome.

We know we need to make certain that the containers in which we place our water are themselves free of parasites or bacteria by cleaning the containers with soap and water—preferably water we know to be good! After rinsing, we know we still need to submerge the containers in a solution of 1 teaspoon of bleach to every quart of water, and then rinse again with a progressively weaker mixture of bleach and water.

We know to strain the water through a cloth to capture large foreign bodies and then let what we've strained settle and gently pour off the water above the sediment, tossing the sediment. *Then* we boil the water, or add chlorine to it in small quantities (yuck), or leave it in full sunlight in a clear container for 6 hours or more.

I make this slight digression not to turn us all into Ranger Rick buddies but to point out that, while this may work for American or European backpackers concerned about giardia or some other major inconvenience, it is just too much trouble to implement in most of the developing world. Worse, the attitude in many parts of the developing world is, "My parents drank that water and lived. I am drinking that water and living. So something else must be making my child sick."

We'll deal with this in greater depth as we begin to discuss investment approaches and opportunities. For now, two approaches that must go hand in hand if we are to make water more potable and safer in much of the world. The UN estimates that some 2.5 billion people on this planet do not have toilets. La toilette is an open ditch next to the creek that provides drinking water. The first step is education, and that doesn't come easily without empirical evidence that things must change. The other element is portable purification systems that will provide that empirical evidence. Although it sounds counterintuitive to any caring, giving aid worker, the first systems should be given to only a few people—those who will actually use them. Quietly let others see that these systems work, and make them come forward to ask for the systems. Trying to change a thousand generations of belief in a week or month is a losing proposition.

It isn't my intent, or within my knowledge and ability, to explain how contaminated water, wastewater, and water carrying terrible diseases may be rendered pure. But I know that pure water comprises 90% or 95% or 99% of all bad water. And I know there are methods to purify it of whatever small percentage of bad stuff is in there. And I also know that lack of water (or dirty water) is by far the largest disease problem in the world; that only 20% of the world's population enjoys the benefits of indoor running water; and that every year, the amount of global water polluted equals the water consumed. That makes this science worth pursuing. The social benefits are there, and the economics are there.

I also know that, in general, there are physical processes like the ones I discussed earlier, biological processes such as the sand-and-charcoal filters I've used in my aquariums, chemical processes such as flocculation and chlorination, and the use of ultraviolet light. (That's the only thing we do to our natural snow water in my own water district—no chemicals, no filters, just UV light.)

All these processes mimic what Mother Nature does over a more extended time frame. Some companies today do this and do it well. Indeed, whole industries have come into existence to purify water on scales both small and large, local and international. With luck and pluck, we may yet be able to vastly increase the amount of potable water available to all—albeit at a higher price than scooping up a handful of freshly fallen snow or catching a raindrop on your tongue.

An even more ambitious endeavor is removing the salts and other minerals from sea water and turning seawater into potable drinking water. This technology is well-proven. Although it too comes at a higher cost than free water falling from the sky, nations such as Saudi Arabia and Yemen have no alternative. Nations such as Israel have some alternatives but want to control the safety *and* purity of their water and have the engineering prowess and technology to do so.

The U.S. Navy (and other navies, as well as a number of commercial vessels) have been desalinating water for a long time. With water weighing over 8 pounds per gallon, the weight of the water that would have to be carried on a vessel, at great cost in fuel and space, to sustain just a 6-week deployment would be too daunting—let alone a 6-month deployment. The average person uses about 120 gallons of water a day, and an aircraft carrier has some 5,000 crew members. And that's just one vessel in a task force. Do the math!

You can see why, for some applications, desalination makes the most *economic* sense.

On the other hand, large-scale desalination typically uses huge amounts of expensive energy, as well as very expensive infrastructure, and incurs relatively high maintenance costs. But it is cost-effective enough that, according to the International Desalination Association, well over 13,080 desalination plants produce more than 12.5 billion gallons of water a day worldwide. That's a bunch of water.

And desalination must be cost-effective in order to make the economies of scale work in this business. Economies of scale yield more R&D, and more R&D yields greater economies of scale, less energy consumption, and a better and cheaper way to ensure a product that tastes just like that raindrop on your tongue.

And they'd better. There is no way you can do this job halfway. I know from personal experience just how dangerous salt water can be. First I'll tell you about the physiology of it all, and then how I know firsthand.

Salt water in nature isn't just the teaspoon of NaCl table salt you pour in a glass of warm water to gargle when you have a sore throat. Salt water in ocean and sea is composed of all kinds of elements and minerals we call "salts": Epsom salts, potassium salts, iodine salts, and lots more. Ocean water is about three times as salty as your blood. So if you ingest ocean water, the water in your body (which makes up 60% to 70% of your weight) floods out of your cells in a fruitless effort to dilute the salt you just ingested. Since all cells need water, this outward flood leaves them perilously dehydrated. Drinking salt water results in cellular dehydration, with symptoms including hallucinations, muddled thinking, seizures, unconsciousness, brain damage, and, finally, as the overwhelmed kidneys shut down, death. Period.

I recently had reason to think about all this a bit more. On a scuba dive on the USS *Vandenberg*, 12 miles off Key West, I found I needed extra weight to descend with a new buoyancy compensator (BC) I hadn't used before. With my dive buddy on the anchor line at the bow, I went to the stern and took off my fins to climb aboard for more weight. The next thing I remember is being 100 yards down-current in 3-foot seas (so, out of sight and earshot of my dive partner) with no fins. It seems that the transom had lifted on a rogue wave and slammed down on the back of my head as I reached down to remove my weight belt to climb aboard.

I'm one of the lucky ones. As a former member of Special Forces, I had the opportunity to attend a special Water Survival School. I was also a Red Cross water safety instructor, and I taught and certified lifeguards. So I'm not as likely to panic just because the back of my head is bruised and I'm all alone 12 miles from shore. Plus, I had a collapsible dive flag and a "sausage"—basically an air sack that stands up in the air—sometimes. Sort of. And I knew my dive partner would alert the cavalry. It was only 2 p.m. So I figured my rescuers would soon be out looking for a diver, or at least the body of one. If push came to shove and the sharks weren't too curious, I could jettison the tank I'd kept to ward off those pesky creatures, and my weight belt, deflate my BC a little, and start kicking. With luck, I could make Key West by midnight.

Now comes the saltwater part. I knew that ingesting salt water would muddle my brain. The waves were so strong that I kept getting seawater in my snorkel. Although I kept spitting it out, I inevitably swallowed some. After 45 minutes out there alone, waving my collapsible dive flag (it stood 6 feet—my head was 2 feet below the waves), I realized I was fascinated by watching my dive flag move back and forth like a metronome. I wondered who was waving a dive flag. Just that short a time and that little seawater, and already I was starting to lose it.

I had 4 ounces of freshwater and a candy bar as emergency supplies in case something like this happened. I'd planned to save them until I needed them for energy on a swim to shore. Instead, I downed both of them right then and there. Either the concern that I was losing it or the dilution of freshwater or the sugar rush got me focused. Seconds later a charter boat came into view less than a half-mile away, and I waved that flag for all it was worth. I'm no expert on saltwater ingestion, but I'm the closest thing I've got. Been there, done that, didn't get the T-shirt, and don't need to do it again.

Desalination using reverse osmosis membrane technology has become a viable option for the development of new water supplies. You may be surprised at the number of countries—and nations—staking their future on desalination. (And, if they ever make a portable desalination model, they'll be richer than Croesus, because every diver and sailor will line up to buy one. I'll be the first in line.) These countries need to test the water and never get nonchalant or lazy about ensuring that the salts that steal the body's fluids and mess with the brain have been completely removed.

No matter the method used, all desalination plants basically mimic Nature in some way. Reverse osmosis is the most complex method, but also one of the most effective (see Figure 8.3).[3] A semi-permeable membrane serves as an extremely fine filter. (Think GORE-TEX fabric, which allows sweat to pass through it but has pores too small to allow rain to penetrate it.) The salty water is put on one side of the membrane, and pressure is applied to stop, and then reverse, the osmotic process. It generally takes a lot of pressure and is fairly slow, but it works.

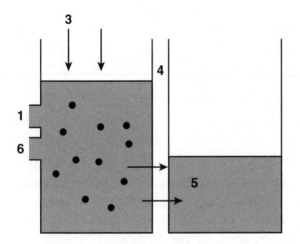

1. Water flows in for the estuary or sea
2. Salt water contains sodium and chloride ions
3. Pressure is applied to force salt water through membrane
4. Semi-permeable membrane with millions of microscopic holes
5. Clean water fit for drinking
6. Saline concentrate flows out

Figure 8.3   Reverse osmosis desalination

Source: BBC News Online

The two biggest desalination plants in the world are in the Middle East. No surprise there. The largest reverse osmosis seawater plant in the world is at Ashkelon, on Israel's southern coast. It provides more than 100 million cubic meters of desalinated water per year at a cost of about US$0.60 per cubic meter. Since one cubic meter equals just over 264 U.S. gallons, and since the average price of water in the U.S. is about $1.50 per 1,000 gallons, it would cost U.S. residents about $0.40 for a cubic meter. (I should point out that this compares Ashkelon's *cost to produce water* to U.S. consumers' *cost to buy* water. Farmers pay considerably less, and Ashkelon's output goes to agriculture as well.)

Still, for consumers at least, if water costs not a penny a gallon, but 2 cents or more, so what? Water is essential, and we will pay what is fair, given our circumstances. Israel's circumstances are that for both security and access to water, it must pay for desalination.

Of the world's water, we know that less than 1% is available as freshwater, polluted or not. And less than 1% of that amount is available to the entire Middle East (yes, that includes the flow from the once-mighty Tigris, Euphrates, and Jordan Rivers). Yet 5% of the world's people live there. Worse, every major river within the Middle East crosses at least one international border. Is it any wonder that Israel chooses not to rely merely on rainwater resident in the Sea of Galilee and the Jordan River, its few aquifers, and recycling? Or that the Golan Heights, which look flat on a sixth-grader's map, actually provide not just the high ground any military commander seeks, but also greater water security for Israel?

The world's largest desalination plant is Jebel Ali (Phase 2) in the United Arab Emirates. Unlike Ashkelon, the technology used here is multistage flash distillation and can produce three times as much— 300 million cubic meters of water per year. (For comparison, the biggest desalination plant in the U.S. is operated by Tampa Bay Water, which produces about 35 million cubic meters of water per year.)

I use these two merely as examples of what can be done when necessity demands it—and the cost can be brought down to not that much more than rainwater if the project is big enough. The politics of water ensures that freshwater sources will be increasingly in doubt for many nations. Desalination remains the only viable alternative. It may not be too big a stretch to suggest that desalination may prevent more wars than the United Nations ever has.

The initial capital investment for desalination is quite expensive, but consider the alternatives. Why have nations moved cautiously? Many have enough freshwater today. Of those that don't, there are environmental considerations. Removing scores of different salts, minerals, and pesticides from brackish or sea water leaves us with the issue of what to do with all that stuff. It can't simply be pumped back into the ocean. As every longtime diver knows, we've done enough harm to our oceans without adding that insult. So all this stuff, some of it benign in minute and necessary concentrations in the oceans but toxic when concentrated, has to be dealt with. And that, too, costs money.

The initial research, which must be proven in larger-scale analysis, is actually heartening. As the U.S.'s National Research Council recently reported, "Limited studies suggest that desalination may be less environmentally harmful than many other ways to supplement water—such as diverting freshwater from sensitive ecosystems.... Desalination also has raised concerns about greenhouse gases because it uses large amounts of energy. Seawater reverse osmosis uses about 10 times more energy than traditional treatment of surface water, for example, and in most cases uses more energy than other ways of augmenting water supplies. Researchers should investigate ways to integrate alternative energy sources—such as the sun, wind, or tides—in order to lower emissions from desalination...."

I am completely in favor of using sun, wind, or tides, but our water problems are pressing now, not in 20 years. What is available now is nuclear and natural gas, and dirty old coal and oil. You want water? Acknowledge that it takes energy, and the energy sources we hope to replace are still the energy sources that we have in abundance—with a transportation and distribution infrastructure already in place.

That's the decision many nations will have to make, and I imagine that's the conclusion many of them will reach. Pure water gives life. Bad water kills. Seawater kills. If we have to use natural gas until these things become more efficient, so be it.

That wraps up where the water is, who's got it and who doesn't, how The Water Cycle has always worked and always will work, and the alternatives that might open new sources of pure water. What could possibly gum up the works? Politics, of course!

Endnotes

[1] The Water Cycle - Water Science for Schools. U.S. Geological Survey. http://ga.water.usgs.gov/edu/watercyclehi.html.

[2] "The Water Cycle: Infiltration." U.S. Geological Survey. http://ga.water.usgs.gov/edu/watercycleinfiltration.html.

[3] Leyne, Jon. "Water factory aims to filter tensions." http://news.bbc.co.uk/2/hi/middle_east/3631964.stm.

9 ————————————

The Politics and Geopolitics of Water

"We never know the worth of water till the well is dry."
—*Thomas Fuller, Gnomologia, 1732*

"When the well is dry, we know the worth of water."
—*Benjamin Franklin (not too proud to borrow),*
Poor Richard's Almanac, 1746

"Anyone who can solve the problems of water will be worthy
of two Nobel prizes—one for peace and one for science."
—*John F. Kennedy*

If current trends continue, there is no doubt that wars will be
fought in the 21st century over water. Not oil. Not ideology. Not the-
ology. Water. Survival.

Figure 9.1 might be a good segue into the politics and geopolitics
of water. There is a reason why Israel and the UAE (and Saudi Arabia
and Libya and almost every other nation in the Middle East) are
spending big money to build desalination plants. The chart shows that
only Lebanon can sustain its agricultural and human-survival level of
water from renewable water resources—and then just barely.

The geopolitical implications of this fact are stunning. We leave
the area of natural resources, discussed in Chapter 7, and the science
of how to increase those resources, discussed in Chapter 8, and move
on to what diplomats, intelligence professionals, and military and
political leaders must consider. What are our vulnerabilities, and how
would an enemy exploit them? What are our enemies' vulnerabilities,

and how might we exploit them? What could we use as a bargaining chip in negotiations? What do they have? Who will use which chip, and who will use it first?

Actual Annual Per Capita Renewable Water Resources

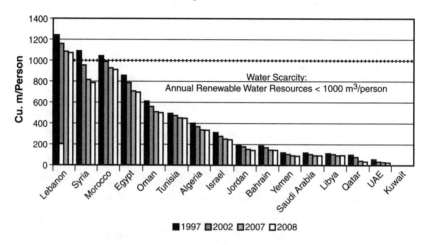

Figure 9.1   Actual annual per capita renewable water resources
Source: USGS

One of the first things that leaps to mind, for example, is that a Middle East so dependent on desalination is remarkably vulnerable in its water supply. What if these single sources of water were contaminated in some way? By definition, they must be located near or have pipes into the sea. Might an enemy's special-operations divers approach undetected underwater and sabotage some key element of a fixed number of plants? Might concentrating so much effort in so few places to provide sustenance to so many mean huge vulnerability to a kinetic (explosive) attack or a cyber attack? If you think the "water planners" in Israel aren't working hand-in-glove with their military and law enforcement personnel to provide the best security, and "red-teaming" various scenarios to anticipate what an underhanded adversary might do, I have a bridge to sell you in New York.

For that matter, if you can identify your enemy's key weaknesses, and one of them is water, a David in terms of size and armament might easily defeat a Goliath with a huge army and the most modern equipment with great logistics and all the fuel in the world. All you have to do is poison, contaminate, blow up, or render inoperable their ability to produce fresh water. Within 3 or 4 days without it, their armies will be laying down their arms and begging to surrender. These are not "think tank" scenarios that I am concocting because of my experience in this area. These are real-world issues borne out by historical example, current veracities of international relations, and, I am quite certain, existing planning being done in many nations' capitals and among their senior-most leaders and war-gamers.

The Pacific Institute, as an adjunct to its annually updated book series, *The World's Water*, maintains an online database of more than 200 examples of conflicts. Some recent ones were local protests resulting in violence; other historical incidents occurred during full-blown warfare. The Institute calls it the Water Conflict Chronology. If you are interested, you can see the entire chronology at http://www.worldwater.org/conflict/. The following list contains a few incidents from the Institute's historical archives and a few more recent events to make the point that you dare not invest in this important sector without understanding the political and geopolitical possibilities, both for good and for ill!

Peter Gleick, editor of *The World's Water*, notes in discussing the chronology, "Water resources are seldom the sole source of violence, but history is rife with tension over water and the use of water systems as weapons, targets, or tools during war. Inequitable access to resources is a critical source of conflict." The following list begins, as so many conflicts have throughout history, in the Middle East, in this case in what is present-day Iraq.

- **Circa 2500 BC:**   Urlama, King of Lagash, diverts water from Lagash to boundary canals, drying up boundary ditches to deprive Umma (today's Iraq) of water.
- **720–705 BC:**   After a successful campaign against the Halidians of Armenia, Sargon II of Assyria destroys their intricate irrigation network and floods their land.
- **600–590 BC:**   Athenian legislator Solon reportedly has roots of helleborus thrown into a small river or aqueduct leading from the Pleistrus River to Cirrha during a siege of this city. The enemy forces become violently ill and are defeated as a result.

- **430 BC:** During the second year of the Peloponnesian War, when plague breaks out in Athens, the Spartans are accused of poisoning the cisterns of the Piraeus, the source of most of Athens' water.

- **537:** The Goths besiege Rome and cut off almost all of the aqueducts leading into the city.

- **1187:** Saladin is able to defeat the Crusaders in 1187 by denying them access to water. In some reports, Saladin sanded all the wells along the way and destroyed the villages of the Maronite Christians, who would have supplied the Christian army with water.

- **1503:** Leonardo da Vinci and Machievelli conspire to divert the Arno River from Pisa during a conflict between Pisa and Florence (although they end up not doing so).

- **1777:** British and Hessians attack the water system of New York: "...the enemy wantonly destroyed the New York water works" during the War for Independence.

- **1860–1865:** William Tecumseh Sherman's memoirs contain an account of Confederate soldiers poisoning ponds by dumping the carcasses of dead animals into them. (Other accounts suggest this tactic was used by both sides.)

- **1907–1913:** The Los Angeles Valley aqueduct/pipeline suffers repeated bombings in an effort to prevent diversions of water from the Owens Valley to Los Angeles.

- **1935:** Arizona calls out the National Guard and militia units to the border with California to protest the construction of Parker Dam and diversions from the Colorado River. The dispute ultimately is settled in court.

- **1938:** Chiang Kai-shek orders the destruction of flood-control dikes on the Huang He (Yellow) River to flood areas threatened by the Japanese army, spilling water across the flat plain. The flood destroys part of the invading army, and its heavy equipment is mired in thick mud. The waters flood an area variously estimated as being between 3,000 and 50,000 square kilometers and kill up to 1 million Chinese.

- **1939–1942:** Japanese chemical and biological weapons activities reportedly include tests by "Unit 731" against military and civilian targets by lacing wells and reservoirs with typhoid and other pathogens.

- **1944:** The German army floods the Pontine Marshes by destroying drainage pumps to contain the Anzio beachhead established by the Allied landings. Over 40 square miles of land are flooded. A 30-mile stretch of landing beaches is rendered unusable for amphibious support forces.

- **1948:** Arab forces cut off West Jerusalem's water supply in the first Arab-Israeli war.

- **1976:** A local militia chief is shot to death in a clash over the damming of the Zhang River. Conflicts over excessive water withdrawals and subsequent water shortages from China's Zhang River will continue for three decades.

- **1978 onward:** Longstanding tensions occur between Egypt and Ethiopia over the Blue Nile, which originates in Ethiopia. Ethiopia's proposed construction of dams on the headwaters of the Blue Nile leads Egypt to repeatedly declare the vital importance of water. According to Anwar Sadat, "The only matter that could take Egypt to war again is water."

- **1990:** The flow of the Euphrates is interrupted for a month as Turkey finishes constructing the Ataturk Dam, part of the Grand Anatolia Project. Syria and Iraq protest that Turkey now has a weapon of war. In mid-1990, Turkish president Turgut Ozal threatens to restrict water flow to Syria to force it to withdraw support for Kurdish rebels operating in southern Turkey.

- **1997:** Malaysia, which supplies about half of Singapore's water, threatens to cut off that supply in retribution for criticisms by Singapore of policy in Malaysia. (To prevent future extortion or control of its citizens, Singapore has embarked on numerous desalination projects.)

- **1999:** Conflicts over excessive water withdrawals and subsequent water shortages from China's Zhang River have been worsening for over three decades. During a clash around the Chinese New Year, farmers from the Hebei and Henan

Provinces fight over limited water resources. Heavy weapons, including mortars and bombs, are used, and nearly 100 villagers are killed. Houses and water facilities are damaged, and the total loss reaches US$1 million. Parties involved are Huanglongkou Village, Shexian County, Hebei Province and Gucheng Village, Linzhou City, Henan Province. Some progress has been made to negotiate a settlement to this dispute, but new projects in the region may fuel new disputes.

- **2000:**   In Kenya, a clash between villagers and thirsty monkeys leaves eight monkeys dead and 10 villagers wounded. The duel starts after water tankers bring water to a drought-stricken area and monkeys desperate for water attack the villagers.

- **2003:**   Four incendiary devices are found in the pumping station of a Michigan water-bottling plant. The Earth Liberation Front (ELF) claims responsibility, accusing Ice Mountain Water Company of "stealing water for profit." Ice Mountain is a subsidiary of Nestle Waters.

- **2004–2006:**   In Ethiopia, at least 250 people are killed and many more are injured in clashes over wells and pastoral lands. Villagers call it the "War of the Well" and describe "well warlords, well widows, and well warriors."

- **2006:**   At least 40 people die in Kenya and Ethiopia in continuing clashes over water, livestock, and grazing land.

- **2009:**   Ethiopian Somalis attack a Borana community in the Oromia region over ownership of a new borehole being drilled on the disputed border between them. Three people from the Oromia village of Kafa are killed and seven are injured, and the entire community is driven from their homes.

- **2009:**   A family in Madhya Pradesh state in India is killed by a small mob for illegally drawing water from a municipal pipe. Drought and inequality in water distribution lead to more than 50 violent clashes in the region in the month of May. The media reports more than a dozen people killed and even more injured since January, mostly fighting over a bucket of water.

You will notice that I selected Ethiopia for many of the final examples. In a study of the world's 25 most populous nations compiled from the United Nations Population Division and the CIA

World Factbook, Ethiopia is predicted to be the nation with the lowest total renewable water resources per person within two generations (see Figure 9.2). It is already the fourth-lowest in the world. Egypt is the second-worst and is projected to remain there. Ethiopia controls the headwaters of the Blue Nile, on which, along with the White Nile, Egypt depends for its survival.

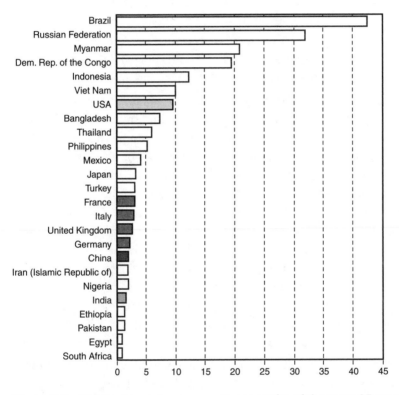

Figure 9.2   Renewable water resources per capita of the most 25 most populous countries in 2009 (in cubic meters per person per year)

Source: World Factbook

Ethiopia-Eritrea-Somalia-Sudan-Egypt is just one flashpoint I see as a possible Water War of this century. Of course, it may not be an issue if funds are found to provide desalination for those with ocean access, which all have except Ethiopia. It would not surprise me to see Ethiopia again at war with Eritrea, which it briefly annexed before those two nations' 30-year war (resulting in Eritrean statehood once more), or with Somalia, or perhaps even tiny Djibouti, if U.S. forces leave it undefended and untreatied.

Another possible flashpoint is the Levant and the ancient areas of Sumeria and Assyria—today's Israel, Jordan, Lebanon, Syria, and Iraq. The continuing conflicts over water resources such as the Jordan, or concerns about Turkey's ability to control the waters of the Euphrates, will always be an issue.

Arguments over who gets what from the Zambezi and Niger Rivers in sub-Saharan Africa will not end, nor will squabbles about downstream use of the Ganges and the Mekong in Southeast Asia.

The troubles are not only between neighbors, but within nations. Since India is the BRIC nation that is second-most-favored by the most analysts, it's worth discussing in this context. With all that crystal-clear snow runoff from the Himalayas into some of the world's most renowned rivers, one would think that what water India has would be exceptional. One would be wrong. According to the World Health Organization, India discharges 95% of its untreated urban sewage directly into surface waters. Of India's 3,119 cities, only 209 have even partial sewage treatment facilities, and just eight have full facilities. Downstream, the polluted water is used for drinking, bathing, and washing. I point out all of this not to alarm but to clarify. In each of these crises, investment opportunity is likely. For instance, if India were to take steps to purify all that dank and malevolent water, how many billions would some lucky companies rake in, doing well by doing good?

China has engaged in military combat with three of its immediate neighbors in the past 50 years and has done its best to influence or control the internal affairs of several more. China "defended" itself against Indian and Russian "incursions" (read: China interpreted its boundaries differently than those other two nations). It also invaded Vietnam to punish it for tossing the Pathet Lao out of Cambodia and attempted to supplant Vietnamese influence there. At one time, more than a million and a half Chinese soldiers were stationed along the old USSR/China border. China has a recent history of either being very paranoid about defending its territory or very truculent in doing so.

China has one-fifth of the world's population. If life were fair, China also would have one-fifth of the world's water. It doesn't. China has just *one-fourteenth* of the world's water supplies. This is the same as Canada, but with 200 times as many people vying for it. And much of that water is rank, dank, and polluted. You think oil is important? Try living without water. Or with water too polluted to drink. And problems have worsened considerably in recent years as the population has burgeoned and factories have dumped toxic pollutants into rivers and lakes. A Chinese bureaucrat recently noted that 90% of China's cities and 75% of its lakes suffer from some degree of water pollution. The Chinese have water—they just can't drink it.

Russia has huge water resources in its sparsely populated eastern provinces commonly thought of as "Siberia," for instance. And all that excess water mostly just drains into the Arctic and Pacific Oceans.

What if? What if China, with 1.3 billion thirsty inhabitants and too little clean water, suggested diverting some of that freshwater southward? Would Russia be wise to barter something for the water or sell it cheaply enough that it wouldn't be worth China's effort or price in blood and treasure to take it?

Declassified documents show that the USSR considered using nuclear weapons against China as long ago as 1969, at the height of their border wars. But it was dissuaded from doing so when the U.S. said it would consider such an act detrimental to American security. The U.S. may have had no recourse but to use its own nuclear arsenal against the then-Soviet Union. "Oh, what a tangled web we weave..." Today it might well be the Russians on the defensive as China's military might grows stronger every day and its desire to project power in what it considers its sphere of influence increases apace.

Of course, numerous water wars could stop well short of actual violence. The whole of Tibet, it seems, is destined to be turned into "nature parks" by the central government in Beijing. Already over 100,000 Tibetan mountain dwellers and nomads have been "resettled" into concrete housing and are excluded from the 34% of Tibet now considered nature parks. These nature parks include the headwaters for three great Asian river systems: the Yangtze, the Yellow, and the Mekong. It is clearly not a shooting war to resettle indigenous populations without representation, but, to many observers, the goal is aggrandizement, and the effect is the same. If another project to divert water from Tibet to northern China is successful (water now flowing to India and Bangladesh), there may be even more unhappy campers in the neighborhood. Is a second India-China war brewing?

Even the most grandiose and international schemes for water procurement and waterway development may one day come under the rubric of Water Wars. Right now there are great plans for a Kazakh-Russian "Eurasia" canal, which would link the Caspian and Azov seas. This would allow landlocked Kazakhstan to ship its oil (estimated to double in the next 5 years to some 150 million tons) by much cheaper waterways to the Azov Sea and on to the Black Sea and then straight to the world's oceans—assuming that the Bosporus Strait stays open during some other conflict, of course.

With some 5% to 10% of the world's oil reserves, Kazakhstan remains the only one of the world's top 20 producers without access to oceangoing ports. Russia would benefit hugely from such a project, because all of the canal portion would be built on Russian soil. This would allow Russia not only to collect transit fees for transport on this new waterway, but also to shut it down or select which traffic passes through if any of its European or Asian neighbors displeases it. "The geopolitics of water" isn't only about drinking water! It's about all the ways in which water may be used as a carrot, stick, or anvil to secure one nation's political objectives over another. In fact, if fellow Caspian neighbors (and large oil and gas exporters) Iran and Azerbaijan were to join with Russia and Kazakhstan, they could form quite the cartel in the energy field, perhaps on par with OPEC.

Who might fund a project of such magnitude? Well, already the Chinese have volunteered. Given that the EU is China's second-largest trading partner and that they have a desperate need for energy, the Chinese have an incentive to get on neighbor Kazakhstan's good side. They may secure Kazakh oil and gas rights in exchange, and they might be able to ship goods to Europe less expensively in the bargain. Shipped from western China by truck across Kazakhstan, and then loaded onto ships and never offloaded until the goods hit the EU in Romania for overland delivery. Quite the dream. If a land and sea "road" were to connect China, Russia, and Kazakhstan and siphon just a 5% market share of current Europe-Asia sea cargo, the transit countries might receive some $3 billion in transit fees annually. (This is according to Kazakh sources in September 2009.)

Heady stuff. Now, I don't see water trading for more per unit than, say, oil. Desalination and purification will keep the threshold well below such figures. But we use a bit more water every day than we do oil! Like about 100 gallons more every day. Trading the amount needed, or withholding the amount needed, of each may be a parity game for some. And the simple geographic ability to withhold water sends a message to a potential adversary that may well prevent them from taking a precipitous action against you.

Now let's take this from the geopolitical to the merely political. Tip O'Neill, former Speaker of the House, once proclaimed that "All politics is local." Well, it's not as if we don't have our own Water Wars and water problems right here in the U.S.

For our first case, let's look at the city where what happens there, stays there—Las Vegas.

Anyone who's ever been there can readily attest that, except for a little snow runoff from Mt. Charleston and its environs, no water is in sight for a hundred miles from the corner of Glitter Gulch and the Strip. But that never stopped an entrepreneur. Las Vegas was founded in 1905 as a sleepy way station. A couple years later, some settlers struck water held for eons in the aquifer beneath the city—and Vegas never looked back. (Or more deeply, as it turns out.)

Back in the day, the groundwater that evaporated or transpired or collected at the surface was just about the same as the amount coming in from Mt. Charleston and the rest of the Spring Mountains. The discovery of the aquifer, however, turned the valley into a desert oasis. In Spanish, Las Vegas means "the meadows."

By 1968, however, Las Vegas residents were pumping an average of 88,000 acre-feet of water every year, while only 25,000 to 35,000 acre-feet of water were naturally recharging the aquifer every year. About the same time, surveyors noticed that the city was sinking. In 1968, three years after I graduated from high school in that little town, Vegas was nothing compared to what it is now. Today, Las Vegas is the fastest-growing metropolitan area in the U.S. It grew from fewer than 200,000 people to 2 million. And some 30 to 40 million tourists pour into the city every year, drinking a little branch water with their bourbon. That aquifer is fast disappearing; some estimates say it will be completely gone in 20 years. Others are slightly more

optimistic. But green irrigated lawns and swimming pools that evaporate an inch a day in the broiling sun do not exactly instill confidence
in hopeful projections.

Still, Vegas is a gambling town. And gamblers aren't known for
their propensity to think much further ahead than the next roll of the
dice. Since gambling fills the city coffers, the attitude is to eat, drink,
and be merry and worry about where to site the next Las Vegas
(maybe Macau?) tomorrow.

Of course, Las Vegas does have another source of water. By order
of the Colorado River Commission, which governs the relationship
between all states downstream of the headwaters of the mighty Colorado, Nevada is allotted 300,000 acre-feet a year from the river.
That's for the whole state, although Vegas and Clark County figure all
those other southern counties can pound sand for a living. Every year,
Southern Nevada exceeds its allotment, according to the Las Vegas
Review-Journal. Within the next 20 years, the *Review-Journal*
reports, the state will likely need 700,000 acre-feet or more per year.
Says Devin Galloway, a groundwater specialist for the USGS Western
Region, "The biggest problem everywhere is groundwater depletion."

A side effect of all this is earth fissures. There's one in the desert
just miles from my old high school (near Nellis Air Force Base). As
Garrett Hardin said way back when (and in Chapter 7), "We can
never do merely one thing." These fissures, due to depleted groundwater causing the rock and soil to lose integrity, are appearing in many
places—at a cost of tens of millions of dollars in damage to existing
structures and automobiles and scaring the bejeezus out of people.

Some parts of the valley sank as much as 6 feet between 1960 and
1990, says John Bell, a research engineering geologist. He and other
researchers also found that the northwest portion of the city continues to sink at about 2.5 to 3 centimeters per year. The city is trying to
"recharge" the aquifer by pumping Colorado River water into the
ground in wintertime and then praying that they won't take out as
much in summer. So far, that approach has had less-than-stellar
results.

All researchers agree that the city's future depends on how much
water it can garner from outside the valley. "I don't think there's
enough water in Las Vegas Valley to sustain the economic activity

taking place there," one of them says. "They really are going to have to look for surface water. In the long run, the groundwater is limited by the natural recharge." Welcome to the Water Wars of the West. Do you really think California and Arizona will give up their agricultural allotments of Colorado River water so that people in Las Vegas can have manicured lawns and kidney-shaped swimming pools?

Of course, often the Water Wars won't be so clearly defined. Sometimes the wars will take place between growing cities and the farmers who feed them.

It takes somewhere between the 3 pounds of grain the National Cattlemen's Beef Association estimates and the 16 pounds some environmentalists and vegetarians claim it takes to produce a single pound of beef. I believe the truth lies closer to the cattlemen's numbers. All the ranchers I know, and I know plenty, graze their cattle where they consume vast quantities of weeds and natural grasses. What rancher wants to buy grain, adding to his cost of doing business?

On northern-clime ranches, however, covered in snow in winter, ranchers have to provide hay or other feed to keep their cattle alive. But often the supplemented feed is the garbage that is left after crops grown for human consumption have been extracted. These are things like almond hulls; tomato, soy, and other pomace; and the soybean meal that comes from the bean flakes remaining after the soy oil is extracted for those who demand only soy oil. (Before any busybody with a need to tell others how to live gets their knickers in a knot, I enjoyed a soy hot chocolate this morning—while contemplating what kind of steak to put on the grill tonight.)

Whether you like the cattlemen's numbers or some other, one fact is inescapable: Whether you are producing grain, meat, fruits, or vegetables, you are using *water*—lots of it. More than 50% of America's fresh water goes to irrigate our crops and provide us with food. Do you like whole grain bread? I do. According to Kansas State University, which knows a thing or two about wheat, it takes 151 gallons of water to produce one pound of wheat. And I've read that it takes 2,000 gallons of water to make one gallon of milk, which sounds awfully high unless you accept that it takes a lot of grain to feed a cow to make that milk. Figure 9.3 shows how many gallons of water are needed to make some common products.

Water Used in Common Products

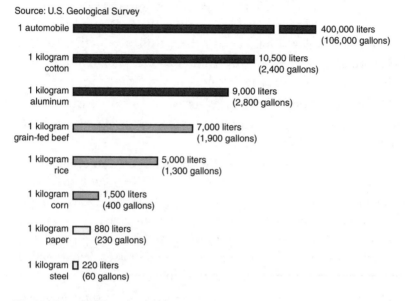

Source: U.S. Geological Survey

1 automobile — 400,000 liters (106,000 gallons)

1 kilogram cotton — 10,500 liters (2,400 gallons)

1 kilogram aluminum — 9,000 liters (2,800 gallons)

1 kilogram grain-fed beef — 7,000 liters (1,900 gallons)

1 kilogram rice — 5,000 liters (1,300 gallons)

1 kilogram corn — 1,500 liters (400 gallons)

1 kilogram paper — 880 liters (230 gallons)

1 kilogram steel — 220 liters (60 gallons)

Figure 9.3   Water used in common products

Source: U.S. Geological Survey

Industrially, it takes nearly *20,000* gallons of water to make one ton of steel. And U.S. power plants alone go through 136 billion gallons a day, meaning that this industry uses more water on a daily basis than do humans for drinking. As countries further industrialize, levels of water consumption will grow, further straining water supply. These trends could potentially force companies to find water in new places and most certainly force all of us to develop more efficient recycling systems.

From this perspective, it is astounding that we haven't run out of water already.

We have not yet reached the point of recycling all wastewater like the Fremen of Arrakis in Frank Hebert's brilliant novel *Dune*. But if we are consigned to endlessly squabble over that fixed 1% in a world where population is anything but fixed, many will die, and many more will suffer.

Finally, before moving on to investment opportunities, let me leave you with Figure 9.4, courtesy of ITT Industries. I first published it in the September 2006 issue of our investment publication, Investor's Edge®. Nothing has changed since then. Oil for water, anyone?

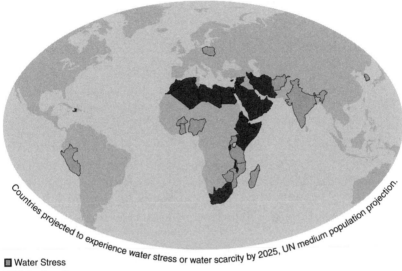

☐ Water Stress
◼ Water Scarcity

Figure 9.4   Nations that are experiencing water stress and water scarcity

Source: United Nations

10

Investment Implications and Opportunities

"Water flows uphill toward money."
—*A common saying, then and now, in the American West*

"What makes the desert beautiful is that somewhere it hides a well."
—*Antoine de Saint-Exupery*

What do you need to find success among the various subsectors, industries, and companies involved in the water sector? I think an understanding of where the water is on this Earth is the best foundation, because most solutions will be local in implementation if not in production. You also should know something about the science of how water is purified and made potable so that you know what to look for in which subsectors of remediation. Finally, you must understand the political and geopolitical issues involved. Only then will you be able to invest knowledgeably and confidently. I think you now have the foundation to understand which areas might provide the best opportunities.

I see the following as the primary areas of possible interest:

- Nations with all the water they need for industry, agriculture, and their citizens, and that can bargain for downstream concessions by being the upstream provider of water.
- The owners (holders) of water rights in nations where property rights are actually respected.

- The water utilities that process the water that farmers, manufacturers, and consumers buy.
- Consumer product companies making money by selling "special" water.
- Companies involved in desalination.
- Companies involved in water remediation and purification.
- Companies involved in infrastructure—making pipes and pumps and other infrastructure products that are used by the water sector, though perhaps not exclusively by the water sector. (Of course, many firms that consider themselves "water" companies are engaged in more than one of these areas. Maybe that's why some people prefer to just buy.)
- ETFs that try to cover the "water" front.

Let's look at each in turn.

Nations with All the Water They Need and That Can Bargain for Downstream Concessions

These countries may or may not be thought of by most as water plays. They are beneficiaries of water because it is one thing they simply don't have to worry about. They may need to clean it or recycle the gray version, but these countries have plenty of water. I have identified them as having other qualities that I want in selecting a macro investment theme.

I have coined the acronym ANBNC to help remember them. There is only one BRIC or emerging nation among them, and it alone does not share the qualities I find in the others—although it has its own unique set of qualifications. ANBNC stands for Australia, Norway, Brazil, New Zealand, and Canada. All have ample water per capita for the foreseeable future. All save Brazil have a long history of delineation and protection of property rights, respect for the rule of law, a tradition of democratically elected governments, a record of entrepreneurialism complemented by a low bureaucracy level that allows the formation of new business, and low to nonexistent levels of bribery, nepotism, and corruption.

Brazil is an exception. The frustration of starting a business in Brazil is extreme, corruption is rampant, and property rights are a relatively new concept. But Brazil also has massive natural resources; fortuitous geography; and a young, optimistic, vibrant spirit that may well catapult it into the ranks of the stellar "Western democracies" in the coming years.

I don't necessarily recommend water investments in these nations, although some investments mentioned in other categories are based in these nations. I'm merely pointing out that countries which have ample water and that have other admirable investment qualities as well are ahead of the game. As we measure "the wealth of nations," these countries start from a higher point.

The Owners of Water Rights in Nations Where Property Rights Are Respected

In this category, I think of the companies, foundations, and individuals who own the "rights" to a particular groundwater under their property or a river that flows through their property.

T. Boone Pickens comes to mind. Via his privately held Mesa Water company, he's buying up water rights in drought- and tornado-prone Roberts County, Texas left and right.[1] He expects to make more than $1 billion on his investment of $75 million in 30 years. He plans to pump water from the Ogallala aquifer and pump about 200,000 acre-feet of groundwater annually to El Paso, Lubbock, San Antonio, and Dallas-Fort Worth.

Here's my problem with investing alongside the holders of water rights. They are granted by law, yes, but the law is subject to interpretation by the government. And what the government gives, it can and usually does take away. So as long as nobody complains about the fact that the Ogallala aquifer doesn't really "belong" to T. Boone, and as long as everybody he sells to is happy with the price, and as long as contiguous landowners don't sue because he's reducing the value of the water under their land by draining it out of his, and as long as the environmentalists don't successfully argue that water rights are not the same as oil rights because they are constantly in motion (albeit slowly at times) as part of The Water Cycle, and as long as the government doesn't decide to expropriate these rights "in the public interest," you might be able to make money in these plays.

Clearly, I don't believe all those rosy scenarios will line up for long. With water at $1,000 an acre-foot, no one will get too excited. But if T. Boone is correct and the value of water rises faster than the economy, I believe other interested groups will suddenly find a reason to change how water laws are written. I believe it may be even worse in other nations. Water facilities have been nationalized in a number of emerging markets already. Further nationalization is always a possibility.

If you disagree, here are a couple of interesting companies you may want to conduct due diligence on:

PICO Holdings (PICO) owns 134,130 acre-feet of water rights in Nevada and Arizona, plus a small amount in Colorado, and is currently negotiating for more.[2] It does this by establishing water rights on property it owns, or by buying someone else's water rights on other property. If you accept the investment thesis, at least PICO is in the right neighborhood. It's hard to find two faster-growing states, increasingly filled with Californians escaping their intrusive state's regulations and taxes, or two more arid geographies. If you make the same assumptions that T. Boone is making for his investment (I don't), you'd value PICO somewhere between $80 and $90 based on its stored water, water rights, and land.

J.G. Boswell (BWEL) is America's largest cotton grower. Cotton is a rather water-intensive crop to grow and no fun to pick, I can tell you from personal experience! BWEL is the country's biggest cotton grower partly because it is the largest landowner in California. That may seem like a booby prize in today's real estate market, but California, for all its overreaching paternalism, is still the most geographically interesting state, with way more than its share of grandeur and natural beauty. When the economy recovers, and it will, Boswell's land will be worth more than its current valuation. Finally, the land

and the cotton need not fear the next drought. BWEL owns the rights to 15% of the water flowing down the magnificent Kings River.[3] If you accept the investment thesis that these water rights are secure from government and public interest (I say again: I *don't* accept this!), BWEL is sitting on an in-perpetuity gift from the gods—or at least the Sierras. As long as there's snow or rain in the Sierras, Boswell has lots of fresh, pure water. If you accept the premise of the syllogism, the water alone is worth the price of the stock, with the land and cotton thrown in for free.

The Water Utilities

This is a far more limited universe than you might imagine. Unlike "America's investor-owned electric utilities," more than 80% of the population is served by municipally owned and operated utility districts, or by municipalities of one sort or another themselves. It's more of a local process. Unlike electric energy utilities, which can send electricity over vast distances relatively cheaply, it costs a lot of money to move something that weighs 8 pounds per gallon. It's simply impractical and ineffective to try.

The relatively few publicly traded entities are regulated utilities, so they enjoy the advantages and disadvantages of all regulated monopolies. Advantages include steady cash-flow generation and, typically, steady dividend flow and dividend increases, as well as steadily granted rate increases to fund capital expenses needed to ensure compliance with the Clean Water Act and Safe Drinking Water Act. Disadvantages include the fact that they are slow, steady, and boring and—for me, anyway—too expensive for what I get. If I decide to pay higher PEs and price/book than I normally might, I want companies with *growth*. That doesn't mean water utilities.

If you disagree, you might do further research on companies such as Aqua America, Inc. (WTR), American Water Works (AWK), the York Water Company (YORK), American States Water (AWR), Connecticut Water Service (CTWS), SJW Corp.—the old San Jose Water Company (SJW), and California Water Service Group (CWT). All provide steady if low yield and probably a lock on future growth in usage.

To provide a little better launch for your due diligence, here's a slightly more in-depth look at one of these American water utilities.

The largest of them all, Aqua America, Inc., provides water and wastewater systems to 2.5 million U.S. customers. It is the biggest acquirer in the sector, having picked up more than 100 smaller firms in the past five years. As the industry leader, WTR is well positioned to benefit from local, state, and federal government infrastructure spending estimated at something like $300 billion over the next 20 years. Current revenues are about $500 million, and annual rate increases typically run 3% to 5%.

As investments, I prefer water remediation and infrastructure firms, but they will be working for these water utilities as they replace aging pipes, pumps, and plants. Many of the old pipes still being used today have a leakage rate of up to 50%; the number of these dwarf the National Highway System four to one. Surely the water utilities will be able to take a little (legal) vigorish as they manage the efforts, award the contracts, inspect the work, and so on. So there may yet be opportunity in American water utilities.

Personally, I prefer the water utilities beyond U.S. borders, where the problems are more acute and the opportunities to move beyond regulated water acquisition, treatment, and delivery are more numerous. Offshore "utilities" may also cross over and function in the remediation, infrastructure, or desalination businesses. The following are some examples.

Consolidated Water Company (CWCO) is a water utility operating in Belize, the Cayman Islands, Barbados, the Virgin Islands, and the Bahamas. Tourists and expatriates have driven growth in demand, especially with developers, who, to attract tourists and expats, have built many golf courses and swimming pools at their resorts and residential communities. Consolidated Water develops and operates seawater desalination plants as well as water distribution systems.

United Utilities PLC (UU), a major British utility, also crosses many national boundaries in providing water and sewage services to a number of current and former Commonwealth countries. UU also conducts a number of unregulated activities in the United Kingdom and overseas.

Then there is Companhia de Saneamento Basico do Estado de Sao Paulo (SBS). SBS is a Brazilian water utility headquartered in Sao Paulo. I mentioned earlier that Brazil was the only high total available renewable water resource country that made it into my ANBNC club. Here's a company that is in Brazil, is in water, and meets my own personal growth and fundamental value criteria.

SBS has been growing at double-digit rates for several years, and it's one of the ways I've decided to enter the Brazilian market. The company provides clean water as well as environmental sanitation services such as treating sewage and recycling gray water via its industrial waste treatment facilities. Founded in 1954, the company has grown with the Sao Paulo state of Brazil. The company treats sewage for 26 million people and also handles rainwater drainage and management.

Warren Buffett likes to talk about moats. One thing all water utilities have are very wide moats. SBS, for example, has no competitors. Its growth depends on the growth of the nation, not taking market share from a rival—or worrying about a rival taking its market share. And, unlike the American water utilities, growth in Brazil is extensive, and SBS will continue to grow as Brazil grows. The company enjoys a high free cash flow of some $2 billion a year, as well as high growth. Revenues of $4.9 billion in 2005 increased to $8.6 billion by the end of 2009.

The next World Cup will have games in Sao Paulo. Wanting to project the best image to the rest of the world, I imagine these games will be a huge boost to SBS's sanitation facilities. Future regional and world events, such as the World Cup and the Olympics, will ensure that Brazil takes appropriate steps to improve water quality, sanitation, and many other infrastructure opportunities.

The company sells at one times revenue, a P/E of 7.1, and well below book value, which is over $100. Before I would buy a low-growth, politically constrained American water utility, I'd take a hard look at SBS and other water utilities in developing nations.

Consumer Product Companies

Anticipating a much bigger recession than most, I wrote an article in June 2007 titled "When Environmental Chic Disintegrates." I noted that the highest-margin business for most beverage companies was not syrupy cola or fine whisky, but bottled water. I found it troubling that in a nation spending itself into a horrible recession, Americans were willing to pay more for bottled water per gallon than they were for gasoline. ($1 for a 16-ounce bottle of water equals $8 per gallon.)

For all we know, that 99-cent bottle of hoity-toity water came out of the tap down the street. It has certainly been shown in many independent tests that most American municipalities' tap water has fewer pollutants and such than most bottled water.

Yet, on those very rare occasions when I dine at the kinds of places where ordinary mortals like me go only occasionally, and only then for your basic $80 lunch, but where Wall Street movers and shakers and Midtown trust fund babies go every day, I hear something like this:

> "Welcome to Tres Snootez. I am Jacques. (I hail from Rapid City and I'm really an actor, not a waiter, and I'm working on my French accent, so) I will be providing you wiz tonight's delectable meanderings from Chef Michel, who may deign to allow you to say you touched one of his extravagant*lee* ovair-priced amusees. Would Monsieur care to begin by clearing his p*alaht* with a Perrier from France, a San Pellegrino from Italy, Fiji water from an aquifer deep below Fiji, or Voss, glacial runoff from the Norwegian fjords?"

OK, snootays of the world. I was partly raised in Norway and, yes indeed, they do have some truly marvelous water. I drink it from the streams, and the taps, whenever I am there. I have been to the town of Voss and dined at the Hotel Fleischer, arguably Voss's most upscale restaurant. And I have never seen a bottle of Voss on the tables. They'll dust one off if you're a tourist who asks for it, but the truth is that tap water in Norway tastes exactly the same and has the same chemical composition as the water in a Voss bottle: H_2O and nothing else.

But here's the even bigger rub: All that fancy imported water has to be transported to Your Town, America. How much does water weigh? About 8.3 pounds per gallon. And how many gallons of carbon-emitting jet fuel or ship's diesel do you think it takes to transport 8 pounds of water from mountains in Norway to mountains in Colorado? Granted, there are a few truly onerous municipal water systems. Except for these, however, in a chemical analysis and a blind tasting of your favorite bottled water versus tap, tap would win.

I wrote in 2007 that "the environmental chic movement is about to go bipolar. It's chic to drink bottled water with funny names. But it's déclassé to increase one's carbon footprint. Oh my, oh my, what's a with-it limousine liberal to do?"

I would have thought that common sense and lowered incomes would win out over Madison Avenue making people feel as if they are bumpkins if they drink tap water. So far, I've been wrong. Bottled water sales are not up, but they're bumping along at close to flat. I guess bringing common sense to a battle with advertising-to-people's-insecurities is like bringing a knife to a gunfight. So I will tell you that the biggest players in selling "special" water to consumers are all names you know well. Coca-Cola (KO) distributes, among others, Dasani. Pepsi-Cola (PEP) distributes, among others, Aquafina (PEP). Danone (DANOY) offers Evian and many others. Nestlé (NSRGY) is the biggest bottled-water purveyor in the world, with Poland Spring and a score of others.

Try as I might, I can't make an investment case for bottled water. I can make an investment case for every one of the fine companies just listed, but not based on their water business. So buy them if you like, for all the reasons your research would lead you to buy them, and take the water business, with its crazy-high margins, as icing on the cake for as long as it lasts. And if you figure out why people prefer tap water in a blind taste test yet purchase bottled water, drop me a line!

If you've been reading only for investment tips, you must be mightily disappointed by now. To make informed investment decisions, I believe we must understand who has the water and who doesn't. Then I asked you to review The Water Cycle to see how we mimic Mother Nature in remediating bad water or desalinating seawater.

Then I tried to warn of at least some of the possibly confiscatory political or—even more dangerous—geopolitical considerations. And now, in the first three investment categories—owners of water rights, water utilities, and those selling special water—I've said, with rare exception, that I wouldn't touch them! Will I ever get to industries and companies within this sector that I believe will do exceedingly well? Yes. Right now.

Companies Involved in Desalination, Water Remediation and Purification, and Infrastructure

Which companies are working to turn saltwater into fresh, clean up our water supplies, help us use less in agriculture and other areas, and prevent loss via transport? With 97.5% of the world's water composed of saltwater, we might get the biggest bang for our buck in companies in that arena.

But some companies working in the fresh-water world will benefit mightily from their technologies and experience today. Pollution, chemical and oil spills, waste, and fertilizers have exaggerated the health impact caused by the lack of clean drinking water. It's the same all over the world. In the U.S., agriculture accounts for more than 70% of water pollution, because the pesticides used in agriculture pollute the groundwater. Industrial pollution also contributes to compromised water quality. At least 70,000 different chemicals are used regularly throughout the world, and between 200 and 400 toxic chemicals contaminate the world's waterways.[4] This industrial waste, when coupled with agricultural runoff, exacerbates the problem of freshwater pollution.

That's why wastewater treatment is big business, processing millions of gallons of water while sending tons of the refuse taken from the water to landfills. However, in much of the world, this process is even more necessary and is just getting started! In many nations, 90% or more of all sewage and almost an equal percentage of all industrial waste are discharged into surface waters without any treatment whatsoever!

Therefore, in demand are companies that provide desalination expertise or services to collect, treat, and monitor water; companies that meter and analyze water and wastewater; companies that provide pipes, pumps, generators, and flow-control systems; and companies that provide efficient irrigation and that recycle gray water. This last area is where I find 90% of the great investment opportunities.

I can't possibly do justice to all these fine companies in the little space remaining. But I can introduce you to them and invite you to research them, as I have done.

First up is TETRA-TECH (TTEK). This company does it all: consulting, engineering, program management, construction, and technical services, all focused on resource management and infrastructure. It is involved in the Big Three going forward: water, the environment, and alternative energy services.

PENTAIR (PNR) has two primary business segments: water and technical products. The Water Group provides products and systems used to move, store, and treat water. (The Technical Products Group is mostly about thermal management, designing standard and custom enclosures for electronics and electrical components.)

ITT Corp. (ITT) is not a pure play but, rather, a conglomerate (sorry—"multi-industry company") that is in three primary areas. Fluid Technology includes water and wastewater treatment systems, the pumps that make it all work, and related technologies. Motion & Flow Control provides products and services for the defense, aerospace, industrial, transportation, computer, telecommunication, and marine industries. Defense Electronics & Services is a high-tech government contractor that deals with certain electronic systems and components, communications systems, and engineering and applied research. All are on the cusp of what this nation needs going forward.

I must also mention the biggest player in all this, even though it is too diverse, and in fields I believe will restrict its future growth, for me to consider its water subsidiaries as capable of overcoming its shortcomings as an investment. The biggest player in water is also the world's biggest factor in nuclear power and a host of other industries: GE. Its Water & Process Technologies Division is the world leader in supplying seawater reverse osmosis membrane desalination systems. GE also pioneered brackish water desalination in the early 1950s.

This is important to the U.S., where decades of overfertilizing has left much groundwater brackish at best. And, coincidentally, GE is no small shakes in nuclear design and development, as well.

One of the smallest players, in terms of market cap but not in terms of expertise or the size of its projects, is Hyflux (HYFXF in the U.S.; the company is located in business-friendly Singapore). Hyflux is a water treatment company, building a massive desalination plant in Algeria. It's also a leading environmental company with operations and projects in China, the Middle East, North Africa, and India.

Then there is Lindsay Corp. (LNN). If you drive or fly across America, you'll see gigantic circular crop irrigators that spew water like huge lawn sprinklers. This is what Lindsay makes: self-propelled center-pivot and lateral-move irrigation systems. These typically move by a computer-controlled mechanism that the farmer can adjust based on rain, elevation, whether the crops are in a gully or on a rise, and a dozen other variables. Basically, these irrigation systems save the farmer money and save all of us water. The company also manufactures and markets infrastructure products, including movable barriers for traffic-lane management, crash cushions, preformed reflective pavement tapes, and other road safety devices. That puts Lindsay in two investing sweet spots.

Veolia Environnement SA (VE) is a big French water services firm, with a large and growing presence in a number of developing markets, and concentrating on China. Veolia has also been targeting the seawater desalination market, setting up operations in North Africa and Middle Eastern countries.

Suez Environnement SA (SZEVY) is another French company primarily engaged in environmental services. The company has two divisions. The Water Division is involved in the treatment and distribution of drinking water and the purification of domestic and industrial water. The Waste Division is involved in waste collection and treatment; recycling; and material, biological, and energy recovery.

Layne Christensen (LAYN) is an interesting drilling and construction company focused on water, mining, and natural gas production. LAYN conducts its business in North and South America, Africa, Australia, and Europe, with three operating segments: Water and Waste Water (76% of 2009 revenues), Mineral Exploration (19%), and Energy (5%). In the water arena, LAYN provides well-drilling services, water and sewer distribution remediation services, and wastewater treatment services. As water management becomes more critical, LAYN's services to repair in situ (in-the-ground) distribution pipes for both water and sewer become more important. Of special interest right now are treatment facilities for water used in natural gas shale fracking processes.

Energy Recovery Inc. (ERII) is a small-cap company that seeks to make desalination more affordable. ERII products reduce the electricity required to separate freshwater from saltwater using the reverse osmosis method. The huge energy cost of reverse osmosis has historically been almost prohibitive in some areas. Enter ERII. ERII's primary product is the PX Pressure Exchanger. This rotary positive displacement pump recycles about 98% of the energy used in the pressure requirements of reverse osmosis, reducing overall project energy requirements by 60% or more. I first came across ERII in a geographic area that had absolutely no need for seawater reverse osmosis. ERII provided a product for a pilot project to generate electricity in the fjords of Norway to capture energy generated by mixing freshwater from river runoffs with seawater. It was just too cool a concept not to stir the imagination and for me to research the company further.

The number of Chinese companies that have sprung up to deal with China's truly horrendous water problems is huge. Here are a few to get you started down that research path if you are so inclined: Tri-Tech Holding (TRIT), China Water Group (CHWG), HollySys (HOLI), and Duoyuan Global Water (DGW). Scores are available to buyers worldwide, and probably hundreds more are available only on Chinese exchanges. My guess is that the Chinese will want to turn to some of the big international firms that have years of expertise in these matters first, and then buy their services and products to copy or reverse-engineer. Therefore, I don't see the Chinese companies as being as attractive as the others mentioned and the following.

Here are a few more for your consideration: Itron (ITRI), Insituform (INSU), Millipore Corporation (MIL), Gorman-Rupp Co. (GRC), Valmont Industries, Inc. (VMI), Badger Meter, Inc. (BMI), Itron, Inc. (ITRI), RWE (RWEOY), Idex (IEX), Flowserve (FLS),

Ameron (AMN), Pall Corp (PLL), Dow Chemical (DOW), Watts Water Technologies (WTS), Siemens (SI), Basin Water (BWTR), Mueller Industries, Inc. (MLI), Mueller Water Products (MWA), Danaher (DHR), Calgon Carbon (CCC), Franklin Electronics (FELE), Fluor (FLR), and Nalco Holding Company (NLC)—the largest global player in the industrial water treatment industry.

I believe if you do your due diligence on these companies, and others like them that will inevitably arise, you will find ample rewards in terms of steady, predictable, outsize growth.

ETFs That Try to Cover the "Water" Front

Currently four ETFs invest heavily in many of the companies just mentioned. Among them, if you're seeking diversification with just one security, you should be able to find a long-term winner.

PowerShares Water Resources (PHO) is the largest water ETF, with $1.5 billion in portfolio holdings. It focuses on U.S. companies, and its largest holding is one of my favorites: Tetra Tech, Inc. (TTEK). This is an equal-weighted ETF, which means that PHO will have a greater bias toward all market caps—a plus in my book. Other names among its top holdings include giant Veolia Environment (VE), flow control equipment specialists Flowserve (FLS), Watts Water (WTS), and Insituform (INSU), whose core product allows damaged water lines to be repaired in place, without requiring expensive excavation.

PowerShares Global Water Resources (PIO) looks not just in the U.S. but globally. It has thus far focused on companies in the U.S., Canada, Finland, and Switzerland. Its largest holding is also Tetra Tech, but it includes companies I haven't mentioned previously, such as Finland's giant wastewater treatment specialists, Kemira Oyj. The U.S. makes up about 30% of its holdings, followed by Japan at 12% and France at 10%. Nearly a quarter of its holdings are in utilities companies. This makes sense, because they are the safest way to play nations that may not enjoy the same transparency as U.S. firms.

Claymore S&P Global Water (CGW) focuses on the U.S., the UK, France, Japan, and Switzerland. Its largest holding is Veolia Environment, but it also holds Switzerland's Geberit AG, which specializes in water sanitary systems and the transportation of water through piping systems. It holds 25 water utilities and infrastructure companies (water supply, water utilities, wastewater treatment, water, sewer and pipeline construction, water purification, well drilling, and water testing). It also holds 25 water equipment and materials companies (water treatment chemicals, water treatment appliances, pumps and pumping equipment, fluid power pumps and motors, plumbing equipment, totalizing fluid meters, and counting devices). This ETF is also diversified among developed markets: nearly 40% of the fund is in U.S. stocks, with 15% in the UK, 14% in France, and 9% in Japan.

Finally, First Trust ISE Water Index Fund (FIW) focuses primarily on the U.S. Its largest holding is Millipore Corporation (MIL). It is a market cap weighted ETF that also counts Veolia Environment and Nalco Holding Company among its primary holdings.

Conclusion

You have learned about water distribution, how water is purified and regenerated both naturally and artificially, and the political and geopolitical environment in which "water decisions" are made by individuals, corporations, municipalities, nations, and regions. I believe this knowledge will help you make the most informed decisions about how to invest in order to profit from your knowledge of the world's desperate need for fresh water. I hope the companies and ETFs described in this chapter will whet your appetite for further research and yield the kinds of returns, without undue risk, that are the mark of every truly successful investor.

Endnotes

1   Mayer, Chris. "Oil Baron Finds New Buried Treasure – But It's Not Oil."
    http://dailyreckoning.com/oil-baron-finds-new-buried-treasure-but-its-not-oil/.

2   Mayer, Chris. "A Refreshing Idea," *Daily Wealth*. http://www.dailywealth.
    com/770/A-Refreshing-Idea.

3   Shaefer, Joseph L., "Positioning for When Water Runs Out." http://www.
    silverbearcafe.com/private/07.09/water2.html.

4   "Water Is the New Oil." http://seekingalpha.com/article/17769-water-is-the-
    new-oil.

Bibliography

Part I, "Investing in Demographics"

Aaron, Henry. "Medium-term Strategies for Long-term Goals," in *Tackling Japan's Fiscal Challenges: Strategies to Cope with High Public Debt and Population Aging*, edited by Keimei Kaizuka and Anne O. Krueger, International Monetery Fund, 2006, 79-104.

Akihiko, Matsutani. *Shrinking Population Economics: Lessons from Japan*. Tokyo: International House of Japan, 2006.

Bernheim, B.D. and Shoven, J.B. "Pension Funding and Saving." NBER Working Paper 1622. Cambridge, MA: NBER Research.

Broda, C. and Weinstein, D.E. "Happy News from the Dismal Science: Reassessing Japanese Fiscal Policy and Sustainability" in T. Ito, H. Patrick, and D.E. Weinstein, eds., *Reviving Japan's Economy: Problems and Prescriptions*. Cambridge: MIT Press, 2005.

Coulmas, Florian. *Population Decline and Aging in Japan: The Social Consequences*. New York: Routledge, 2007.

Coulmas, Florian and Conrad, H., eds. *The Demographic Challenge: A Handbook About Japan*. Boston: Brill Academic Publishers, 2008.

Fehr, H., Jokisch, S., and Kotlikoff, L.J. "The Role of Immigration in Dealing with the Developed World's Demographic Transition." *FinanzArchiv* 60 (2004): 296-324.

Feldstein, Martin. "Japan's Savings Crisis." *Daily News Egypt*, October 1, 2010. Online. December 10, 2010. http://belfercenter.ksg.harvard.edu/publication/20397/japans_savings_crisis.html.

Fukawa, T. and Izumida, N. "Japanese Health Care Expenditures in a Comparative Context." *Japanese Journal of Social Security Policy* 3 (2004): 51-61.

Hubbard, R.G. and Ito, T. "Overview of the Japanese Debt Question" (in Kaizuka and Krueger, 2006).

Ihori, T. and Sato, M., eds. *Government Deficit and Fiscal Reform in Japan.* Boston: Kluwer Academic Publishers, 2002.

Ihori, T. and H. Kondo. "Japanese Fiscal Reform: Fiscal Reconstruction and Fiscal Policy." *Japan and the World Economy*, vol. 14, 351-370.

Ihori, T., Kato, R., and Kawade, M. "Public Debt and Economic Growth in an Aging Japan." Working paper, Faculty of Economics, University of Tokyo (2005).

Kaizuka, Keimei and Krueger, Anne O., eds. *Tackling Japan's Fiscal Challenges: Strategies to Cope with High Public Debt and Population Aging.* New York: Palgrave Macmillan, 2006.

Katz, Richard. *Japan, the System That Soured: The Rise and Fall of the Japanese Economic Miracle.* Armonk: M.E. Sharpe, 1998.

Kingston, Jeff. *Contemporary Japan: History, Politics, and Social Change Since the 1980s.* New York: Wiley-Blackwell, 2010.

Kotlikoff, L.J. and Burns, S. *The Coming Generational Storm.* Cambridge: MIT Press, 2004.

Lincoln, Edward J. *Arthritic Japan: The Slow Pace of Economic Reform.* Washington D.C.: Brookings Institution Press, 2001.

Moriguchi, Chiaki and Ono, H. "Japanese Lifetime Employment: A Century's Perspective." EIJS Working Paper Series No. 205 (2006).

Most, Carl. *Japanese Economic Development: Markets, Norms, Structures.* New York: Routledge, 2007.

National Institute of Population and Social Security Research. "Population Pyramid 1955, 2010, 2055." Extracted from NIPSSR website, December 10, 2010. http://www.ipss.go.jp/sitead/TopPageData/Pyramid_a.html.

Pym, Hugh. "Japan: Debt, Demographics and Deflation." *BBC News (Business).* BBC, November 30, 2010. Online. December 10, 2010. http://www.bbc.co.uk/news/business-11867257.

Rogoff, Kenneth and Reinhart, Carmen M. *This Time Is Different: Eight Centuries of Financial Folly*. Princeton: Princeton University Press, 2009.

Traphagan, John W. and Knight, J. *Demographic Change and the Family in Japan's Aging Society*. Albany: SUNY Press, 2003.

Tricks, Henry (for *The Economist*). "Into the Unknown: A Special Report on Japan." *The Economist*, November 20, 2010.

Vogel, Ezra. *Japan as Number One: Lessons for America*. Bloomington: IUniverse, 1999.

Wattenberg, Ben J. *Fewer: How the Demography of Depopulation Will Shape Our Future*. Lanham: Ivan R. Dee Publisher, 2005.

Whipp, Lindsay (for *The Financial Times*). "Japan Looks at Pension Fund to Cover Shortfall." *Financial Times*, November 30, 2010. Online. December 8, 2010. http://www.ft.com/cms/s/0/76330324-fcba-11df-bfdd-00144feab49a.html#axzz18gi4sEER.

Yashiro, N. "Aging of the Population in Japan and its Implications to the Other Asian Countries." *Journal of Asian Economics* 8 (2002):245-261.

Yaukey, David, Anderton, Douglas L., and Lundquist, Jennifer Hickes. *Demography: The Study of Human Population*. Long Grove: Waveland Press, 2007.

Part II, "The Tuna Trade"

Adam, M.S., J. Sibert, D. Itano, and K. Holland. 2003. Dynamics of bigeye (*Thunnus obesus*) and yellowfin (*T. albacares*) tuna in Hawaii's pelagic fisheries: analysis of tagging data with a bulk transfer model incorporating size-specific attrition. *Fishery Bulletin* 101:215-228.

Adler, J. 2002. The great salmon debate. *Newsweek* 140(18):54-56.

Allain, V. 2005. What do tuna eat? A tuna diet study. *SPC Fisheries Newsletter* 112:20-22.

Allen, S. and D.A. Demer. 2003. Detection and characterization of yellowfin and bluefin tuna using passive-acoustical techniques. *Fisheries Research* 63:393-403.

Allport, S. 2006. *The Queen of Fats: Why Omega-3s Were Removed from the Western Diet and What We Can Do to Replace Them.* University of California Press.

Altringham, J.D. and B.A. Block. 1997. Why do tuna maintain elevated slow muscle temperatures? Power output of muscle isolated from endothermic and ectothermic fish. *Journal of Experimental Biology* 200:2617-2627.

Altringham, J.D. and R.E. Shadwick. 2001. Swimming and muscle function. In B.A. Block and E.D. Stevens, eds. *Tuna: Physiology, Ecology, and Evolution.* 313-344. Academic Press.

Amoe, J. 2005. Fiji tuna and billfish fisheries. *Fisheries Department, Ministry of Fisheries and Forests, Fiji* FR/WP-12:1-6.

Amorim, A.F. and C.A. Arfelli. 2001. Analysis of Santos (São Paulo), fleet from southern Brazil. *Col. Vol. Sci. Pap. ICCAT* 54(4):263-271.

Anderson, J.L. 2002. Aquaculture and the future: why fisheries economists should care. *Marine Resources Economics* 17:133-151.

Anderson, J.M. and N.K. Chhabra. 2002. Maneuvering and stability performance in a robotic tuna. *Integrative and Comparative Biology.* 42:118-126.

Anonymous. 1986. Eating fish vital to health. *SAFISH* 10(3):17-18.

Anonymous. 2004. Farmed fish vex sushi lovers. *Yomiuri Shimbun* 27 December.

Anonymous. 2005. National report: Japan. *Technical Compliance Committee. Commission for the Conservation and Management of Highly Migratory Fish Stocks in the Eastern and Central Pacific Ocean.* 10 pp.

Anuska-Pereira, M., A.F. Amorin, and C.A. Arfelli. 2005. Tuna fishing in the south and southeast off Brazil from 1971 to 2001. *Col. Vol. Sci. Pap. ICCAT* 58(5):1715-1723.

Apple, R.W. 2002. How to grow a giant tuna. *New York Times* April 3:F1-2.

Archer, F., T. Gerrodette, A. Dizon, K. Abella, and S. Southern. 2001. Unobserved kill of nursing dolphin calves in a tuna purse-seine fishery. *Marine Mammal Science* 17(3):540-54.

Associated Press. 2001. "Giant tuna sells for record $173,600." http://www.flmnh.ufl.edu/fish/InNews/GiantTuna.htm.

Baker, C.S. and P.J. Clapham. 2004. Modelling the past and future of whales and whaling. *Trends in Ecology and Evolution Trends Ecol. Evol.* 19(7):365-371.

Baker, C.S., G.M. Lento, F. Cipriano, M.L. Dalebout, and S.R. Palumbi. 2000. Scientific whaling: source of illegal products for market? *Science* 290:1695-1696.

Bandini, R. 1939. *Veiled Horizons: Stories of Big Game Fish of the Sea.* Derrydale Press.

Bardach, J. 1968. *Harvest of the Sea.* Harper & Row.

Batalyants, K.Y. 1989. On spawning of skipjack tuna (*Katsuwonus pelamis* L.) *Col. Vol. Sci. Pap. ICCAT* 30(1):20-27.

Baum, J.K., J.M. McPherson, and R.A. Myers. 2005. Farming need not replace fishing if stocks are rebuilt. *Nature* 437:26.

Bayliff, W.H. 1993. A review of the biology and fisheries for northern bluefin tuna, *Thunnus thynnus*, in the Pacific Ocean. In R.S. Shomura, J. Majkowski, and S. Langi, eds., *Interactions of Pacific Tuna Fisheries Vol. 2: Papers on Biology and Fisheries.* FAO, Rome.

Beardsley, G.L. 1975. A review of the status of the stocks of Atlantic bluefin tuna. *Col. Vol. Sci. Pap. ICCAT* 4:161-172.

Bearzi, G., E. Politi, S. Agazzi, and A. Azzellino. 2006. Prey depletion caused by overfishing and the decline of marine megafauna in the eastern Ionian Sea coastal waters (central Mediterranean). *Biological Conservation* 127:373-582.

Beckett, J.S. 1974. High recovery rates of small bluefin tuna (*Thunnus thynnus*) tagged in the northwest Atlantic. *Col. Vol. Sci. Pap. ICCAT* 2:232-233.

Bergin, A. and M. Howard. 1994. Southern bluefin tuna fishery: recent developments in international management. *Marine Policy* 18(3):263-273.

Bernal, D., K.A. Dickson, R.E. Shadwick, and J.B. Graham. 2001. Analysis of the evolutionary convergence for high performance swimming in lamnid sharks and tunas. *Comparative Biochemistry and Physiology* 129:695-726.

Bernal, D., C. Sepulveda, O. Mathieu-Costello, and J.B. Graham. 2003. Comparative studies of high performance swimming in sharks. I. Red muscle morphometrics, vascularization and ultrastructure. *Journal of Experimental Biology* 206:2831-2843.

Berners, J. 1486. *The Book of St. Albans*. Westminster. 1966 reprint, Abercrombie & Fitch; University Microfilms.

Bestor, T.C. 2000. How sushi went global. *Foreign Policy* 121:54-63.

—————. 2004. *Tsukiji: The Fish Market at the Center of the World*. University of California Press.

Bigelow, H.B. and W.C. Schroeder. 1953. Fishes of the Gulf of Maine. *U.S. Fish Wildl. Serv. Fish. Bull.* 74:1-577.

Blake, R.W., K.H.S. Chan, and E.W.Y. Kwok. 2005. Finlets and the steady swimming performance of *Thunnus albacares*. *Journal of Fish Biology* 67(5):1434-1445.

Blanc, M., A. Desurmont, and S. Beverly. 2005. *Onboard Handling of Sashimi-Grade Tuna: A Practical Guide for Crew Members*. Secretariat of the Pacific Community (Fisheries).

Blank, J.M., J.M. Morrisette, P.S. Davie, and B.A. Block. 2002. Effects of temperature, epinephrine, and Ca^{2+} on the hearts of yellowfin tuna. *Journal of Experimental Biology* 205:1881-1888.

Blank, J.M., J.M. Morrisette, A.M. Landeira-Fernandez, S.B. Blackwell, T.D. Williams, and B.A. Block. 2004. *In situ* performance of Pacific bluefin tuna hearts in response to acute temperature change. *Journal of Experimental Biology* 207:881-890.

Block, B.A. and F.G. Carey. 1985. Warm brain and eye temperatures in sharks. *Comparative Biochemistry and Physiology* 156:229-236.

Block, B.A., D. Booth, and F.G. Carey. 1992. Direct measurement of swimming speeds and depth of blue marlin. *Journal of Experimental Biology* 166:267-284.

Block, B.A., J.R. Finnerty, A.F.R. Stewart, and J. Kidd. 1993. Evolution of endothermy in a fish: mapping physiological traits on a molecular phylogeny. *Science* 260:210-214.

Block, B.A. and J.R. Finnerty. 1994. Endothermy in fishes: a phylogenetic analysis of constraints, predispositions, and selection pressures. *Environmental Biology of Fishes* 40(3):283-302.

Block, B.A., J.E. Keen, B. Castillo, H. Dewar, E.V. Freund, D.J. Marcinek, R.W. Brill, and C. Farwell. 1997. Environmental preferences of yellowfin tuna (*Thunnus albacares*) at the northern extent of its range. *Marine Biology* 130(1):119-132.

Block, B.A., H. Dewar, C. Farwell, and E.D. Prince. 1998. A new satellite technology for tracking the movements of Atlantic bluefin tuna. *Proceedings of the National Academy of Sciences* 95(16): 9384-89.

Block, B.A., H. Dewar, S.B. Blackwell, T.D. Williams, E.D. Prince, C.J. Farwell, A. Boustany, S.L.H. Teo, A. Seitz, A. Walli, and D. Fudge. 2001. Migratory movements, depth preferences, and thermal biology of Atlantic bluefin tuna. *Science* 293:1310-14.

Block, B.A., A. Boustany, S. Teo, A. Walli, C.J. Farwell, T. Williams, E.D. Prince, M. Stokesbury, H. Dewar, A. Seitz, and K. Wong. 2003. Distribution of western tagged Atlantic bluefin tuna determined from archival and pop-up satellite tags. *Col. Vol. Sci. Pap. ICCAT* 55(3):1127-1139.

Block, B.A., S.L.H. Teo, A. Walli, A. Boustany, M.J.W. Stokesbury, C.J. Farwell, K.C. Weng, H. Dewar, and T.D. Williams. 2005. Electronic tagging and population structure of Atlantic bluefin tuna. *Nature* 434:1121-1127.

Bohnsack, B.L., R.B. Ditton, J.R. Stoll, R.J. Chen, R. Novak, and L.S. Smutko. 2002. The economic effects of the recreational bluefin tuna fishery in North Carolina. *N.A. Journal of Fisheries Management* 22:165-176.

Borgstrom, G. 1964. *Japan's World Success in Fishing*. Fishing News (Books).

Bransden, M.P., C.G. Carter, and B.F. Nowak. 2001. Alternative methods for nutrition research on the southern bluefin tuna, *Thunnus maccoyii* (Castelnau): evaluation of Atlantic salmon, *Salmo salar* L., to screen experimental feeds. *Aquaculture Research* 32(1):174-182.

Bregazzi, R.M. 2004. *The Tuna Ranching Intelligence Unit—September 2004*. Advanced Tuna Ranching Technologies. Madrid.

————. 2005. *The Tuna Ranching Intelligence Unit—Special November 2005 ICCAT Sevilla-Spain Meeting Edition*. Advanced Tuna Ranching Technologies. Madrid.

————. 2006. *The Plunder of Bluefin Tuna in the Mediterranean and East Atlantic in 2004 and 2005: Uncovering the Real Story*. World Wide Fund for Nature.

Brill, R.W. 1996. Selective advantages conferred by the high performance physiology of tunas, billfishes, and dolphin fish. *Comparative Biochemistry and Physiology* 113A(1):3-15.

Brill, R.W., B.A. Block, C.H. Boggs, K.A. Bigelow, E.V. Freund, and D.J. Marcinek. 1999. Horizontal movements and depth distribution of large adult yellowfin tuna (*Thunnus albacares*) near the Hawaiian Islands, recorded using ultrasonic telemetry: implications for the physiological ecology of pelagic fishes. *Marine Biology* 133:395-408.

Brill, R.W. and P.G. Bushnell. 2001. The cardiovascular system of tunas. In B.A. Block and E.D. Stevens, eds. *Tuna: Physiology, Ecology, and Evolution*. 79-120. Academic Press.

Brill, R.W. and M.E. Lutcavage. 2001. Understanding environmental influences on movements and depth distributions of tunas and billfishes can significantly improve population assessments. *American Fisheries Society Symposium* 25:179-198.

Brill, R.W., M. Lutcavage, G. Metzger, P. Bushnell,, M. Arendt, L. Lucy, C. Watson, and D. Foley. 2001. Horizontal and vertical movements of juvenile bluefin tuna (*Thunnus thynnus*), in relation to oceanographic conditions of the western North Atlantic, determined by ultrasonic telemetry. *Fishery Bulletin* 100:155-167.

Brill, R.W., K.A. Bigelow, M.K. Musyl, K.R. Fritsches, and E.J. Warrant. 2005. Bigeye tina (*Thunnus obesus*) behavior and physiology and their relevance to stock assessments and fishery biology. *Col. Vol. Sci. Pap. ICCAT* 57(2):142-161.

Browder, J.A. and G.P. Scott. 1992. History of the western Atlantic U.S. yellowfin fishery. *Col. Vol. Sci. Pap. ICCAT* 38:195-202.

Browder, J.A., B.E. Brown, and M.L. Parrack. 1991. The U.S. longline fishery for yellowfin tuna in perspective. *Col. Vol. Sci. Pap. ICCAT* 36:223-240.

Bruni, F. 2004. Sushi at Masa in a Zen thing. *New York Times* December 29.

Buck, E.H. 1995. *Atlantic Bluefin Tuna: International Management of a Shared Resource*. Congressional Research Service. Washington, D.C.

Bullis, H.R. and F.J. Mather. 1956. Tunas of the genus *Thunnus* of the northern Caribbean. *American Museum Novitates* 1765:1-12.

Bundy, A. 2001. Fishing on ecosystems: the interplay of fishing and predation in Newfoundland-Labrador. *Can. Jour. Fish. Aquat. Sci.* 58(6):1153-67.

Bundy A., G.R. Lilly, and P.A. Shelton. 2000. A new balance model of the Newfoundland-Labrador Shelf. *Can. Tech. Rep. Fish. Aquat. Sci.* 2301:1-157.

Burros, M. 2003. Issues of purity and pollution leave farmed salmon looking less rosy. *New York Times* May 28:F1-F5.

——————. 2006. Advisories on fish and pitfalls of good intent. *New York Times* February 15:F5-6.

Bushnell, P.G. and D.R. Jones. 1994. Cardiovascular and respiratory physiology of tuna: adaptations for support of exceptionally high metabolic rates. *Environmental Biology of Fishes* 403:303-318.

Butler, M.J.A. 1977. The trap (mackerel) and impoundment (bluefin) fishery in St. Margaret's Bay, Nova Scotia: its development. *Col. Vol. Sci. Pap. ICCAT* 6(2):237-241.

——————. 1978. St. Margaret's Bay Bluefin Research Programme: a progress report. *Col. Vol. Sci. Pap. ICCAT* 7(2):371-374.

——————. 1982. Plight of the bluefin tuna. *National Geographic* 162(2):220-39.

Butler, M.J.A. and J.A. Mason. 1978. Behavioural studies on impounded bluefin tuna. *Col. Vol. Sci. Pap. ICCAT* 7(2):379-382.

Butler, M.J.A. and D. Pincock. 1978. Ultrasonic monitoring of bluefin tuna impounded in St. Margaret's Bay. *Col. Vol. Sci. Pap. ICCAT* 7(2):375-378.

Byatt, A., A. Fothergill, and M. Holmes. 2001. *The Blue Planet.* BBC Worldwide Limited.

Campbell, D., D. Brown, and T. Battaglene. 2000. Individual transferable catch quotas: Australian experience in the southern bluefin tuna fishery. *Marine Policy* 24:109-117.

Carey, F.G. 1973. Fish with warm bodies. *Scientific American* 228(2):36-44.

Carey, F.G. and J.M. Teal. 1966. Heat conservation in tuna fish muscle. *Proc. Nat. Acad. Sci.* 56(5):1464-69.

Carey, F.G. and K.D. Lawson. 1973. Temperature regulation in free-swimming bluefin tuna. *Comparative Biochemistry and Physiology* 44(2):375-378.

Carey, F.G., J.W. Kanwisher, O. Brazier, G. Gabrielson, J.G. Casey, and H.L. Pratt. 1982. Temperature and activities of a white shark, *Carcharodon carcharias. Copeia* 1982(2):254-260.

Carey, F.G. and R.J. Olson. 1982. Sonic tracking experiments with tunas. *Col. Vol. Sci. Pap. ICCAT* 17(2):458-466.

Carey, F.G. and Q.H. Gibson. 1983. Heat and oxygen exchange in the rete mirabile of the bluefin tuna, *Thunnus thynnus. Comparative Biochemistry and Physiology* 74(2):333-342.

Carey, F.G., J.W. Kanwisher, and E.D. Stevens.1984. Bluefin tuna warm their viscera during digestion. *Journal of Experimental Biology* 109:1-20.

Carey, F.G., J.G. Casey, H.L. Pratt, D. Urquhart, and J.E. McCosker. 1985. Temperature, heat production and heat exchange in lamnid sharks. *Memoirs S. Cal. Academy of Sciences* 9:92-108.

Carroll, M.T., J.L. Anderson, and J. Martínez-Garmendia. 2001. Pricing U.S. North Atlantic bluefin tuna and implications for management. *Agribusiness* 17(2):243-254.

Carson, R.L. 1943. Food from the sea: fish and shellfish of New England. *U.S. Dept. Interior Cons. Bull.* 33: 1-74.

Castro, J.J., J. A. Santiago, and A.T. Santana-Ortega. 2002. A general theory on fish aggregation to floating objects: an alternative to the meeting point hypothesis. *Reviews in Fish Biology and Fisheries* 11:255-277.

Caton, A.E. 1993a. Commercial and recreational components of the southern bluefin tuna (*Thunnus maccoyii*) fishery. In R.S. Shomura, J. Majkowski, and S. Langi, eds., *Interactions of Pacific Tuna Fisheries Vol. 2: Papers on Biology and Fisheries*. FAO, Rome.

—————. 1993b. Review of aspects of southern bluefin tuna biology, population, and fisheries. In R.S. Shomura, J. Majkowski, and S. Langi, eds., *Interactions of Pacific Tuna Fisheries Vol. 2: Papers on Biology and Fisheries*. FAO, Rome.

—————. 2000. The Commonwealth-managed fisheries of Australia: An overview. *Infofish* 6:58-62.

Cayre, P. 1991. Behaviour of yellowfin tuna (*Thunnus albacares*) and skipjack tuna (*Katsuwonus pelamis*) around fish aggregating devices (FADs) in the Comoros Islands as determined by ultrasonic tagging. *Aquatic Living Resources* 4(1):1-12.

Chase, B.C. 2002. Differences in diet of Atlantic bluefin tuna (*Thunnus thynnus*) at five seasonal feeding grounds on the New England continental shelf. *Fisheries Bulletin* 100:168-180.

Chavez, F.P., J. Ryan, S.E. Lluch-Cota, and M. Ñiquen. 2003. From anchovies to sardines and back: multidecadal change in the Pacific Ocean. *Science* 299:217-221.

Cheshire, A. and J. Volkman. 2004. Australians net benefits of sustainable fish farming. *Nature* 432:671.

Chivers, C.J. 1998. Empty waves. *Wildlife Conservation* 101(4):36-44.

Chow, S., H. Okamoto, N. Miyabe, K. Hiramatsu, and N. Barut. 2000. Genetic divergence between Atlantic and Indo-Pacific stocks of bigeye tuna (*Thunnus obesus*) and admixture around South Africa. *Molecular Ecology* 9(2):221-243.

Christensen, V., S. Guénette, J.J. Heymans, C.J. Walters, R. Watson, D. Zeller, and D. Pauly. 2002. Estimating fish abundance of the North Atlantic, 1950 to 1999. In S. Guénette, V. Christensen, and D. Pauly, eds., *Fisheries Impacts on North Atlantic Ecosystems: Models and Analyses.* Fisheries Centre Research Reports 9(4):1-25.

Clarkson, T.W. 1998. Human toxicology of mercury. *Journal of Trace Elements in Experimental Medicine.* 11(2-3):303-317.

—————. 2002. The three modern faces of mercury. *Environmental Health Perspectives* 110 (Suppl. 1):11-23.

Clarkson, T.W. and J.J. Strain. 2003. Nutritional factors may modify the toxic action of methyl mercury in fish-eating populations. *Journal of Nutrition* 133:1539-1543.

Clayton, M. 2006. New questions about safety of tuna imports. *Christian Science Monitor* July 12.

Clean Seas. 2005. *Prospectus.* Clean Seas Tuna Ltd.

Clover, C. 2006. *The End of the Line: How Overfishing Is Changing the World and What We Eat.* New Press.

Coan, A.L., G.T. Sakagawa, D. Prescott, P. Williams, and G. Yamasaki. 1999. *The 1998 U.S. Tropical Tuna Purse Seine Fishery in the Central Western Pacific Ocean.* South Pacific Regional Tuna Treaty, March 24-30, 1999. Koror, Republic of Palau. 23 pp.

Coghlan, A. 2002. Extreme mercury levels revealed in whale meat. *New Scientist* 173:11.

—————. 2003. Shops in Japan are selling mercury-ridden dolphin flesh as whale meat. *New Scientist* 178:7.

—————. 2006. Diabetes spotlight falls on fish. *New Scientist* 197:18.

Collette, B.B. and C.E. Nauen. 1983. FAO *Species Catalogue, Vol. 2. Scombrids of the World: An Annotated and Illustrated Catalogue of Tunas, Mackerels, Bonitos, and Related Species Known to Date.* FAO Fisheries Synopsis 125(2) Rome.

Collette, B.B., C. Reeb, and B.A. Block. 2001. Systematics of the tunas and mackerels (scombridae). In B.A. Block and E.D. Stevens, eds. *Tuna: Physiology, Ecology, and Evolution*. 5-33. Academic Press.

Cone, M. 2006. Warning on tuna cans is rejected. *Los Angeles Times* May 13.

Corriero, A., S. Karakulak, N. Santamaria, M. Deflorio, D. Spedicato, P. Addis, S. Desantis, F. Cirillo, A. Fenech-Farrugia, R. Vassallo-Agius, J.M. de la Serna, Y. Oray, A. Cau, P. Megalofonou, and G. Metrio. 2005. Size and age at sexual maturity of female bluefin tuna (*Thunnus thynnus* L. 1758) from the Mediterranean Sea. *Journal of Applied Ichthyology* 21(6):483-486.

Cort, J.L. 1991. Age and growth of the bluefin tuna *Thunnus thynnus* (L.) of the northeast Atlantic. *Col. Vol. Sci. Pap. ICCAT* 35(2):213-230.

Cort, J.L. and F.X. Bard. 1980. Description of the bluefin tuna fishery in the Bay of Biscay. *Col. Vol. Sci. Pap. ICCAT* 11:168-173.

Cushing, D.H. 1988. *The Provident Sea*. Cambridge University Press.

Dagorn, L. and P. Fréon. 1999. Tropical tuna associated with floating objects: a simulation study of the meeting point hypothesis. *Canadian Journal of Fisheries and Aquatic Sciences*. 56(6):984-993.

Dagorn, L., E. Josse, and P. Bach. 2000. Individual differences in horizontal movements of yellowfin tuna (*Thunnus albacares*) in nearshore areas in French Polynesia, determined using ultrasonic telemetry. *Aquatic Living Resources* 13(4):193-220.

Dagorn, L., P. Bach, and E. Josse. 2004. Movement patterns of large bigeye tuna (*Thunnus obesus*) in the open ocean, determined using ultrasonic telemetry. *Marine Biology* 136(2):361-371.

Dai, X., L. Zhao, and L. Xu. 2003. A review of available bluefin tuna information for China: 1994-2001. *Col. Vol. Sci. Pap. ICCAT* 55(3):1233-1241.

Dalton, R. 2002. US pushes fish farming into deep water. *Nature* 420:451.

—————. 2004a. Plan to cull aquarium tuna dead in the water. *Nature* 431:233.

—————. 2004b. Fishing for trouble. *Nature* 431:502-504.

—————. 2004c. Plans to track tuna canned amid claims of cash shortfall. *Nature* 432:539.

—————. 2005a. Satellite tags give fresh angle on tuna quota. *Nature* 434:1056-1057.

—————————. 2005b. Bill on deep-sea fish farms brings wave of disapproval. *Nature* 435:1014.

—————————. 2006. Fish futures. *Conservation in Practice* 7(3):22-27.

Darby, A. 2006. Revealed: how Japan caught and hid $2 billion worth of rare tuna. *Sydney Morning Herald* August 12.

Davidson, P.W., G.J. Meyers, C. Cox, C. Axtell, C. Shamlaye, J. Sloan-Reeves, E. Cernichiari, L. Needham, A. Choi, Y. Wang, M. Berlin, and T.W. Clarkson. 1998. Effects of prenatal and postnatal methylmercury exposure from fish consumption on neurodevelopment: outcomes at 66 months of age in the Sychelles Development Study. *Jour. Amer. Assoc. Medicine* 280(8):701-707.

Davis, J.E. 2005. Not a fish story. *San Francisco Chronicle* August 3:B9.

Davis, T.L.O. and J.H. Farley. 2001. Size distribution of southern bluefin tuna (*Thunnus maccoyii*) by depth on their spawning ground. *Fishery Bulletin* 99:381-386.

Davis, T.L.O. and C.A. Stanley. 2002. Vertical and horizontal movements of southern bluefin tuna (*Thunnus maccoyii*) in the Great Australian Bight observed with ultrasonic telemetry. *Fishery Bulletin* 100:448-465.

Dean, C. 2006a. Fish farms also harbor deadly lice. *New York Times* October 3:F3.

—————————. 2006b. Study sees 'global collapse' of fish species. *New York Times* November 3:7.

Debelle, P. 2006. Fishy behavior doesn't worry the millionaires of Port Lincoln. *The Age* August 19.

Dekker, A. and K. Truelove. 1994. Australia plays a leading role in SBT Convention. *Australian Fisheries* July 1994:6-7.

de Leiva, J.I. and J. Majkowski, 2005. *Tuna resources*. FAO. Rome.

Delgado, C.L., N. Wada, M.W. Rosegrant, S. Meijer, and M. Ahmed. 2003. *The Future of Fish: Issues and Trends to 2020*. International Food Policy Research Institute.

De Metrio, G., I. Oray, G.P. Arnold, M. Lutcavage, M. DeFlorio, J.L. Cort, S. Karakulak, N. Anbar, and M. Ultanur. 2004. Joint Turkish-Italian research in the eastern Mediterranean: bluefin tuna tagging with pop-up satellite tags. *Col. Vol. Sci. Pap. ICCAT* 56(3):1163-1167.

De Metrio, G., G.P. Arnold, J.M. de la Serna, B.A. Block, P. Megalofonou, M. Lutcavage, I. Oray, and M. DeFlorio. 2005. Movements of bluefin tuna (*Thunnus thynnus* L.) tagged in the Mediterranean Sea with pop-up satellite tags. *Col. Vol. Sci. Pap. ICCAT* 58(4):1337-1340.

Dewar, H. and J.B. Graham. 1994a. Studies of tropical tuna swimming in a large water tunnel. I. Energetics. *Journal of Experimental Biology* 192:13-31.

————. 1994b. Studies of tropical tuna swimming in a large water tunnel. III. Kinematics. *Journal of Experimental Biology* 192:45-59.

Dewar, H., J.B. Graham, and R.W. Brill. 1994. Studies of tropical tuna swimming in a large water tunnel. II. Thermoregulation *Journal of Experimental Biology* 192:33-44.

Dickson, K.A. 1995. Unique adaptations of the metabolic chemistry of tunas and billfishes for life in the pelagic environment. *Environmental Biology of Fishes* 42(1):65-97.

Dickson, K.A. and J.B. Graham. 2004. Evolution and consequences of endothermy in fishes. *Physiological and Biochemical Zoology* 77(6):998-1018.

Dizon, A.E. and R.W. Brill. 1979. Thermoregulation in tunas. *American Zoologist* 19(1):249-265.

Donley, J.M., C.A. Sepulveda, P. Konstantinitis, S. Gemballa, and R.E. Shadwick. 2004. Convergent evolution in mechanical design of lamnid sharks and tunas. *Nature* 429:31-33.

Donoghue, M., R.R. Reeves, and G.S. Stone (eds.). 2003. *Report of the Workshop on Interaction Between Cetaceans and Longline Fisheries*. New England Aquarium Press.

Earle, S.A. 1991. Sharks, squids, and horseshoe crabs—the significance of marine biodiversity. *BioScience* 41(7):506-509.

————. 1995. *Sea Change: A Message of the Oceans*. Fawcett Columbine.

Ellis, R. 1982. *Dolphins and Porpoises*. Knopf.

————. 1987. Australia's Southern Seas. *National Geographic* 171(3):286-319.

————. 2003a. *The Empty Ocean*. Island Press.

—————. 2003b. End of the line: eating the tuna out of existence. *The Ecologist* 33(8):43-55.

—————. 2005a. *Tiger Bone & Rhino Horn: The Destruction of Wildlife for Traditional Chinese Medicine*. Island Press.

—————. 2005b. *Singing Whales and Flying Squid: The Discovery of Marine Life*. Lyons Press.

Essington, T.E., D.E. Schindler, R.J. Olson, J.F. Kitchell, C. Boggs, and R. Hilborn. 2002. Alternative fisheries and the predation rate of yellowfin tuna in the eastern Pacific Ocean. *Ecological Applications* 12(3):724-734.

Fabricant, F. 2001. Sashimi that isn't: a star is born. *New York Times* September 12.

Faiella, G. 2003. *Fishing in Bermuda*. Macmillan Caribbean.

Farley, J.H. and T.L.O. Davis. 1998. Reproductive dynamics of southern bluefin tuna, *Thunnus maccoyii*. *Fishery Bulletin* 96(2):223-236.

Farwell, C.J. 2001. Tunas in captivity. In B.A. Block and E.D. Stevens, eds. *Tuna: Physiology, Ecology, and Evolution*. 391-412. Academic Press.

Farrington, S.K. 1937. *Atlantic Game Fishing*. Kennedy Brothers.

—————. 1942. *Pacific Game Fishing*. Coward-McCann.

—————. 1949. *Fishing the Atlantic, Offshore and On*. Coward-McCann.

—————. 1953. *Fishing the Pacific, Offshore and On*. Coward-McCann.

—————. 1971. *Fishing with Hemingway and Glassell*. McKay.

—————. 1974. *The Trail of the Sharp Cup*. Dodd, Mead.

Fierstine, H.L. and V. Walters. 1968. Studies in locomotion and anatomy of scombroid fishes. *Memoirs of the Southern California Academy of Sciences* 6:1-31.

Fisheries Agency of Japan. 2005. Report on the progress in the implementation of the measures to eliminate illegal unreported and unregulated large scale tuna longline fishing vessels. *Col. Vol. Sci. Pap. ICCAT* 58(5):1776-1780.

Fisheries Data Analysis Division, Southeast Fisheries Center (NMFS). 1980. A description of the fishery for Atlantic bluefin tuna by United States fishermen. *Col. Vol. Sci. Pap. ICCAT* 11:186-192.

Fitch, J.E. and R.J. Lavenberg. 1971. *Marine Food and Game Fishes of California*. University of California Press.

Fonteneau, A., J. Ariz, D. Gaertner, V. Nordstrom, and P. Pillares. 2000. Observed changes in the species composition of tuna schools in the Gulf of Guinea between 1981 and 1999, in relation with the Fish Aggregating Device fishery. *Aquatic Living Resources* 13:253-257.

Fréon, P and L. Dagorn. 2004. Review of fish associative behaviour: toward a generalization of the meeting point hypothesis. *Reviews in Fish Biology and Fisheries*. 10(2):183-207.

Fritsches, K.A. and E. Warrant. 2004. Do tuna and billfish see colors? *PFRP Newsletter* 9(1):1-4.

Fromentin, J.M. 2003. The East Atlantic and Mediterranean bluefin tuna stock management: uncertainties and alternatives. *Scientia Marina* 67(Suppl. 1):51-62.

—————. 2006. Size limits regulation for tuna: should we also consider the protection of large fish? *Vol. Sci. Pap. ICCAT* 59(2):590-592.

Fromentin, J.M. and A. Fonteneau. 2001. Fishing effects and life history traits: a case study comparing tropical versus temperate tunas. *Fisheries Research* 53(2):133-150.

Fromentin, J.M., H. Farrugio, M. Deflorio, and G. De Metrio. 2003. Preliminary results of aerial surveys of bluefin tuna in the western Mediterranean Sea. *Col. Vol. Sci. Pap. ICCAT* 55(3):1019-1027.

Fromentin, J.M. and J.E. Powers. 2005. Atlantic bluefin tuna: population dynamics, ecology, fisheries and management. *Fish and Fisheries* 6(4):281-298.

Fromentin, J.M. and C. Ravier. 2005. The East Atlantic and Mediterranean bluefin tuna stock: Looking for sustainability in a context of large uncertainties and strong political pressures. *Bulletin of Marine Science* 76(2): 353-361.

Fromentin, J.M., A. Fonteneau, and V. Restrepo. 2006. Ecosystem approach to fisheries: a brief overview and some considerations for its application to ICCAT. *Col. Vol. Sci. Pap. ICCAT* 59(2):682-689.

Garcia, A., J.M. de la Serna, J.L. López-Jurado, F. Alemany, and E. Rodriguez-Marin. 2002. Bluefin tuna egg and larval survey in the Balearic Sea, June 2001 (TUNIBAL 06/01). *Col. Vol. Sci. Pap. ICCAT* 54(2):425-431.

Garcia, S.M. and R.J.R. Grainger. 2005. Gloom and doom? The future of marine capture fisheries. *Philosophical Transactions of the Royal Society B.* 360:21-46.

Garrell, M.H. 1993. The pursuit of bluefins meets reality. *Sea Frontiers* 31(6):18-21.

Gerrodette, T. 2002. Tuna-dolphin issue. 1269-73 in W.F. Perrin, B. Würsig, and J.G.M. Thewissen, eds., *Encyclopedia of Marine Mammals.* Academic Press.

Gerrodette, T. and J. Forcada. 2005. Non-recovery of two spotted and spinner dolphin populations in the eastern tropical Pacific Ocean. *Marine Ecology Progress Series* 291:1-21.

Goadby, P. 1975. *Big Fish and Blue Water: Gamefishing in the Pacific.* Angus & Robertson. Sydney.

Godsil, H.C. 1938. The high seas tuna fishery of California. *Cal. Fish and Game Fish Bulletin 51:1-44.*

Goldburg, R. and R. Naylor. 2005. Future seascapes, fishing, and fish farming. *Frontiers in Ecology and Environment* 3(1):21-28.

Gorton, S. 2005. Fishery shut, 19 dolphins killed. *Port Lincoln Times* August 30.

Graham, J.B. and K.A. Dickson. 2001. Anatomical and physiological specializations for endothermy. In B.A. Block and E.D. Stevens, eds. *Tuna: Physiology, Ecology, and Evolution.* 121-165. Academic Press.

—————. 2004. Tuna comparative physiology. *Journal of Experimental Biology* 207:4015-4024.

Graham, J.B., H. Dewar, N.C. Lai, W.R. Lowell, and S.M. Arce. 1990. Aspects of shark swimming performance determined using a large water tunnel. *Journal of Experimental Biology* 151:175-192.

Graham-Rowe, D. 2006. China and its friends push tiger farm idea. *New Scientist* 92:16-17.

Gray, J. 1933. Studies in animal locomotion. I. The movements of fish with special reference to the eel. *Journal of Experimental Biology* 10:88-104.

Greenberg, P. 2006a. Green to the gills. *New York Times Magazine* June 18.

—————. 2006b. Other fish to fry. *New York Times* September 8:A29.

Grey, L. 1982. *Angler's Eldorado: Zane Grey in New Zealand*. Walter J. Black.

Grey, R.C. 1930. *Adventures of a Deep-Sea Angler*. Harper & Brothers. (2002 Edition, Derrydale Press.)

Grey, Z. 1919. *Tales of Fishes*. Harper & Brothers. (1990 Edition, Derrydale Press.)

——————. 1925. *Tales of Fishing Virgin Seas*. Harper & Brothers.

——————. 1927. *Tales of Swordfish and Tuna*. Harper & Brothers.

——————. 1931. *Tales of Tahitian Waters*. Harper & Brothers. (1990 Edition, Derrydale Press.)

Guerra, A.S. 1980. Description of the bluefin tuna fishery (*Thunnus thynnus*) in the Canary Islands. *Col. Vol. Sci. Pap. ICCAT* 11:174-177.

Gunn, J. and B.A. Block. 2001. Advances in acoustic, archival and satellite tagging of tunas. In B.A. Block and E.D. Stevens, eds. *Tuna: Physiology, Ecology, and Evolution*. 167-224. Academic Press.

Günther, A.C.L.G. 1880. *An Introduction to the Study of Fishes*. Adam and Charles Black.

Hampton, J., A. Lewis, and P. Williams. 2002. *The Western and Central Pacific Tuna Fishery: 2000 Overview and Status of Stocks*. Tuna Fisheries Assessment Report/Secretariat of the Pacific Community. Oceanic Fisheries Programme Report No. 3:59.

Hampton, J., J.R. Sibert, P. Kleiber, M.N. Maunder, and S.J. Harley. 2005. Decline of Pacific tuna exaggerated? *Nature* 434:E1-E2.

Hanrahan, B. and F. Juanes. 2001. Estimating the number of fish in Atlantic bluefin tuna (*Thunnus thynnus*) schools using models derived from captive school observations. *Fishery Bulletin* 99:420-431.

Harada, Y. 1999. A flag-waving squabble. *Sumudra* 24:30-31.

——————. 2002. Tuning tuna. *Sumudra* 33:32-34.

Harder, B. 2003. Whale meat in Japan is loaded with mercury. *Science News* 163(23):365.

Hardin, G. 1968. The tragedy of the commons. *Science* 162:1243-48.

Hayden, T. 2003. Empty oceans: why the world's seafood supply is disappearing. *U.S. News and World Report* 134(20):38-45.

Hayes, E.A. 1997. *A Review of the Southern Bluefin Tuna Fishery: Implications for Ecologically Sustainable Management*. TRAFFIC Oceania.

Hazin, F.H.V., J.R. Zagaglia, M.K. Broadhurst, P.E.P. Travassos, and T.R.Q. Bezerra. 1998. Review of small-scale pelagic longline fishery off northeastern Brazil. *Marine Fisheries Review* 60(3):1-8.

Hazin, F.H.V., M.K. Broadhurst, and H.G. Hazin. 2000. Preliminary analysis of the feasibility of transferring new longline technology to small artisinal vessels off northeastern Brazil. *Marine Fisheries Review* 62(1):27-34.

Hearn, W.S. and T. Polacheck. 2003. Estimating long-term growth-rate changes of southern bluefin tuna (*Thunnus maccoyii*) from two periods of tag-return data. *Fishery Bulletin* 101:58-74,

Heilner, V.C. 1953. *Salt Water Fishing*. Knopf.

Hempel, G. and D. Pauly. 2002. Fisheries and fisheries science in their search for sustainability. In J.G. Field, G. Hempel, and C.P. Summerhayes. 2002. *Oceans 2020: Science, Trends, and the Challenge of Sustainability*. 109-35. Island Press.

Hespe, M. 2004. Bluefin Tuna: Australian Port Lincoln's Crop. *Japan Times* Sept 17.

Hester, F. 2002. Atlantic bluefin tuna: some considerations on mixing on the feeding grounds. *Col. Vol. Sci. Pap. ICCAT* 54(2):400-406.

Hibbein, J. 1998. Fish consumption and major depression. *The Lancet* 351:1213.

Hilborn, R., T.A. Branch, B. Ernst, A. Magnusson, C.V. Minte-Vera, M.D. Scheuerell, and J. L. Valero. 2003. State of the world's fisheries. *Annual Review of Environment and Resources*. 28:359-399.

Hisada, K., C. Shingu, and T. Yonemori. 1989. Recent status of the southern bluefin tuna stock. *Col. Vol. Sci. Pap. ICCAT* 8(2):454-460.

Hites, R.A., J.A. Foran, D.O. Carpenter, M.C. Hamilton, B.A. Knuth, and S.J. Schwager. 2004. Global assessment of organic contaminants in farmed salmon. *Science* 303:226-229.

Hobsbawn, P.I., J.D. Findlay, S. Rowcliffe, and A. Bodsworth. 2005. Australia's annual review of the southern bluefin tuna fishery. *Working Paper CCSBT-EC/051/SBT Fisheries Australia presented at the Second Meeting of the Extended Commission of the Commission for the Conservation of Southern Bluefin Tuna*. Attachment 8-1:1-13.

Holland, K.N., R.W. Brill, and R.K.C. Chang. 1990. Horizontal and vertical movements of yellowfin and bigeye tuna associated with fish aggregating devices. *Fishery Bulletin* 88(3):493-507.

Holland, K.N., R.W. Brill, R.K.C. Chang, J.R. Sibert, and D.A. Fournier. 1992. Physiological and behavioral thermoregulation in bigeye tuna (*Thunnus obesus*). *Nature* 358:410-412.

Holland, K.N., P. Kleiber, and S.M. Kajiura. 1999. Different residence times of yellowfin tuna, *Thunnus albacares*, and bigeye tuna, *T. obesus*, found in mixed aggregations over a seamount. *Fishery Bulletin* 97:392-395.

Holland, K.N. and J.R. Sibert. 2005. Physiological thermoregulation in bigeye tuna, *Thunnus obesus. Environmental Biology of Fishes* 40(3):317-327.

Holloway, M. 2002. Blue revolution [Fish farming]. *Discover* 23(9):57-63.

Holt, S.J. 1969. The food resources of the ocean. *Scientific American* 221(2):178-194.

Honma, M. 1973. Overall fishing intensity and catch by length class of yellowfin tuna in Japanese Atlantic longline fishery, 1956-1970. *Col. Vol. Sci. Pap. ICCAT* 1:59-77.

————. 1976. Catch statistics of Japanese Atlantic purse seine fishery, 1974 and 1975. *Col. Vol. Sci. Pap. ICCAT* 5(1):23-25.

Honma, M. and Z. Suzuki. 1974a. Catch statistics and sample length composition in Japanese Atlantic tuna purse seine fishery, 1967-1969. *Col. Vol. Sci. Pap. ICCAT* (2):10-14.

————. 1974b. Catch statistics and sample length composition in Japanese Atlantic tuna purse seine fishery, 1971 and 1972, with a brief review of the fishery since 1964. *Col. Vol. Sci. Pap. ICCAT* 2:15-24.

Hori, T. 1996. *Tuna and the Japanese.* Japan External Trade Organization.

Hosaka, E.Y. 1944. *Sport Fishing in Hawaii.* Bond's.

Hsieh, C.H., C.S. Reiss, J.R. Hunter, J.R. Beddington, R.M. May, and G. Sugihara. 2006. Fishing elevates variability in the abundance of exploited species. *Nature* 443:859-862.

Humston, R., J.S. Ault, M.E. Lutcavage, and D.B. Olson. 2000. Schooling and migration of large pelagic fishes relative to environmental data. *Fisheries Oceanography* 9:136-146.

Hurley, P.C.F. and T.D. Iles. 1980. A brief description of Canadian fisheries for Atlantic bluefin tuna. *Col. Vol. Sci. Pap. ICCAT* 11:93-97.

International Game Fish Association. 2006. *World Record Game Fishes*. IGFA. Dania Beach, Florida.

Itano, D.G. 2000. *The Reproductive Biology of Yellowfin Tuna (Thunnus albacares) in Hawaiian Waters and the Western Tropical Pacific Ocean: Project Summary*. Joint Institute for Marine and Atmospheric Research Contribution 00-328: 75 pp.

Itoh, T. 2006. Sizes of adult bluefin tuna *Thunnus orientalis* in different areas of the western Pacific Ocean. *Fisheries Science* 72:53-62.

Itoh, T., S. Tsuji, and A. Nitta. 2003a. Migration patterns of young Pacific bluefin tuna (*Thunnus orientalis*) determined with archival tags. *Fishery Bulletin* 101(3):514-534.

—————. 2003b. Swimming depth, ambient water temperature preference, and feeding frequency of young Pacific bluefin tuna (*Thunnus orientalis*) determined with archival tags. *Fishery Bulletin* 101(3):535-544.

IUCN. 2006. *2006 IUCN Red List of Threatened Species*. http://www.iucnredlist.org. Downloaded on October 19, 2006.

Jackson, J.B.C. and K.G. Johnson. 2001. Measuring past biodiversity. *Science* 293:2401-03.

Jackson, J.B.C., M.X. Kirby, W.H. Berger, K.A. Bjorndal, L.W. Botsford, B.J. Bourque, R.H. Bradbury, R. Cooke, J. Erlandson, J.A. Estes, T.P. Hughes, S. Kidwell, C.B. Lange, H.S. Lenihan, J.M. Pandolfi, C.H. Peterson, R.S. Steneck, M.J. Tegner, and R.R. Warner. 2001. Historical overfishing and the recent collapse of coastal ecosystems. *Science* 293:629-38.

Jordan, D.S. and B.W. Evermann. 1902. *American Food and Game Fishes*. Doubleday, Page & Co.

—————. 1926. A review of the giant mackerel-like fishes, tunnies, spearfishes, and swordfishes. *Occasional Papers Calif. Acad. Sci*.12:1-113.

Joseph, J. 1994. The tuna-dolphin controversy in the eastern Pacific Ocean: biological, economic and political impacts. *Ocean Development and International Law* 25(1):1-30.

—————. 1998a. A brief history of tuna research. *Col. Vol. Sci. Pap. ICCAT* 50(1):183-193.

—————. 1998b. On scientific advice and tuna management. *Col. Vol. Sci. Pap. ICCAT* 5(2):855-861.

Joseph, J. and J.W. Greenough. 1979. *International Management of Tuna, Porpoise, and Billfish*. University of Washington Press.

Joseph, J., W. Klawe, and P. Murphy. 1988. *Tuna and Billfish: Fish Without a Country*. Inter-American Tropical Tuna Commission.

Josse, E., A. Bertrand, and L. Dagorn. 1999. An acoustic approach to study tuna aggregated around fish aggregating devices in French Polynesia: methods and validation. *Aquatic Living Resources* 12(5):303-313.

Josse, E., L. Dagorn, and A. Bertrand. 2000. Typology and behaviour of tuna aggregations around fish aggregating devices from acoustic surveys in French Polynesia. *Aquatic Living Resources* 13:183-192.

Josupeit. H. and C. Catarci. 2004. The world tuna industry—an analysis of imports, prices, and of their combined impact on tuna catches and fishing capacity. FAO. Rome.

Kaji, T., M. Tanaka, Y. Takahishi, M. Oka, and N. Ishibashi. 1993. Preliminary observations on development of Pacific bluefin tuna *Thunnus thynnus thynnus* (Scombridae) raised in the laboratory, with special reference to the digestive system. *Marine and Freshwater Research* 47(2):261-269.

Karakulak, S., I. Oray, A. Corriero, A. Aprea, D. Spedicato, D. Zubani, N. Santamaria, and G. De Metrio. 2004. First information on the reproductive biology of the bluefin tuna (*Thunnus thynnus*) in the eastern Mediterranean. *Col. Vol. Sci. Pap. ICCAT* 56(3):1158-1162.

Kataviae, I., V. Tièina, and V. Franièviae. 2002. A preliminary study of the growth rate of bluefin tuna from Adriatic when reared in the floating cages. *Col. Vol. Sci. Pap. ICCAT* 54(2):472-476.

Katz, S.L., D.A. Syme, and R.E. Shadwick. 2001. Enhanced power in yellowfin tuna. *Nature* 410:770-771.

Kawamura, G., S. Masuma, N. Tezuka, M. Koiso, T. Jimbo, and K. Namba. 2003. Morphogenesis of sense organs in the bluefin tuna *Thunnus orientalis*. 123-135 in H.I. Browman and A.B. Skiftesvik, eds., *The Big Fish Bang: Proceedings of the 26th Annual Larval Fish Conference, Os, Norway, July 22-26, 2002*. Institute of Marine Research, Bergen.

Keith-Reid, R. 2002. Yellow fin tuna under threat. *Pacific* February: 22-28.

Kessler, A. 1976. The hunt for tuna. *Oceans* 9(4):50-57.

Kitagawa, T., S. Kimura, H. Nakata, and H. Yamada. 2004. Overview of research on tuna thermo-physiology using electric tags. *Mem. Natl. Polar Res. Spec. Issue* 58:69-79.

Klawe, W., I. Barrett, and B.M.H. Klawe. 1963. Hemoglobin content of the blood of six species of scombroid fishes. *Nature* 96.

Kleiner, K. 2002. All fished out. *New Scientist* 173(2331):11.

Klimley, A.P. and C.F. Holloway. 1999. School fidelity and homing synchronicity of yellowfin tuna, *Thunnus albacares*. *Marine Biology* 133:307-317.

Klimley, A.P., S.J. Jorgensen, A. Muhlia-Melo, and S.C. Beavers. 2003. The occurrence of yellowfin tuna (*Thunnus albacares*) at Espiritu Santo Seamount in the Gulf of California. *Fishery Bulletin* 101:684-692.

Kluger, J. 2006. Mercury rising. *Time* 168(10):52-55.

Kobayashi, N., R.J. Barnard, S.M. Henning, D. Elashoff, S.T. Reddy, P Cohen, P. Leung, J. Hong-Gonzalez, S.J. Freedland, J. Said, D. Gui, N.P. Seeram, L.M. Popoviciu, D. Bagga, D. Heber, J.A. Glaspy, and W.J. Aronson. 2006. Effect of altering dietary omega-6/omega-3 fatty acid ratios on prostate cancer membrane composition, Cyclooxygenase-2, and Prostaglandin E_2 *Clinical Cancer Research* 12:4662-4670.

Kondo, I. 2001. Rise and Fall of the Japanese Coast Whaling. Sanyosha.

Korsmeyer, K.E. and H. Dewar. 2001. Tuna metabolism and energetics. In B.A. Block and E.D. Stevens, eds. *Tuna: Physiology, Ecology, and Evolution*. 36-78. Academic Press.

Krkosek, M., A. Morton, and J.P. Volpe. 2005. Nonlethal assessment of juvenile pink and chum salmon for parasitic sea lice infections and fish health. *Transactions of the American Fisheries Society* 134:711-716.

Krkosek, M., M.A. Lewis, A. Morton, L.N. Frazer, and J.P. Volpe. 2006. Epizootics of wild fish induced by farm fish. *Proceedings of the National Academy of Sciences*.

Kwei, E.A. 1991. Pricing of yellowfin and other tunas. *Col. Vol. Sci. Pap. ICCAT* 36:506-514.

La Mesa, M., M. Sinopoli, and F. Andaloro. 2005. Age and growth rate of juvenile bluefin tina (*Thunnus thynnus*) from the Mediterranean Sea (Sicily, Italy.) *Scientia Marina* 69(2):241-249.

La Monte, F. 1945. *North American Game Fishes*. Doubleday.

—————. 1952. *Marine Game Fishes of the World*. Doubleday.

—————. 1965. *Giant Fishes of the Open Sea*. Holt, Rinehart and Winston.

Lato, D. 2003. $6m tuna lost as cage collapses. *GROWfish*. http://www.growfish.com.au/grow/pages/News/2003/mar2003/56603.htm.

Lee, M. (ed.). 2000. *Seafood Lover's Almanac*. National Audubon Society.

Linthicum, D.S. and F.G. Carey. 1972. Regulation of brain and eye temperatures by the bluefin tuna. *Comparative Biochemistry and Physiology* 43(2):425-430.

Lipton, J. 1968. *An Exaltation of Larks*. Viking.

Lo, N.C.H. and T.D. Smith. 1986. Incidental mortality of dolphins in the Eastern tropical Pacific, 1959-72. *Fishery Bulletin* 84(1):27-34.

Loew, E.R., W.N. McFarland, and D. Margulies. 2002. Developmental changes in the visual pigments of the yellowfin tuna, *Thunnus albacares*. *Marine and Freshwater Behaviour and Physiology* 35:235-246.

Lowe, T.E., R.W. Brill, and K.L. Cousins. 2004. Blood-binding characteristics of bigeye tuna (*Thunnus obesus*), a high-energy demand teleost that is tolerant of low ambient oxygen. *Marine Biology* 136(6):1087-1098.

Lund, E., D. Engeset, E. Alsaker, G. Skeie, A. Hjartaker, A.K. Lundebye, and E. Niebor. 2004. Cancer risk and salmon intake. *Science* 305:477.

Lutcavage, M. 2001. Bluefin spawning in Central North Atlantic? *Pelagic Fisheries Research Program Newsletter* 6(2):1-3.

Lutcavage, M. and S. Kraus. 1995. The feasibility of direct photographic assessment of giant bluefin tuna, *Thunnus thynnus*, in New England waters. *Fishery Bulletin* 93:495-503.

Lutcavage, M.E., R.W. Brill, G.B. Skomal, B.C. Chase, J.L. Goldstein, and J. Tutein. 2000. Tracking adult North American bluefin tuna (*Thunnus thgynnus*) in the northwestern Atlantic using ultrasonic telemetry. *Marine Biology* 137(2):347-358.

Lutcavage, M.E., R.W. Brill, J. Porter, P. Howey, E. Murray, A. Mendillo, W. Chaprales, M. Genovese, and T. Rollins. 2001. Summary of pop-up satellite tagging of giant bluefin tuna in the joint US-Canadian program, Gulf of Maine and Canadian Atlantic. *Col. Vol. Sci. Pap. ICCAT* 52(1): 759-770.

MacLeish, W.H. 1989. *The Gulf Stream: Encounters with the Blue God*. Houghton Mifflin.

Maggio, T. 2001. *Mattanza: The Ancient Sicilian Ritual of Bluefin Tuna Fishing*. Penguin.

Magnuson, J.J., C. Safina, and M.P. Sissenwine. 2001. Whose fish are they anyway? *Science* 293:1267-68.

Margulies, D., V.P. Scholey, J.B. Wexler, R.J. Olson, A. Nakazawa, and J.M. Suter. 1997. Captive spawning of the yellowfin tuna and the development of their eggs and larvae. *Tuna Newsletter* (NMFS Southwest Fisheries Center) 126:4-5.

Margulies, D., V. Scholey, S. Hunt, and J. Wexler. 2005. Achotines Lab studies diets for larval, juvenile yellowfin tuna. *Global Aquacul. Advocate* 8(2): 87.

Marra, J. 2005. When will we tame the oceans? *Nature* 436:175-176.

Martínez-Garmendia, J. and J.L. Anderson. 2005. Conservation, markets, and fisheries policy: the North Atlantic bluefin tuna and the Japanese sashimi market. *Agribusiness* 21(1):17-36.

Martínez-Garmendia, J., J.L. Anderson, and M.T. Carroll. 2000. Effect of harvesting alternatives on the quality of U.S. North American bluefin tuna. *N.A. Journal of Fisheries Management* 20:908:922.

Mason, J.H. 1975. U.S. Atlantic bluefin tuna tagging, October 1971 through October 1974. *Col. Vol. Sci. Pap. ICCAT* 4:133-140.

Mather, F.J. 1954. Northerly occurrences of warmwater fishes in the Western Atlantic. *Copeia* 1954(4):292-293.

——————. 1960. Recaptures of tuna, marlin and sailfish tagged in the western North Atlantic. *Copeia* 1960(2):149-151.

——————. 1980a. Note on the relationship between recently acquired mark-recapture data and existing age estimates for Atlantic bluefin tuna. *Col. Vol. Sci. Pap. ICCAT* 9(2):470-477.

——————. 1980b. A preliminary note on migratory tendencies and distributional patterns of Atlantic bluefin tuna based on recently acquired and cumulative tagging results. *Col. Vol. Sci. Pap. ICCAT* 9(2):478-490.

Mather, F.J. and C.G. Day. 1954. Observations of the pelagic fishes of the tropical Atlantic. *Copeia* 1954(3):179-188.

Mather, F.J. and R.H. Gibbs. 1957. Distributional records of fishes from the waters off New England and the Middle Atlantic states. *Copeia* 1957(3):242-244.

——————. 1958. Distribution of the Atlantic bigeye tuna, *Thunnus obesus*, in the western North Atlantic and the Caribbean Sea. *Copeia* 1958(3):237-239.

Mather, F.J. and J.M. Mason. 1973. Recent information on tagging and tag returns for tunas and billfishes in the Atlantic Ocean. *Col. Vol. Sci. Pap. ICCAT* 1:501-531.

—————. 1976. Results of United States cooperative tagging of Atlantic bluefin tuna October 1974 through October 1975. *Col. Vol. Sci. Pap. ICCAT* 11:180-183.

Mather, F.J. and H.A. Schuck. 1951. A blackfin tuna (*Parathunnus atlanticus*) from North Carolina waters. *Copeia* 1951(3):248.

—————. 1952. Additional notes on the distribution of the blackfin tuna (*Parathunnus atlanticus*). *Copeia* 1952(4):267.

Mather, F.J., W.R. Bartlett, and J.S. Beckett. 1967. Transatlantic migrations of young bluefin tuna. *Journal of the Fisheries Research Board of Canada* 24(9):1991-1997.

Mather, F.J., B.J. Rothschild, and G.J. Paulik. 1973. Preliminary analysis of bluefin tagging data. *Col. Vol. Sci. Pap. ICCAT* 1:413-444.

Mather, F.J., J.H. Mason, and A.C. Jones. 1974. Distribution, fisheries and life history relevant to the identification of Atlantic bluefin tuna stocks. *Col. Vol. Sci. Pap. ICCAT* 2:234-258.

Matsen, B. 1990. *Deep Sea Fishing: The Lure of Big Game Fish.* Thunder Bay Press.

Matsuda, Y. 1998. History of the Japanese tuna fisheries and a Japanese perspective on Atlantic bluefin tuna. *Col. Vol. Sci. Pap. ICCAT* 50(2):733-751.

Matthiessen P. 1959. *Wildlife in America.* Viking.

McClane, A.J. 1965. *McClane's Standard Fishing Encyclopedia.* Holt, Rinehart, and Winston.

McDowell, N. 2002. Stream of escaped farm fish raises fear for wild salmon. *Nature* 416:571.

McGhee, K. 2004. Taking stock: southern bluefin on the line. *ECOS (CSIRO Newsletter)*:119:24-27.

McPherson, G.R. 1991. Reproductive biology of yellowfin tuna in the eastern Australian Fishing Zone, with special reference to the north-western Coral Sea. *Marine and Freshwater Research* 42(5):465-477.

Migdalski, E.C. 1958. *Angler's Guide to the Salt Water Game Fishes, Atlantic and Pacific.* Ronald Press.

Migdalski, E.C. and G.S. Fichter. 1976. *The Fresh & Salt Water Fishes of the World*. Knopf.

Milius, S. 2000. Carnivorous fish nibble at farming gain. *Science News* 158(1):7.

Minasian, S. 1977. Dolphins and/or tuna. Oceans 10(3):60-63.

Miyabe, N. 2003. Description of the Japanese longline fishery and its fishery statistics in the Mediterranean Sea during recent years. *Col. Vol. Sci. Pap. ICCAT* 55(1):131-137.

Miyabe, N., M. Ogura, T. Matsumoto, and Y. Nishikawa. 2004. *National Tuna Fisheries Report of Japan as of 2004*. SCTB17 Working Paper NFR-11. National Research Institute of Far Seas Fisheries, Shizuoka. 24 pp.

Miyabe, N. and H. Okamoto. 2005. Documentation of data provision and processing for the Japanese tuna fisheries in the eastern Pacific Ocean. *IATTC Document* DC-1-02a:1-6.

Miyake, P.M. 1987. Historical review of Atlantic tuna catches and some thoughts on tuna management. *Col. Vol. Sci. Pap. ICCAT* 26(2):433-455.

—————. 2006. Why do we have to control the global fishing capacity? *OPRT Newsletter* 10:1-4.

Miyake, P.M., J.M. De la Serna, A. Di Natale, A. Farrugia, I. Katavic, N. Miyabe, and V. Ticina. 2003. General review of bluefin tuna farming in the Mediterranean area. *Col. Vol. Sci. Pap. ICCAT* 55(1):114-124.

Miyake, P.M., N. Miyabe, and H. Nakano, 2004. *Historical Trends in Tuna Catches in the World*. FAO Fisheries Technical Paper. No. 467. FAO, Rome. 74 pp.

Miyashita, S., Y. Sawada, N. Hattori, H. Nakatsukasa, T. Okada, O. Murata, and H. Kumai. 2000. Mortality of northern bluefin tuna *Thunnus thynnus* due to trauma caused by collision during growout culture. *Jour. World Aquaculture Society* 31(4):632-639.

Morgan, R. 1955. *World Sea Fisheries*. Pitman.

Mori, M., T. Katsukawa, and H. Matsuda. 2001. Recovery plan for an exploited species, southern bluefin tuna. *Population Ecology* 43:125-132.

Mowat, F. 1984. *Sea of Slaughter*. Atlantic Monthly Press.

Moyle, P.B. and J.J. Cech. 2004. *Fishes: An Introduction to Ichthyology*. Prentice-Hall.

Musyl, M.K., R.W. Brill, C.H. Boggs, D.S. Curran, T.K. Kazama, and M.P. Seki. 2003. Vertical movements of bigeye tuna (*Thunnus obesus*) associated with islands, buoys, and seamounts near the main Hawaiian islands from archival tagging data. *Fisheries Oceanography* 12(3):152-168.

Myers, R.A. and C.A. Ottensmeyer. 2005. Extinction risk in marine species. 58-79 in E. Norse and L.B. Crowder, eds., *Marine Conservation Biology*. Island Press.

Myers, R.A. and B. Worm. 2003. Rapid worldwide depletion of predatory fish communities. *Nature* 423:280-283

————. 2005. Extinction, survival or recovery of large predatory fishes. *Philosophical Transactions of the Royal Society B*. 360:13-20.

Mylonas, C. 2005. Research breakthrough—saving the bluefin tuna. Hellenic Centre for Marine Research website. http://www.hcmr.gr/english_site/news/archive/show_news2.php3?id=46.

Nagai, T., S. Hayasi, and T. Yonemori. 1987. A proposal to management of bluefin tuna stock in the western Atlantic based on information obtained by September, 1986. *Col. Vol. Sci. Pap. ICCAT* 26(2):276-282.

National Research Council. 1992. *Dolphins and the Tuna Industry*. National Academy Press.

————. 1994. *An Assessment of Atlantic Bluefin Tuna*. National Academy Press.

Naylor, R.L. 2006a. Environmental safeguards for open-ocean aquaculture *Issues in Science and Technology*. Spring 2006:53-58.

————. 2006b. Offshore aquaculture legislation. *Science* 313:1363.

Naylor, R.L., R.J. Goldburg, H. Mooney, M.C.M. Beveridge, J. Clay, C. Folke, N. Kautsky, J. Lubchenko, J. Primavera, and M. Williams. 1998. Nature's subsidies to shrimp and salmon farming. *Science* 282:883-884.

Naylor, R.L., R.J. Goldburg, J.H. Primavera, N. Kautsky, M.C.M. Beveridge, J. Clay, C. Folke, J. Lubchenko, H. Mooney, and M. Troell. 2000. Effect of aquaculture on world fish supplies. *Nature* 405:1017-24.

Naylor, R.L. and M. Burke. 2005. Aquaculture and ocean resources: raising tigers of the sea. *Annual Review of Environment and Resources* 30:185-218.

Neill, W.H., R.K.C. Chang, and A.E. Dizon. 1976. Magnitude and ecological implications of thermal inertia in skipjack tuna, *Katsuwonus pelamis* (Linnaeus). *Environmental Biology of Fishes* 1(1):61-80.

Nestle, M. 2006. *What to Eat.* North Point.

Newlands, N.K., M.E. Lutcavage, and T.J. Pitcher. 2004. Analysis of foraging movements of the Atlantic bluefin tuna (*Thunnus thynnus*): individuals will switch between two modes of search behaviour. *Population Ecology* 46:39-53.

Nicoll, R. 1993. Port Lincoln carves out a bright future. *Australian Fisheries Newsletter* November:14-20.

Nishida, T., S. Chow, and P. Grewe. 1998. Review and research plan on the stock structure of yellowfin tuna (*Thunnus albacares*) and bigeye tuna (*Thunnus obesus*) in the Indian Ocean. *Indian Ocean Tuna Commission Proceedings* 1:230-236.

Nootmorn, P. 2004. Reproductive biology of bigeye tuna in the eastern Indian Ocean. *Indian Ocean Tuna Commission Proceedings* 7:1-6.

Norman, J.R. and F.C. Fraser. 1938. *Giant Fishes, Whales and Dolphins.* W.W. Norton.

Norman, J.R. and P.H. Greenwood. 1963. *A History of Fishes.* Hill and Wang.

Northridge, S. P. 1991. *Driftnet Fisheries and their Impact on Non-Target Species: A Worldwide Review.* FAO Fisheries Technical Paper 320:1-115.

Olson, R.J., and V.P. Scholey. 1990. Captive tunas in a tropical marine research laboratory: growth of late-larval and early-juvenile black skipjack *Euthynnus lineatus. Fishery Bulletin* 88:821-828.

Onishi, N. 2006. Farming bluefin tuna, through thick stocks and thin. *New York Times* September 26:A4.

Oppian, N.D. *Halieutica.* (1928 translation by A.W. Mair. Loeb Classical Library, Harvard University.)

Oray, I.K. and F.S. Karakulak. 1997. Some remarks on the bluefin tuna (*Thunnus thynnus* L. 1758) fishery in Turkish waters in 1993, 1994, 1995. *Col. Vol. Sci. Pap. ICCAT* 46(2):357-362.

Parfit, M. 1995. Diminishing returns: exploiting the ocean's bounty. *National Geographic* 188(5):2-37.

Parrack, M.L., S.L. Brunenmeister, and S. Nichols. 1979. An analysis of Atlantic bluefin catches, 1960-1976. *Col. Vol. Sci. Pap. ICCAT* 8(2):391-420.

Parrack, M.L. and P.L. Phares. 1979. Aspects of the growth of the Atlantic bluefin tuna determined from mark-recapture data. *Col. Vol. Sci. Pap. ICCAT* 8(2):356-366.

Paul. L. 1997. *Marine Fishes of New Zealand.* Reed.

Paul, L.M.B. 1994. *High Seas Driftnetting: A Plunder of the Global Common.* Earthtrust.

Pauly, D. 1995. Anecdotes and the shifting baseline syndrome of fisheries. *Trends in Ecology and Evolution* 10(10):430.

Pauly, D., V. Christensen, J. Dalsgaard, R. Froese, and F. Torres. 1998. Fishing down marine food webs. *Science* 279:860-63.

Pauly, D., V. Christensen, R. Froese, and M.L. Palomares. 2000. Fishing down aquatic food webs. *American Scientist* 88(1):46-51.

Pauly, D. and J. Maclean. 2002. *In a Perfect Ocean: The State of Fisheries and Ecosystems in the North Atlantic Ocean.* Island Press.

Pauly, D., J. Alder, E. Bennett, V. Christensen, P. Tyedmers, and R. Watson. 2003. The future for fisheries. *Science* 302:1359-1361.

Pauly, D. and R. Watson. 2003. Counting the last fish. *Scientific American* 289(1):42-47.

Pauly, D. and M.L. Palomares. 2005. Fishing down marine food web: It is far more pervasive than we thought. *Bulletin of Marine Science* 76(2):197-212.

Perrin, W.F. 1968. The porpoise and the tuna. *Sea Frontiers* 14(3):166-174.

———. 1969. Using porpoise to catch tuna. *World Fishing* 18(6):42-45.

Peterson, C.L., W.L. Klawe, and G.D. Sharp. 1973. Mercury in tunas: a review. *Fishery Bulletin* 71(3):603-613.

Pierce, W.G. 1989. *Going Fishing: The Story of the Deep-Sea Fishermen of New England.* International Marine.

Pliny, N.D. *Natural History.* 10 Vols. Loeb Classical Library. Harvard University Press.

Polovina, J.J. 1996. Decadal variation in the trans-Pacific migration of the northern bluefin tuna (*Thunnus thynnus*) coherent with climate-induced change in prey abundance. *Fisheries Oceanography* 5(2):114-119.

Porch, C.E. 2005. The sustainability of Western Atlantic bluefin tuna: A warm-blooded fish in a hot-blooded fishery. *Bulletin of Marine Science.* 76(2):363-384.

Porch, C.E., S.C. Turner, and R.D. Methot. 1994. Estimates of the abundance and mortality of west Atlantic bluefin tuna using the stock synthesis model. *Col. Vol. Sci. Pap. ICCAT* 42(1):229-239.

Porch, C.E. and S.C. Turner. 1999. Virtual population analyses of Atlantic bluefin tuna with alternative models of transatlantic migration. *Col. Vol. Sci. Pap. ICCAT* 49(X):291-305.

Porch, C.E., S.C. Turner, and J.E. Powers. 2001. Virtual population analyses of Atlantic bluefin tuna with alternative models of transatlantic migration: 1970-1997. *Col. Vol. Sci. Pap. ICCAT* 52(1):1022-1045.

Powell, K. 2003. Eat your veg. *Nature* 426:378-379.

Powers, J.E. and J. Cramer. 1996. An exploration of the nature of Atlantic tuna mixing. *Col. Vol. Sci. Pap. ICCAT* 45(2):173-181.

Preikshot, D. and D. Pauly. 2005. Global fisheries and marine conservation: is coexistence possible? 185-197 in E. Norse and L.B. Crowder, eds., *Marine Conservation Biology.* Island Press.

Preston, G.L., L.B. Chapman, and P.G. Watt. 1998. *Vertical Longlining and Other Methods of Fishing Around Fish Aggregating Devices (FADs): A Manual for Fishermen.* Secretariat of the Pacific Commission.

Radcliffe, W. 1921. *Fishing from the Earliest Times.* John Murray. (1974 reprint, Ares Publishers, Chicago.)

Raloff, J. 2005. Empty nets. *Science News* 167(23):360-362.

Ravier, C. and J.M. Fromentin. 2001a. Long-term fluctuations in the eastern Atlantic and Mediterranean bluefin tuna population. *ICES Journal of Marine Science* 58(6):1299-1317.

————. 2001b. Trends in NE Atlantic and Mediterranean bluefin abundance. *PFRP Newsletter* 6(4):1-6.

————. 2004. Are the long-term fluctuations in Atlantic bluefin tuna (*Thunnus thunnus*) population related to environmental changes? *Fisheries Oceanography* 13(3):145-156.

Ray, J.C., K. Redford, R. Steneck, and J. Berger. (eds.) 2005. *Large Carnivores and the Conservation of Biodiversity.* Island Press.

Reid, T.R. 1995. Tsukiji: The great Tokyo fish market. *National Geographic* 188(5):38-55.

Reiger, G. 1973. *Profiles in Saltwater Angling*. Prentice-Hall.

————. 1976. The Bluefin tuna. *Motorboat* November:47.

Reischauer, E.O. 1974. *Japan: The Story of a Nation*. Tuttle.

Relini, O., L.F. Garibaldi, C. Cima, and G. Palandri. 1995. Feeding of the swordfish, the bluefin and other pelagic nekton in the western Ligurian Sea. *Col. Vol. Sci. Pap. ICCAT* 44(1):283-286.

Rembold, C.M. 2004. The health benefits of eating salmon. *Science* 305:475.

Revkin, A.C. 2003. Commercial fishing is cited in decline of oceans' big fish. *New York Times* May 14.

————. 2005. Tracking the imperiled bluefin from ocean to sushi platter. *New York Times* May 3:F1-4.

————. 2006. Farms' output grows closer to matching fishing harvests. *New York Times* September 4:A6.

Richards, W.J. 1976. Spawning of bluefin tuna (*Thunnus thynnus*) in the Atlantic Ocean and adjacent seas. *Col. Vol. Sci. Pap. ICCAT* 5(2):267-278.

————. 1977. A further note on Atlantic bluefin tuna spawning. *Col. Vol. Sci. Pap. ICCAT* 6(2):335-336.

Richardson, S. 1994. Warm blood for cold water. *Discover* 15(1):42-43.

Ringle, K. 1986. Seafood summit: Tokyo's Tsukiji fishmarket. *Oceans* 19(5):12-17.

Rivas, L.R. 1953. The pineal apparatus of tunas and related scombrid fishes as a possible light receptor controlling phototactic movements. *Bull. Mar. Sci. Gulf and Carib.* 3: 168-80.

————. 1977. Age composition anomalies as evidence for transoceanic migrations by intermediate age groups of the North Atlantic bluefin tuna (*Thunnus thynnus.*) *Col. Vol. Sci. Pap. ICCAT* 5(2):290-296.

————. 1979. Proposed terminology for size groups of the North Atlantic bluefin tuna (*Thunnus thynnus*). *Col. Vol. Sci. Pap. ICCAT* 8(2):441-446.

Rivas, L.R. and F.J. Mather. 1976. A comparison of Eastern and Western Atlantic bluefin tuna (*Thunnus thynnus*) with reference to stock differences. *Col. Vol. Sci. Pap. ICCAT* 5(2):290-296.

Rivkin, M. 2005. *Big Game Fishing Headquarters: A History of the IGFA.* IGFA Press.

Robbins, M.W. 2006. The catch. *Mother Jones* 31(2):49-53.

Roberts, C.M. 1997. Ecological advice for the global fisheries crisis. *Trends in Ecology and Evolution* 12(1):35-38.

Robins, C.M. and A.E. Caton. 1998. Review of Australian tuna fisheries in the Indian Ocean. *Proceedings Indian Ocean Tuna Consultation* 1:76-78.

Rodriguez-Marín, E., J.M. de la Serna, A. Garcia, C. Pla, and A. Gracia. 2004. Spanish bluefin tuna research activities. *Col. Vol. Sci. Pap. ICCAT* 56(3):1175-1181.

Rodriguez-Roda, J. 1980. Description of the Spanish bluefin (*Thunnus thynnus*) trap fishery. *Col. Vol. Sci. Pap. ICCAT* 11:180-183.

Roe, S. and M. Hawthorne. 2005. How safe is tuna? *Chicago Tribune* December 13.

Romanov, E.V. and V.V. Zamorov. 2002. First record of a yellowfin tuna (*Thunnus albacares*) in the stomach of a longnose lancetfish (*Alepisaurus ferox.*) *Fishery Bulletin* 100(2):386-389.

Rosenthal, E. 2006a. Fishing depletes Mediterranean tuna, conservationists say. *New York Times* July 16:A13.

—————. 2006b. In Europe it's fish oil after heart attacks, but not in U.S. *New York Times* October 3:F5.

Roughley, T.C. 1951. *Fish and Fisheries of Australia.* Angus and Robertson.

Russell, D. and B. Keating. 1984. Sushi today, gone tomorrow: the plight of the bluefin tuna. *Amicus Journal* Winter:38-46.

Ryther, J.H. 1981. Mariculture, ocean ranching, and other culture-based fisheries. *BioScience* 31(3):223-230.

Safina, C. 1993. Bluefin tuna in the West Atlantic: Negligent management and the making of an endangered species. *Conservation Biology* 7(2):229-233.

——————. 1995. The world's imperiled fish. *Scientific American* 273(5):46-53

——————. 1997. *Song for the Blue Ocean.* Henry Holt.

——————. 1998a. Scorched-earth fishing. *Issues in Science and Technology* 14(3):33-36.

——————. 1998b. Fish market mutiny. *New York Times.* April 14.

——————. 2001. Tuna conservation. In B.A. Block and E.D. Stevens, eds. *Tuna: Physiology, Ecology, and Evolution.* 413-459. Academic Press.

Safina, C., A. Rosenberg, R.A. Myers, T.J. Quinn, and J.S. Collie. 2005. U.S. ocean fish recovery: staying the course. *Science* 309:707-708.

Sakagawa, G.T. and A.L. Coan. 1974. A review of some aspects of the bluefin tuna (*Thunnus thunnus thynnus*) fisheries of the Atlantic Ocean. *Col. Vol. Sci. Pap. ICCAT* 2:259-313.

Samson, J. 1973. Line Down! The Special World of Big-Game Fishing. Winchester.

Sara, R. 1980. Bluefin tuna trap fishing in the Mediterranean. *Col. Vol. Sci. Pap. ICCAT* 11:129-144.

——————. 1998. A route three-thousand years long: Genetic grouping, social manifestations, body language of bluefin tuna, through the underwater filming of the Favignana trap fishery (video). *Col. Vol. Sci. Pap. ICCAT* 50(2):493.

Schaefer, K.M. 1984. Swimming performance, body temperature and gastric evacuation times of the black skipjack. *Euthynnus lineatus. Copeia* 4:1000-1005.

——————. 2000. Assessment of skipjack tuna (*Katsuwonus pelamis*) spawning activity in the eastern Pacific Ocean. *Fishery Bulletin* 99:343-350.

——————. 2001. Reproductive biology of tunas. In B.A. Block and E.D. Stevens, eds. *Tuna: Physiology, Ecology, and Evolution.* 225-270. Academic Press.

Schick, R. S., J. Goldstein, and M.E. Lutcavage. 2004. Bluefin tuna (*Thunnus thynnus*) in relation to sea surface temperature fronts in the Gulf of Maine (1994-96). *Fisheries Oceanography* 13(4):225-238.

Schiermeier, Q. 2002. How many more fish in the sea? *Nature* 419:662-65.

————. 2003. Fish farms' threat to salmon stocks exposed. *Nature* 425:753.

Schindler, D.E., T.E. Essington, J.F. Kitchell, C. Boggs, and R. Hilborn. 2002. Sharks and tunas: fisheries impacts on predators with contrasting life styles. *Ecological Applications* 12(3):735-748.

Scholey, V., D. Margulies, J. Wexler, and S. Hunt. 2003. Panamanian lab hosts research on tuna, other marine species. *Global Aquacult. Advocate* 6(1): 75-76.

————. 2004. Larval tuna research mimcs ocean conditions in lab. *Global Aquacul. Advocate* 7(1): 38.

Scholey, V.P., D. Margulies, R.J. Olson, J.B. Wexler, J.M. Suter, and S. Hunt. 2001. Lab culture and reproduction of yellowfin tuna in Panama. *Global Aquacult. Advocate* 4(2): 17-18.

Scott, T.D., C.J.M. Glover, and R.V. Southcott. 1974. *The Marine and Freshwater Fishes of South Australia.* Government Printer, South Australia.

Seabrook, J. 1994. Death of a giant: stalking the disappearing bluefin tuna. *Harper's* 288(1729): 48-56.

Secor, D.H. 2002. Is Atlantic bluefin tuna a metapopulation? *Col. Vol. Sci. Pap. ICCAT* 54(2):390-399.

Sepulveda, C.A., K.A. Dickson, and J.B. Graham. 2003. Swimming performance studies on the eastern Pacific bonito, *Sarda chiliensis*, a close relative of the tunas (family Scombridae). *Journal of Experimental Biology* 206:2739-2748.

Shadwick, R.E. 2005. How tunas and lamnid sharks swim: an evolutionary convergence. *American Scientist* 93(6):524-531.

Sharp, G.D. 2001. Tuna oceanography—an applied science. In B.A. Block and E.D. Stevens, eds. *Tuna: Physiology, Ecology, and Evolution*. 345-389. Academic Press.

Shelly, K.C. 2003. *Lynn Bogue Hunt: A Sporting Life*. Derrydale.

Shingu, C. and K. Hisada. 1977. A review of the Japanese Atlantic longline fishery for bluefin tuna and the consideration of the present status of the stock. *Col. Vol. Sci. Pap. ICCAT* 6(2):366-384.

————. 1978. Recent status of the medium and large bluefin tuna population in the Atlantic Ocean. *Col. Vol. Sci. Pap. ICCAT* 7(2):266-275.

——————. 1979. Analysis of the Atlantic bluefin tuna stock caught by longline fishery, based on the data up to 1978. *Col. Vol. Sci. Pap. ICCAT* 8(2):421-429.

——————. 1980. Analysis of the Atlantic bluefin tuna stock. *Col. Vol. Sci. Pap. ICCAT* 9(2):595-600.

Shingu, C., K. Hisada, S. Kume, and M. Honma. 1975. Biological information on Atlantic bluefin tuna caught by longline fishery and some views on the management of the resource. *Col. Vol. Sci. Pap. ICCAT* 4:145-160.

Sibert, J.R., M.K. Musyl, and R.W. Brill. 2003. Horizontal movements of bigeye tuna (*Thunnus obesus*) near Hawaii determined by Kalman filter analysis of archival tagging data. *Fisheries Oceanography* 12(32):141-151.

Silvani, L., M.Gazo, and A. Aguilar. 1999. Spanish driftnet fishing and incidental catches in the Mediterranean. *Biol. Cons.* 90(1):79-85.

Sissenwine, M.P., P.M. Mace, J.E. Powers, and G.P. Scott. 1998. A commentary on Western Atlantic bluefin tuna assessments. *Transactions of the American Fisheries Society* 127:838-855.

Sloan, S. 1993. The "Connie Jean" incident. *The Edge Big Game Fishing Report*. Fall 1993:22-23.

——————. 2003. *Ocean Bankruptcy: World Fisheries on the Brink of Disaster*. Lyons.

Small, M. 2002. The happy fat. *New Scientist* 175(2357):34-37.

Smith, P. 1973. The bluefin tuna: the fat man who won't dance. *Sports Afield* June:54-55,108-112.

Smith, P.J., L. Griggs, and S. Chow. 2001. DNA identification of Pacific bluefin tuna (*Thunnus orientalis*) in the New Zealand fishery. *N.Z. Journal of Freshwater and Marine Research* 35:843-850.

Smith, T.D. (ed.) 1979. Report of the status of porpoise stocks workshop (August 27-31, 1979, La Jolla, California). *NMFS Southwest Fisheries Center AdministrativeReport LJ-79-41.* 62 pp.

——————. 2001. Examining cetacean ecology using historical fishery data. 207-214 in P. Holm, T.D. Smith, and D.J. Starkey (eds.) 2001. *Research in Maritime History No. 21.* International Maritime History Association/Census of Marine Life.

Steele, J.H. and M. Schumacher. 1999. On the history of marine fisheries: Report of the Woods Hole workshop. *Oceanography* 12(3):28-29.

—————. 2000. Ecosystem structure before fishing. *Fisheries Research* 44:201-205.

Steneck, R.S. 1998. Human influences on coastal ecosystems: does overfishing create trophic cascades? *Trends Ecol. Evol.*13(11):429-30.

Stevens, E.D., F.G. Carey, and J. Kanwisher. 1978. Changes in visceral temperature of Atlantic bluefin tuna. *Col. Vol. Sci. Pap. ICCAT* 7(2):383-388.

Stevens, E.D. and F.G. Carey. 1981. One why of the warmth of warm-bodied fish. *American Journal of Regulatory, Integrative and Comparative Physiology* 240(3):151-155.

Stokesbury, M.J.W., S.L.H. Teo, A. Seitz, R.K. O'Dor, and B.A. Block. 2004. Movement of Atlantic bluefin tuna (*Thunnus thynnus*) as determined by satellite tagging initiated off New England. *Canadian Journal of Fisheries and Aquatic Sciences* 61(10):1976-1987.

Sugano, M. and F. Hirahara. 2000. Polyunsaturated fatty acids in the food chain in Japan. *Amer. Jour. Clinical Nutrition* 71(1):189-196.

Summers, A.P. 2004. Fast fish. *Nature* 429:31-33.

Sun, C.L., W.R. Wang, and S. Yeh. 2005. Reproductive biology of yellowfin tuna in the central and western Pacific Ocean. *Western and Central Pacific Fisheries Commission* WCPFC-SCI/B1/WP-1.15pp.

Susca, V., A. Corriero, M. Delflorio, C.R. Bridges, and G.DeMetrio. 2001. New results on the reproductive biology of the bluefin tuna (*Thunnus thynnus*) in the Mediterranean. *Col. Vol. Sci. Pap. ICCAT* 52(2):745-751.

Suzuki, Z. 1980. Bluefin fisheries and stocks in the Atlantic, 1970-81. *Col. Vol. Sci. Pap. ICCAT* 20(2):399-416.

—————. 1992. Critical review of the stock assessment of bluefin tuna in the western Atlantic. *Col. Vol. Sci. Pap. ICCAT* 39(3):710-716.

—————. 1993. A review of the biology and fisheries for yellowfin tuna (*Thunnus albacares*) in the western and central Pacific Ocean. In R.S. Shomura, J. Majkowski, and S. Langi, eds., *Interactions of Pacific Tuna Fisheries Vol. 2: Papers on Biology and Fisheries*. FAO, Rome.

Syme, D.A. and R.E. Shadwick. 2002. Effects of longitudinal body position and swimming speed on mechanical power of deep red muscle from skipjack tuna (*Katsuwonus pelamis*). *Journal of Experimental Biology* 205:189-200.

Takagi, M. T. Okamura, S. Chow, and N. Taniguchi. 2001. Preliminary study of albacore (*Thunnus alalunga*) stock differentiation inferred from microsatellite DNA analysis. *Fishery Bulletin* 99:697-701.

Taylor, L.R. 1970. Untaxing taxonomy. *Oceans* 3(6):104-106.

Teal, J. and M. Teal. 1975. *The Sargasso Sea*. Atlantic-Little, Brown.

Terry, P., P. Lichtenstein, M. Feychting, A. Ahlbom, and A. Wolk. 2001. Fatty fish consumption and risk of prostate cancer. *The Lancet* 357:1764-66.

Thiele. C. 1969. *Blue Fin*. Harper & Row.

Ticina, V., L. Grubisic, I. Katavic, I. Jeftimijades, and V. Franicevic. 2003. Tagging of small bluefin tuna in the growth-out floating cage—report of the research activities on tuna farming in the Adriatic Sea during 2002. *Col. Vol. Sci. Pap. ICCAT* 55(3):1278-1281.

Tinsley, J.B. 1984. *The Sailfish: Swashbuckler of the Open Seas*. University of Florida Press.

Triantafyllou, M.S. and G.S. Triantafyllou. 1995. An efficient swimming machine. *Scientific American* 272(3):64-72.

Triantafyllou, M.S., A.H. Techet, Q. Zhu, D.N. Beal, F.S. Hover, and D.K.P. Yue. 2002. Vorticity control in fish-like propulsion and maneuvering. *Integrative and Comparative Biology* 42:1026-1031.

Trivedi, B. 2006. The good, the fad and the unhealthy. *New Scientist* 191(2570):42-49.

Tudela, S. 2002a. Tuna farming in the Mediterranean: the 'coup de grâce' to a dwindling population? *World Wildlife Fund Mediterranean Program Office*, Rome.

—————. 2002b. Grab, cage, fatten, sell. *Samudra* July:9-17.

Tudela, S., A.K. Kai, F. Maynou, M. El Andalossi, and P. Guglielmi. 2005. Driftnet fishing and biodiversity conservation: the case study of the large-scale Moroccan driftnet fleet operating in the Alboran Sea (SW Mediterranean). *Biological Conservation* 121:65-78.

Tuomisto, J.T., J. Tuomisto, M. Tainio, M. Niittynen, P. Verkasalo, Vartiainen, H. Kiviranta, and J. Pekkanen. 2004. Risk-benefit analysis of eating farmed salmon. *Science* 305:476.

Uozumi, Y. 2006. Crisis for tuna resources triggered by biased scientific paper—an argument over Myers paper. *OPRT Newsletter* 9:1-3.

Vaughan, H. 1982. *The Australian Fisherman's Companion*. Landsdowne Press.

Volpe, J.P. 2005. Dollars without sense: the bait for big-money tuna ranching around the world. *BioScience* 55(4):301-302.

von Brandt, A. 1972. *Revised and Enlarged Fish Catching Methods of the World*. Fishing News (Books).

Waldman, P. 2005. Mercury and tuna: U.S. advice leaves lots of questions. *Wall Street Journal* August 1:A1-A6.

Walters, V. and H. Fierstine. 1964. Measurements of swimming speeds of yellowfin tuna and wahoo. *Nature* 202:208-209.

Ward, P. and R.A. Myers. 2005. Shifts in open-ocean fish communities coinciding with the commencement of commercial fishing. *Ecology* 86(4):835-847.

Ward, R.D., N.G. Elliott, and P.M. Grewe. 1995. Allozyme and Mitochondrial DNA separation of the Pacific northern bluefin tuna, *Thunnus thunnus orientalis* (Temminck and Schlegel), from southern bluefin tuna, *Thunnus maccoyii* (Castelnau). *Marine and Freshwater Research* 46:921-30.

Watson, R. and D. Pauly. 2001. Systematic distortions in world fisheries catch trends. *Nature* 414:534-36.

Weaver, D.E. 2004. Contaminant levels in farmed salmon. *Science* 305:478.

Webber, H.H. 1968. Mariculture. *BioScience* 18(10):940-945.

Weber, P. 1993. *Abandoned Seas: Reversing the Decline of the Oceans*. Worldwatch.

——————. 1994. *Net Loss: Fish, Jobs, and the Environment*. Worldwatch.

Weng, K.C. and B.A. Block. 2004. Diel vertical migration of the bigeye thresher shark (*Alopias superciliosus*) a species possessing orbital retia mirabilia. *Fishery Bulletin* 102(1):221-229.

Westneat, M.W. and S.A. Wainwright. 2001. Mechanical design for swimming: muscle, tendon and bone. In B.A. Block and E.D. Stevens, eds. *Tuna: Physiology, Ecology, and Evolution*. 271-311. Academic Press.

Wexler, J.B., D. Margulies, S. Masuma, N. Tezuka, K. Teruya, M. Oka, M. Kane Matsu, and H. Nikaido. 2001. Age validation and growth of yellowfin tuna, *Thunnus albacares*, larvae reared in the laboratory. *IATTC Bulletin* 22(1):52-71.

Wexler, J.B., V.P. Scholey, R.J. Olson, D. Margulies, A. Nakazawa, and J.M. Suter. 2003. Tank culture of yellowfin tuna, *Thunnus albacares*: developing a spawning population for research purposes. *Aquaculture* 220: 327-353.

Whitehead, S.S. 1931. Fishing methods for the bluefin tuna (*Thunnus thynnus*) and an analysis of the catches. *Cal. Fish and Game Fish Bulletin* 33:1-34.

Whynott, D. 1995. *Giant Bluefin*. North Point Press.

————. 1999. The most expensive fish in the sea. *Discover* 20(4):80-85.

————. 2000. Something's fishy about this robot. *Smithsonian* 31(5):54-60.

Wild, A. 1993. A review of the biology and fisheries for yellowfin tuna, *Thunnus albacares*, in the eastern Pacific Ocean. In R.S. Shomura, J. Majkowski, and S. Langi, eds., *Interactions of Pacific Tuna Fisheries Vol. 2: Papers on Biology and Fisheries*. FAO, Rome.

Williams, J.G., F.P. Chavez, J. Ryan, S.E. Lluch-Cota, and M. Ñiquen C. 2003. Sardine fishing in the early 20th century. *Science* 300:2032-2033.

Wilson, S.G., M.E. Lutcavage, R.W. Brill, M.P. Genovese, A.B. Cooper, and A.W. Everly. 2005. Movements of bluefin tuna (*Thunnus thynnus*) in the northwestern Atlantic Ocean recorded by pop-up satellite archival tags. *Marine Biology* 146:409-423.

Worm, B., M. Sandow, A. Oschlies, H.K. Lotze, and R.S. Myers. 2005. Global patterns of predator diversity in the open ocean. *Science* 309:1365-1369.

Worm, B., E.B. Barbier, N. Beaumont, J.E. Duffy, C. Folke, B.S. Halpern, J.B.C. Jackson, H.K. Lotze, F. Micheli, S.R. Palumbi, E. Sala, K.A. Selkoe, J.J. Stachowicz, and R. Watson. 2006. Impacts of biodiversity loss on ocean ecosystem services. *Science* 314:787-790.

Wright, K. 2005. Our preferred poison [mercury]. *Discover* 26(3):58-65.

Wylie, P. 1990. Crunch and Des: Classic Stories of Saltwater Fishing. Lyons.

Yang, P.T. 1980. National report of China (Taiwan), 1978. *Col. Vol. Sci. Pap. ICCAT* 9(3):675-676.

Yao, M. 1988. A note on Japanese longline fisheries in the Atlantic Ocean. *Col. Vol. Sci. Pap. ICCAT* 27:222-229.

Young, J.W., R.W. Bradford, T.D. Lamb and V.D. Lyne. 1996. Biomass of zooplankton and micronekton in the southern bluefin tuna fishery grounds off eastern Tasmania, Australia. *Marine Environmental Progress Series* 138:1-14.

Young, J.W., T.D. Lamb, D. Le, R.W. Bradford, and A.W. Whitlaw. 1997. Feeding ecology and interannual variations in diet of southern bluefin tuna, *Thunnus maccoyii*, in relation to coastal and oceanic waters of eastern Tasmania, Australia. *Environmental Biology of Fishes* 50:275-291.

Yuen, H.S.H. 1966. Swimming speeds of yellowfin and skipjack tuna. *Transactions of the American Fisheries Society* 95:203-209.

—————. 1970. Behavior of skipjack tuna, *Katsuwonus pelamis*, as determined by tracking with ultrasonic telemetry. *Journal of the Fisheries Research Board of Canada* 27:2071-2079.

Zharov, V.L., N.F. Paliy, V.I. Sauskan, and V.G. Yurov. 1973. Results of Soviet fisheries investigations on Atlantic tuna. *Col. Vol. Sci. Pap. ICCAT* 1:549-555.

Part III, "Investing in Demographics"

Gleick, Peter H., ed. 1993 *Water in Crisis: A Guide to the World's Fresh Water Resources*. Oxford University Press.

American Society of Civil Engineers. http://www.asce.org/asce.cfm.

Wastewater Report: Report Card for America's Infrastructure. http://www.infrastructurereportcard.org/fact-sheet/wastewater.

EPA: Various Water Statistics. http://www.epa.gov/ebtpages/water.html.

Water On Tap: What You Need to Know. http://water.epa.gov/drink/guide/upload/book_waterontap_full.pdf.

OECD - Working Party on Agricultural Policies and Markets. http://www.oecd.org/officialdocuments/displaydocumentpdf/?cote=TAD/CA/APM/WP(2009)12/FINAL&doclanguage=en and http://www.unece.org/.

General Reference on Water. http://www.unece.org/env/water/text/text_protocol.htm and http://www.win-water.org/.

Water Infrastructure Now. http://www.win-water.org/reports/winow.pdf.

Clean & Safe Water for the 21ˢᵗ Century. http://www.win-water.org/reports/winow.pdf.

World Water Council. http://www.worldwatercouncil.org/.

A New Water Politics: World Water Council Strategy 2010-2012. http://www.worldwatercouncil.org/fileadmin/wwc/Library/Publications_and_reports/New_Water_Politics.pdf.

Financing Water for All. http://www.financingwaterforall.org/.

Water Crisis. http://www.worldwatercouncil.org/index.php?id=25.

INDEX

Q–R

Rabbit Island, 90, 140
rain, 183, 194, 196
Rainbow Warrior, 129, 144
ramp-up risk, 68
ranch-fattened tuna, 146
ranching, tuna, 138-146,
  156, 167
raw fish, eating, 148. *See
  also* tuna
Red Cross, 203
Red Data Book, 153
Red List of Threatened
  Animals, 108
regulations. *See also* laws
  harvesting tuna, 138
  life settlements, 70
reinsurance, 27, 31
relationships between
  longevity risks and mortality
  risks, 24
renewable water resources,
  210. *See also* water
Republic of Korea, 107
Republic of Panama, 109
requirements of farmed
  fish, 157
resources, water, 181. *See
  also* water
restaurants, 171
  demand for tuna, 147-148
  tuna prices, 173
retirement, 14
  ages, 18
reverse equity transactions, 55
  life settlements, 56-64, 67-72
  reverse mortgages, 71-78
reverse mortgages, 18, 28,
  71-78

reverse osmosis
  desalination, 204
  membrane technology, 203
Review-Journal, 220
risks
  life settlements, 67-69
  longevity, 14, 19, 25
  mortality, 14, 19, 25
    *Japan, 35-45, 49-53
    longevity, 27-34*
  reverse mortgages, 77-78
rivers, 183
Roberts County, Texas, 227
Rocky Mountains, 195
rotifers, 172
Russia, 218
  water, 217
RWE (RWEOY), 237
Ryther, J.H., 156

S

Sadat, Anwar, 213
Safe Drinking Water Act, 229
Safina, Carl, 103, 168
sailfishes, 96
Saladin, 212
salmon, 85, 133
  farming, 157
  wild Atlantic, 157
salt water, 202. *See also* water
San Antonio, Texas, 227
sand-and-charcoal filters, 201
Santic, Tony, 93
Sargon II of Assyria, 211
sashimi, 88, 146, 169, 171. *See
  also* tuna
  popularity of, 171
  prices, 147
Saudi Arabia, politics of
  water, 209

X–Z